Kyle

Since you'll be
recruiting in Oak
Town this is to help you
get to know "hood".

SKYLINE

SKYLINE

One Season, One Team, One City

TIM KEOWN

Macmillan Publishing Company
New York

Maxwell Macmillan Canada
Toronto

Maxwell Macmillan International
New York   Oxford   Singapore   Sydney

Macmillan Publishing Company   Maxwell Macmillan Canada, Inc.
866 Third Avenue   1200 Eglinton Avenue East, Suite 200
New York, NY 10022   Don Mills, Ontario M3C 3N1

Macmillan Publishing Company is part of the Maxwell Communication Group of Companies.

Library of Congress Cataloging-in-Publication Data
Keown, Tim.
    Skyline : one season, one team, one city / Tim Keown.
        p.   cm.
    Includes index.
    ISBN 0-02-562305-2
    1. Skyline High School (Oakland, Calif.)—Basketball—History.   I. Title
GV885.43.S58K46   1994
796.323'62'0979466—dc20   93-37777
CIP

Macmillan books are available at special discounts for bulk purchases for sales promotions, premiums, fund-raising, or educational use. For details, contact:

        Special Sales Director
        Macmillan Publishing Company
        866 Third Avenue
        New York, NY 10022

10 9 8 7 6 5 4 3 2 1

Printed in the United States of America

To Miriam, Brandt and Thomas.
And for my father.

ACKNOWLEDGMENTS

THE LIST OF PEOPLE WHO HAD A PART IN THIS PROJECT COULD NEVER FIT in the alloted space. That, of course, is a cliche. It is also true.

I would like to thank my editor at Macmillan, Rick Wolff, whose guidance and optimism are an integral part of this work. Rick saw the idea clearly from the beginning, then improved upon it. Sincere thanks to Steve Delsohn, a fine agent and editor, who believed in it and made it happen. Also to Frank Weimann, Steve's partner.

I appreciate the efforts of John Curley, my boss at *The San Francisco Chronicle*, for making it easy for me to pursue this project.

More than anything, I would like to express my deepest gratitude to the players and families of the 1992-93 Skyline High School basketball team. I thank them for letting me become part of their lives, and I thank them for sharing their stories. I hadn't cheered at a sporting event in at least three years, but that all changed. I rooted unabashedly for these young men, both on the court and off, and I will continue to do so. I can't imagine a better group of people.

A special thanks to Shawn Donlea, who took a chance by allowing me to invade and observe six months of his life. We started out as strangers and ended up as good friends.

Thanks to Stella Blackwell, Elaine Feemster, the Albert family and Maggie Wimberly. And to Franklin Shelton, my gratitude for the conversation, the company and the insight. It would be hard for a writer to find a better source.

Additional thanks to: Don Lippi, whose experiences started this in motion; Rob McMahon at Macmillan; John Beam; Dave Armstrong for his legal assistance; Tod Golding for the computer work; Sean Colter; Bruce Mills at the Contra Costa District Attorney's office; the good and generous people at the Contra Costa County Clerk's Office; Heather McCracken; Beverly Palley; Joe Panella; Lou Jones; Gloria Govan; Dr. Alan Young; the Oakland

Unified School District Research Department; William Patterson of the NAACP; Willie Hearnton; Greg Brown; Charles Davis; Sean Payton and Curtis Johnson; Bud Geracie, Larry Stone and Don Bosley for their moral support.

And my infinite gratitude to Brandt, Thomas and Miriam (the in-house copy editor), for putting up with me.

Finally, a very special thanks to my 1978 Honda, which made the 100-mile round trip from my home to Oakland, and made it every day.

AUTHOR'S NOTE

THE CHILDREN FROM THE BAYVIEW/HUNTERS POINT NEIGHBORHOOD IN San Francisco begin playing baseball in the dirt parking lot above Candlestick Park as soon as summer vacation begins. They are probably no older than ten, and they play with an unapologetic happiness. They use rocks for bases and only a few wear baseball gloves. The field is bald dirt and narrow strips of dried weeds. The ground is packed hard by the parked cars and swept clean by the area's howling winds.

I have driven past this scene countless times on my way to Candlestick to cover San Francisco Giants baseball games. As I slow down to watch the children play, I find myself thinking these are the real games, more important than those that take place inside the stadium.

Those thoughts set the idea for this book in motion. The lives of young men and women in America's inner cities are all too often reported in bland, monotonous statistics. We hear dropout rates, murder rates, addiction rates and welfare rates until they coalesce into the same anesthetizing blur. To too many of us, the children of the inner city live nameless, faceless lives. I set out to attach names and faces, and to tell their stories. They deserve to be heard.

I wanted to go where athletics and life intertwine, and where the line separating the two sometimes blurs. I wanted to meet young people whose lives are dependent, at least in part, by what they accomplish and learn through athletic competition. I wanted to see first-hand how athletics, and especially basketball, can help kids in ways that far outreach the boundaries of a court. It seemed like a simple, naive idea, yet I knew the reality existed.

I wanted to tell the stories of people such as former Skyline High School basketball coach Don Lippi and Dwhawn Edwards, one of his players. Lippi saw enormous basketball talent in Edwards, and he saw a desire that burned with white-hot intensity. He also saw a student who would never be eligible, whose grade-point average was consistently deficient. Edwards would not always attend classes, but he would make it to the offseason and summer basketball practices, every day, carrying a change of clothes in a paper grocery sack.

Lippi wondered how Edwards, so dedicated to basketball, could find school such a burden. He found that Edwards, like many inner-city students, was unable to get up in time for school in the morning. He didn't own an alarm clock, and there was nobody in his house to wake him. If he missed the first period of the day, Edwards was too proud and discouraged to arrive late. So he stayed home.

Lippi took a chance on changing Edwards' life. He bought an alarm clock, placed it inside a canvas athletic bag and gave it to Edwards. With the alarm clock beside his bed, Edwards began making it to class on time in the morning. His grades became more than respectable. He made the basketball team at Skyline and eventually went on to Hartnell Junior College in Salinas, where he was one of the top scorers in California as a freshman. Now Dwhawn Edwards, the kid with the poor grades and the paper grocery sack, is being recruited by Division I colleges.

Lippi's experiences were the catalyst for this work. It could be said this book was written because Don Lippi gave a young man a duffel bag, an alarm clock and a chance.

Oakland is a dangerous place, statistically the most violent city in California. It is a tough place to grow up, and an even tougher place to grow up and leave. A man who coaches youth baseball in Oakland told me that one of the first lessons the children are taught is how to hit the ground and protect themselves when they hear gunfire coming from a nearby housing project. Sadly, the coach said most of them know exactly what to do even before they are told.

My life has always been easy and comfortable, and maybe that was why places such as the flatlands of Oakland have always held a fascination for me. It isn't my world, but it is a world I wanted to understand. And I wanted to pass along that understanding.

Oakland is surrounded by freeways, many of them elevated. As I drove through and past the city, I would look down at the people going about their daily lives—lives far removed from my own—and wonder about their dreams and hopes. The freeways afford a distant, Olympian perspective, and one not altogether different from my knowledge of the inner city. I had read the statistics. I knew which offramps were considered safe, and which were not. Then I decided to take all the offramps, to walk into the flatland neighborhoods. I found a place where hope still runs ahead of despair, and where dreams remain vivid.

I attended nearly every game and every practice during the 1992–93 basketball season at Skyline High School. All of the events in this book are real and factual, but some names have been changed or altered in order to provide the subjects a measure of privacy. The shooting incident involving Eric Albert was re-created through court transcripts, police reports and interviews.

The first day I walked onto the Skyline High campus—just a guy with a tape recorder, a notepad and the seeds of a vision—I felt sorely out of place. As the season wore on, that changed. The players and I began to understand each other, and each side began teaching the other about two vastly different worlds. Mostly, I listened to their stories, stories that were entrusted to me by the players and their families. I can only hope I did them justice.

INTRODUCTION

The black man's body, the game, basketball, bearing his body's imprint, is used to sell everything from breakfast cereal to automobiles. Our current popular culture would be incomprehensible to an outsider unless he or she understood basketball as the key to deciphering speech styles, clothing styles, metaphors employed by kids, politicians and housewives. Yet that same iconized, commodified black man's body is beaten, incarcerated, the nightmare thief, rapist, addict that Americans arm themselves against.

JOHN EDGAR WIDEMAN

ACROSS THE STREET FROM SKYLINE HIGH SCHOOL, IN THE EXCLUSIVE Oakland hills, a house is for sale with the asking price of $1.55 million. It is a Southwestern-style estate, coral pink stucco with a red tile roof. A deck runs the width of the house in the back, overlooking a sheer cliff. The view is astonishing, stretching uninterrupted for at least one hundred miles. The skyline of San Francisco sits in the middle, like the centerpiece of an elaborate table. The house—described in advertisements as "an architectural masterpiece"—is surrounded on Skyline Boulevard by other houses in the same price range, many of them for sale.

Inside the gymnasium at Skyline High School, about 400 yards from the house, there are no doors on any of the four toilet stalls in the boys bathroom. There are no mirrors on the walls, no toilet paper, no paper towels in the dispensers. At the end of the school day, before the unenviable custodial work begins, the stench is overpowering. It travels through the hall and across the basketball court. Pools of urine lay on the concrete floor around the toilets, which are plugged with paper and excrement and whatever else has accumulated throughout the day.

The boys locker room is dank and gray, a colorless pit of stale air. Several rows of gunmetal gray lockers, about five feet high, are attached to the gray concrete floors. Thin wooden benches run between the stands of lockers. Many of the fluorescent tube lights affixed to the tall ceiling are broken or burned out. There are small skylights on the ceiling. The glass is opaque, allowing only a dull glow of light to penetrate the room.

In the showers, same thing: gray, cold, concrete. Neither the students in physical education classes nor the athletes on the school's sports teams use the showers. It is considered better to go to class or home sweaty and hot than to stand underneath these showers, in this room. Most of the students don't use the bathroom, either, unless it's an emergency. Many of them walk up the hill, where the classrooms are located, and use the faculty bathroom.

"You don't go to the bathroom at this school," one student said. "You go before you leave home or you wait till after school. You just have to be organized. If you have to go at school, go in the faculty bathroom. If they're going to suspend me for taking a crap, that's OK with me."

There is graffiti everywhere in the gym, "tags" from Jinx and Entro, gang identifications and neighborhood boasts. They can't paint fast enough to keep up with the graffiti, and they have long since stopped trying. One of the two metal doors separating the hallway and the gymnasium has a hole where the knob once was. A teacher says the knob was sent to the Oakland Unified School District for repairs in January 1990—nearly three years before— and hasn't been seen since.

The coaches' office is between the locker room and the gym. The walls are beige tiles, the floor the same endless concrete. There are bulletin boards with photographs of children, team schedules and daily reminders. One wall of the coaches' office is covered with eight-by-ten photographs of former Skyline athletes, those who are playing or have played at major colleges, or in the NBA, the NFL or major-league baseball. The Wall of Fame includes basketball player Gary Payton and baseball's Bip Roberts.

The gymnasium is used by the girls volleyball team, the boys

and girls basketball teams (both varsity and junior varsity) and
sometimes the track teams. Jinx and Entro have been inside here,
too: their tags, written in thick black marker, adorn the walls. The
school's colors are black and red, and the gym is one of the few
places on campus where that is apparent. The walls are painted red
from the floor to about fifteen feet above. Behind one basket, tall
white letters form the word SKYLINE inside the red. Behind the
other basket is the word TITANS.

The gym floor is dirty and slick. The rubber-soled squeak of the
stop/start, one of the pure sounds of basketball, is impossible to
produce on this floor. Coaches and administrators at Skyline have
been trying to get the floor refinished for at least five years, but the
money hasn't been available. An attempt was made to repaint the
lines on the floor several years ago, but it was a dismal failure. The
paint was applied on top of the lacquered finish, with a paint brush,
and the resulting look is nearly comical, the texture like flat paint
on glass. The Skyline players spend much of their time on the court
rubbing the soles of their shoes with their hands in an attempt to
remove some of the grit and improve their footing. At times it is
like playing basketball on ice.

Empty candy wrappers and soda cans have been swept into a
corner behind the visiting team's bench. It is a cold, windswept
December night in the Oakland hills, and game time is twenty minutes away.

On that night, the night of December 10, 1992, a Thursday, the
Skyline High basketball team played its first and only home night
game of the season. It was against Hogan High School, a school
located in Vallejo, about a thirty-minute drive to the north. It is
Skyline's eighth preseason game and their third game in four days.
Because it is difficult to find preseason opponents willing to play in
Oakland, they will not play another home game for nearly a month.

Skyline is a member of the Oakland Athletic League, a fiercely
competitive league that consists of the six Oakland public high
schools. It is a league where basketball games sometimes mesh
with turf wars, where spectators must pass through metal detectors before entering the gym, and where league games are held in

the afternoons, when the threat of violence isn't exacerbated by the temptations of the dark.

The Oakland Unified School District, like every urban district in California, is strapped financially. Administrators within the district blame the decay of the inner-city schools on the neglect of state government; local money is limited if not nonexistent, and the local funds that do exist often are siphoned off to law enforcement and other city services. The schools are left to handle their situations as best they can. Layoff threats are an annual rite in the City of Oakland, and in 1993, Mayor Elihu Harris called the city's financial condition the worst since the Depression.

Money *is* spent for security at high school sporting events, though. The six schools in the Oakland Athletic League receive $30,000 for boys athletics—$5,000 for each school. According to the district, that total—for uniforms, equipment and travel—has not changed in more than thirty years. However, during the 1992-93 school year, the district will spend $25,000 attempting to provide a safe environment for its athletes and spectators.

On February 2, 1989, an event occurred on the McClymonds High School campus in West Oakland that provided both incentive and rationale for the strict security at OAL basketball games. On that afternoon, with McClymonds playing Oakland High, a group of young men out for revenge sat together on the home team's side of the gym. What followed was one of grimmer scenes in the league's history.

As the game neared its conclusion, the young men, as if in a hurry to leave, filtered toward the court and surrounded the two metal exit doors. They wore jackets to hide the heavy chains and padlocks they carried. When the game ended, they slung the chains over the long door handles and slipped on the padlocks. The operation was carried out with military precision.

More than 300 people were trapped inside as the aggressors turned the court into a battleground. The gangsters let loose with a wild, frenzied blur of feet and fists and the quick flash of at least one knife. They attacked players, fans, anybody.

Some of the Oakland High players tried to fight their way out. Some ran. Some hid. Most of the spectators stood and watched in horror, utterly defenseless. Basketball games in the OAL had always operated under a tenuous social contract; now it had ripped at the seams.

The genesis of the nightmarish scene occurred two weeks before, when McClymonds lost at Oakland High. There was gloating on the Oakland High side. Looks were exchanged, maybe a few words—in a charged atmosphere, nothing more is needed. Retribution was promised and delivered.

Throughout the league, word spread like ripples on a lake: one Oakland High student was stabbed, dozens were beaten. The game was over and McClymonds had won, but that wasn't enough; the final payment had to be exacted in blood.

When they finally reached their bus, the Oakland High players found its windows broken. News reports the following day centered on the inevitability of such a confrontation. The Oakland Unified School District issued one terse statement: "Some students did get a little physical after the game." The shock was limited to those who believed there was a sacred distinction between the chaos of the streets and the noble pursuits of high school athletes.

The police officers and campus security personnel that work the entrances and exits at every high school basketball game in the city owe their presence, at least in part, to the melee at McClymonds. Before that altercation, it had become increasingly apparent that greater safeguards were necessary; after it, no further evidence was needed.

Even within this setting, the OAL remains the crucible of some of the best high school basketball in the nation. Coaches struggle to impose discipline onto a game ruled by freedom of expression. Players struggle to get to practice, to make grades, to survive.

Shawn Donlea is the Skyline coach. He is a 28-year-old white man with a boyish face, brown hair and brown eyes. He stands 5-foot-11 with a medium build. There is nothing about his appearance or his background that would make his presence here seem plausible. He grew a Fu Manchu mustache and a goatee to coincide with the beginning of the basketball season, his first at Skyline. The facial hair is meant to exude a certain street-wise toughness that, admittedly, he does not possess.

"I'm trying," he said, laughing. "Besides, it can't hurt my social life any, since I don't have one."

Donlea has a master's degree in sports psychology from the University of Iowa and an undergraduate psychology degree from UCLA. He has worked as a low-level assistant coach at two universities. On this dreary December night, with his team in shambles and his life not far from it, he is wondering just what the hell he is doing here.

Donlea coaches both the varsity and the junior varsity teams at Skyline, a feat of patience, endurance and—according to some—lunacy that is considered unprecedented by everyone associated with Oakland basketball. The two jobs will pay him roughly $3,300. He will get the check in March, after the season has been completed. He works as a substitute teacher during the week and as a freelance referee—anywhere, anytime—on the weekends. He lives in an apartment in Mountain View, a small community fifty miles south of Oakland. He has no close friends in the Bay Area, no girlfriend and no prospects. What he does have is basketball.

Skyline comes to the game with a 4–3 preseason record—they had lost three of the last four games—and a gradual rift between Donlea and the players is threatening to widen into a chasm. He is admittedly naive, a white man in a black world, and he is being tested. He expected as much, but still, he struggles to deal with it. Skyline has a rich basketball history, and Donlea aspires to enrich it further. But right now, he would be happy to make it through the evening.

"I don't have anything to say to the varsity," Donlea said as the junior varsity game neared its end. "What can I say? They don't listen, and I'm all talked out. I've said it all. We might not win another game. We're going to get to league games, and we're going to get blown out."

Donlea is a basketball technician and an idealist. He set out to fight the conventional reality of inner-city basketball. The game, at its most basic, is a street fight, a struggle of self-reliance. It is you against me, the city game.

Donlea's game is five interchangeable parts, five energetic cogs of perpetual motion. Five guys who play defense as one, five guys who play offense with the ingrained knowledge of where everybody is at all times. He is a coach who looks upon the game as a geometric proof. He is a man who looks upon the children of the inner city as being ignored and unchallenged.

"I just have to keep reminding myself that the first year's always the toughest," he said.

Before the junior varsity game, Donlea spent more than an hour attempting to make the floor playable. He swept it by pushing a wet towel with a dirty mop. This job of basketball coach is more than he expected: he is coach, trainer, custodian and policeman.

There is no first-aid kit, not even a single roll of athletic tape. A member of the junior varsity team entered the coaches' office before the game and asked Donlea for some tape. His right index finger was sprained, and he wanted to stabilize it by taping it to his middle finger. It is a modest request, and one that would be handled by a certified athletic trainer at most suburban high schools. But at Skyline, Donlea searches the room, unable to find any tape. The player is looking, too. They look through desks and cabinets, finding old newspapers and broken pencils. The player is in a corner, crouched, looking through the dust and cobwebs of a bottom cabinet. He pops his head out and holds up a half-used roll of dirty beige masking tape.

He is smiling and displaying the tape like a proud father holding a newborn in the delivery room.

"This'll work, coach," he says.

The Oakland Athletic League has produced some phenomenal athletes (basketball's Bill Russell and Gary Payton, baseball's Joe Morgan, Frank Robinson and Rickey Henderson), and there are those who believe Will Blackwell has the ability to ascend to that exalted pantheon.

Blackwell is a senior at Skyline, the ultimate big man on campus. He is a *Parade* All-America football player, a wide receiver with strong hands and uncommon elusiveness. One publication listed him as the thirteenth-best high school football player in the nation.

He is not cast in the typical wide-receiver mold. Blackwell is a fraction under six feet tall, and he weighs a sturdy 190 pounds. His legs cover forty yards in 4.5 seconds. He has bright eyes that dart with the speed of a squirrel's, a quick laugh, and a strong, jutting chin that is partially covered by whiskers. But whatever Blackwell is in repose changes when he is faced with competition. His movements on the football field combine strength with fluidity, and, when in motion, his body removes any doubts about size or strength. Desire wins out.

He can also play basketball. Blackwell is in uniform for the Hogan game, the first time this season he has been with the basketball team. His presence has elevated the intensity of the whole team, almost as if his teammates were waiting for his OK in order to get serious. He isn't supposed to be playing basketball, but he has suited up as a symbolic gesture. An ankle and heel injury limited him to six football games, yet he still managed more than 650 receiving yards. The injury was still healing, but he has promised to be back to full strength by the start of the OAL basketball season.

"Football's more of a natural thing for me, but I love basketball," Blackwell said. "I know what I can do in football, and I know if I stay healthy there's no question I can make it. It's automatic. Basketball's more intense, more pressure. It's fun for me, because I love that. It's talkin' and runnin' and gettin' in somebody's face."

Nearly every Division I football program in the nation has made an attempt to procure Blackwell's services for fall Saturdays. The recruiters arrive at his door or on the Skyline campus trumpeting their football programs and their universities with the earnestness and fervor of television evangelists selling salvation. Blackwell has two large manila envelopes in the trunk of his car, both filled with letters from college recruiters. At home, on 104th Street in the heart of East Oakland, in one of America's most dangerous neighborhoods, there is a laundry bag filled with more letters.

He has visited four college campuses, spending two nights at each in luxurious hotel rooms, sometimes suites. His mother went along on most of the trips. By the end of the high school football season, he had eliminated all but five schools: UCLA, USC, Arizona State, California and San Diego State. He leaves open the possibility that another school could enter the picture, but staying on the West Coast is a strict priority.

"I got a way to deal with the recruiters," he said. "You look 'em dead in the eye, and if they look away, they're making promises they can't keep. I had a few guys who never looked at me straight. That's when I knew I didn't want to go to their schools."

He says none of the schools has offered him any illegal inducements to gain his services. "I did wonder what would happen if I asked, though," he said, laughing.

Blackwell played varsity basketball as a sophomore at Skyline, but not varsity football. John Beam, Skyline's football coach, wanted Blackwell to move up from the junior varsity, but other factors prohibited it. The Blackwells—Will, his mother Stella, his younger brother Marcus and his sister Roshanda—lived in the Brookfield Village housing project at the time. Brookfield, like many of Oakland's public housing projects, is a dangerous place, a self-contained clot of violent crime. Will couldn't practice on Monday afternoons because he had to leave Skyline immediately after school and take the city bus to Brookfield Elementary School, where Marcus would be waiting for his big brother to walk him home. It was the only day of the week that Stella or Roshanda couldn't get there, and Marcus was not allowed to walk home alone. To play varsity, he had to attend every practice, but walking his brother home from school was a family obligation that superseded the pursuit of athletic dreams.

Blackwell has lived in Oakland since the seventh grade, when he moved from Arkansas after his parents divorced. His mother had family in nearby Richmond, and she wanted a new start. The Blackwells have lived in West Oakland and East Oakland and points in between. Will has been both a witness and a victim of violent crime. When he was a 10th grader at Skyline, he and some friends were sitting at a bus stop near MacArthur Boulevard in East Oakland, next to a church. A carload of students from another Oakland high school pulled up next to Blackwell and his friends.

"What school you guys go to?" they were asked.

"Skyline."

The car circled the block and returned to the bus stop. One of the passengers got out, pointed a gun at Blackwell and demanded his jacket.

He laughs about it now, saying he shouldn't have told them he went to Skyline, which carries connotations of privilege. He laughs for another reason, too: He has learned that guns and crime are an intrinsic part of growing up in Oakland.

When asked about the dangers of life in Oakland, Blackwell cocks his head to the side and says, "My family, they can handle themselves anywhere. Any neighborhood. I don't worry about that."

There is a supreme, fearless confidence inherent in everything Blackwell does—the way he moves, the things he says, the entire attitude. Right now, the world is his own private joke. He is always on stage, always performing. It is, in some ways, his duty as the school's reigning athletic king. He is impenetrable and invincible. The way his teammates treat him borders on reverence. He has it made, they say. He's got a way out.

When they first met, Donlea and Blackwell had a discussion about the basketball talent on the Skyline campus. Donlea was lamenting the high number of tremendous players who, because of problems with grades or the law, will never play at Skyline.

"There's a whole Division I team on campus," Donlea said, "and it's too bad I haven't met any of them."

And he asked Blackwell: "Who do you think is the best basketball player at this school?"

Blackwell tilted his head to the side and looked at Donlea. He waited, staring at his coach with a wincing expression of exaggerated puzzlement. Donlea stared back, awaiting an answer.

"You serious?" Blackwell finally asked.

"Yeah. I just want your opinion."

"Coach, you ain't been around much, have you? You're lookin' at the best basketball player in this school. It's me—just wait and see."

Before the game against Hogan, Blackwell strode through the locker room with his home-white shorts pulled up almost to his chest, in direct and intentional contradiction of the prevalent style. In fact, in the world of low-riding jeans (underwear visible) and baggy basketball trunks, the high-ride look Blackwell was sporting was probably the quickest way to become a social pariah.

"You can't play basketball if your shorts are hanging off yo' ass," he said. "I see some guys, they be runnin' up the court worrying more about their shorts than the game."

David Strom, Skyline's point guard, is the only white player in the Oakland Athletic League. He is an exceptional student (a 3.6 grade-point average, 1280 on the SAT), but basketball is central to his life. It is a black game, in a black city, yet Strom has managed to survive, and excel, through the sheer force of his will. He is 5-foot-11, of slight build, with a close-cut burr haircut. He is in every way a survivor. He plays whenever and wherever he can ("He plays more than anybody in California, and that's not an exaggeration," says a former coach), and he seems to have a schedule of every open gym in the East Bay embedded in his mind.

Strom has missed the last four games with a severe ankle sprain, but the pain hasn't bothered him as much as the inactivity. Skyline has lost three of the four games Strom has missed, and nobody confused the convergence of those two facts with mere coincidence. He was, in many ways, the team's conscience.

"I'm not used to not playing," he said. "I always play. I can't sit around."

It is nearing game time, and Strom has finished taping his ankle, with tape he has purchased himself. Asked if he needed help with his ankle, he said, "No. I'm going to have to learn how to do it myself, anyway." He has backed away from the noise and restlessness of his teammates. He sat down and closed his eyes. He told himself to be calm and focused, to give his best and leave nothing behind. He told himself to do justice to himself and this game, this addictive game that has embedded itself in the marrow of his being. He opened his eyes, got up and took his spot at the front of the line.

Nobody paid much attention to Jason Wright as he prepared himself to play. He was off to the side, adjusting his shorts—thirty-eight waist on his 6-foot-3, 170-pound body—for the perfect low-ride, funk-and-dunk look. He was sporting new Nikes, too, and he wore tennis-style socks that stopped at the top of his shoes, giving the impression that he wore no socks at all.

There is no mirror anywhere, so Wright had to rely on his own judgment. He adjusted his shorts, then shook his hips to make sure the waistband was tight enough to keep his pants from falling down. It is a fine line, because the objective is to keep the shorts low on the hips, and at the same time be able to run and jump and dive for a loose ball without worrying about losing vital coverage.

When he finished, when everything—shoes, socks, shorts, white undershirt, uniform top and warmup top—was socially acceptable, Wright joined his teammates near the door that connected the locker room to the gym entrance. He moved with acute slowness, stopping every couple of steps to readjust his waistband. He began talking to his teammates, telling them what he was going to do that night.

"Man, J Wright, you sure you're all ready?" asked senior Darren Albert, one of Skyline's starting guards.

Jason nodded quickly, smiling. He and Blackwell went back and forth, jawing at each other, Blackwell telling Wright in no uncertain terms that he would school him on the court once his foot heals. Blackwell stayed on him, criticizing him and teasing him, because he thought it was the only way to bring out the best in Jason Wright.

A junior with immense physical talent—he was dunking with two hands as a 5-foot-10 sophomore—Wright was a potential heir to Blackwell's throne. Wright had grown five inches in the past eight months. Along with his jumping ability—his "hops"—and his left-handed jump shot, Wright had the kind of talent that could earn him a Division I scholarship.

But Wright wasn't getting it. He was lost in Donlea's offensive system. He felt like an automated player, a robot who ran from spot to spot on the floor for no discernible reason. He couldn't comprehend exactly what this offense—called "Brown"—was meant to accomplish. To him, basketball was a celebration of athletic ability—fast, free-wheeling and, above all, fun. So far, his junior season has been none of the three.

"I'm trying to stay with it," Wright said. "I just don't know. I don't think coach knows what I can do, and what other guys can do. I mean, you see me at the playground, then you see me out here? Man, ain't no comparison. I ain't the same guy."

Eric Govan pulled his uniform out of his backpack, which had the words "Go-Go Juice" written on it in thick black felt-tip. He pulled out a headset and tape player, slapped a rap tape inside and began the process of getting ready. He dressed quickly, and when he was finished he began to work on his hair. Govan, a senior forward, is half black and half Hispanic, and his hair—thick, dark and big on top—dominates his appearance.

This was something of a pregame ritual for Govan. He removed the headset and pulled the hair up from the temples with both hands. His head is neatly shaved on both sides to just above the ear, then explodes into a mushroom-cloud riot on top. He stood and pulled it, as if trying to yank it out by its roots. He bent forward, finger-teasing it out over the front of his forehead. The idea was to make it stick up as high as possible. When he felt that that had been accomplished, Govan put the headset back on and started jumping up and down, over and over, to get his legs ready for the game ahead.

He shifted his head back and forth to the beat of the hard-bass tunes emanating from the headset. Occasionally he stopped jumping to lift his arms and give an open-palm hip-hop gyration. The overriding effect was that everything—the hair tease, the jumping, the dancing—was one fluid, constant motion, all done to the same rhythm. Sometimes Govan couldn't help himself; sometimes the music was just too good to ignore.

Eric Govan, at 6-foot-3, was a player. A step too slow to play in the backcourt and a few inches too short to play inside, he nonetheless managed to do both. He had a lithium-light touch from the outside and his post-up moves were unparalleled in the Oakland Athletic League. Strong and smart on the court, he was the son of a coach who had taught his son well.

Bryant Johnson roamed the room, the gentle swish of his vinyl warmup pants following him as he walked and talked. He spoke in an italicized blur, which is exactly how he plays the game. His clothes hung loosely on his thin, whiplike frame. The words spilled out in a mad rush.

"Got to do it, fellas," he said. "We *gotta* do it. Gotta teach those fools somethin'. Just *got* to."

Earlier in the week, several Skyline players sat in the bleachers before practice and argued over who attended the toughest junior high school. Naturally, each player thought his was the toughest.

Johnson said there was no doubt; the winner had to be his junior high, King Estates.

Johnson stood in front of his teammates, punctuating his words with his hands, stopping for affect at the appropriate moments. His head bobbed back and forth, as if dodging invisible punches. His energy level was unparalleled. He was always smiling, always talking, always at the top of his game.

"Man, King was the toughest by far," Johnson said. "If there wasn't a fight going on at King, something was *wrong*. And King had the best dice games. Nobody's close. *Nobody*. The security guards used to roll with us; *that's* how deep it was."

He stopped and smiled. He had most of his audience doubled over in laughter. The case was made. Whether they believed it or not, Johnson's presentation closed the argument. King was the toughest.

Johnson was fifteen years old, the youngest player on the team. One of his nicknames is "Midnight," a reference to his skin color. A junior, his game and his appearance had evoked comparisons to Gary Payton by the time he was in the eighth grade. Nobody who saw him play could name a faster player—at any level—from baseline to baseline. He expressed himself on the court with the same loose, imaginative style that marked his conversation. Guarding him in the open court seemed to be a physical impossibility, and his passes—behind the back, over the head, from any angle imaginable—were as implausible as they were brilliant. His game impressed spectators and sometimes inspired the awe of his teammates. It also had a tendency to drive Donlea nuts.

The junior varsity's game against Hogan was almost over. The restless energy in the locker room was building, taking on a weight and volume that made it nearly tangible. One player jumped up and touched one of the light fixtures that hung from the ceiling. The fluorescent tube, already burned out, tilted from horizontal to vertical and dropped to the floor like a felled tree. Shards of paper-thin glass flew in all directions. Johnson and sophomore guard Rod Ponder, neither of whom were responsible, raced into the janitor's office and grabbed a broom and a dustpan. Within seconds, the mess was gone and the junior varsity players began to filter in.

Donlea walked into the frigid locker room and looked over his team. The players were lined up with Strom at the front. They clapped out a staccato rhythm and punctuated it with the sounds of the rap music that was so much a part of their lives. Donlea walked down the line, patting each player on the back.

Donlea believed in motivation through preparation. Before every game to this point, he had stood before his team and hit them with a litany of technical points. He discussed defenses (31, 13, 21, the Up press, Down press) and variations of the Brown offense (B-Moe, D-Brown, Peanut Butter). Many of the players grew anxious as the talks progressed, especially when the talk cut their warmup time short. Now the players stood before him, clapping and waiting for him to begin. He walked back to the front of the line.

"Let's go," he said and pointed out the door.

They jogged onto the court, the bounce of a single basketball resonating through the building. The gym was nearly empty. Hogan was represented by fewer than ten spectators. There were no cheerleaders. Two police officers leaned against the wall, and three campus security guards kept a lonely vigil at the gym's entrance. Two Skyline students, both players who were academically ineligible, had been recruited to keep the scorebook and the clock. In the corner of the bleachers, behind the Skyline bench, four or five young black men sat in a row, two of them rolling joints they would soon smoke in the unlit lot behind the gym.

Donlea didn't even want his team to play this game. There were too many games in too short a period of time. He would have preferred to have his team alone in the gym to work on the things it would need to compete in the brutally tough OAL. He sat down on the bench and expected the worst.

It was no contest: Skyline ran Hogan ragged.

After the game, Donlea spoke privately with Strom. He asked Strom how the team's performance could change so drastically in such a short period of time.

"You didn't talk before the game," Strom said.

SKYLINE

CHAPTER ONE

SKYLINE HIGH SCHOOL IS AN INNER-CITY SCHOOL TUCKED INTO THE hills. It has a lacrosse team and a Jewish Student Union. It has National Merit scholars as well as students who bring guns to school and steal cars to sell later. It has students who are sometimes afraid to go to school and phenomenal athletes who battle cultural wars to reach 700 on the Scholastic Aptitude Test.

Even something as intrinsically American as the high school dance has vanished from the landscape at Skyline High. There are no dances held on campus. The parking lot is poorly lighted, and it is too difficult to monitor the school's entrances.

Of the six high schools in the Oakland Unified School District, Skyline is seen as the jewel, the lofty institution on the hill. Its test scores are significantly higher than the other five Oakland high schools, a greater percentage of its graduates more successful. Many of its students wind up in prestigious universities. Many others wind up in jail or on the streets.

Oakland is a city separated by elevation, with the wealthy and mostly white citizens living in the hill areas, and the mostly poor and mostly nonwhite living in the flatlands below. When Skyline High School opened its doors in 1961, it seemed a glorious idea. Here was the shining school on the hill, tucked away in the stately Monterey pines and the sturdy eucalyptus, providing a safe campus for the children of the wealthy residents of the Oakland hills. The campus rises up gently from Skyline Boulevard, with the football stadium at the bottom, the gym and outside basketball courts on the next level and the classrooms at the top. Behind the school is Redwood Regional Park, with its oak-studded hills and horse stables. It is a different world from the flatland neighborhoods, where some of the most prominent landmarks are Asian grocery stores and billboards pushing cigarettes and malt liquor.

Skyline was supposed to have altered the chemistry of the Oakland Unified School District, providing it with a cultural—and safe—oasis. It would attract the best teachers and the best students, making it essentially a publicly funded private school. The idea seemed perfect.

Not everyone, however, was thrilled with the notion of Skyline as a world apart. The National Association for the Advancement of Colored People took exception, calling Skyline a separate, unequal member of the Oakland Unified School District. The NAACP and other concerned black citizens felt that their children—the flatland children—should be given an equal chance to partake of Skyline's rich curriculum and safe hallways.

They railed against Skyline's gerrymandered boundaries, which managed to encompass all of the hills area and none of the flatlands. The boundaries ran north and south, in stark contrast to the boundaries of the other five high schools, which ran in east-west strips from San Francisco Bay to the hills. Skyline High School was created to be an educational oasis, unburdened by the city's problems.

William Patterson, the president of the NAACP in Oakland, said his organization challenged the boundaries out of a simple belief in fairness.

"They were taking the top socio-economic strata, the top configuration of the city, and putting it in one school," Patterson said. "They were taking the better families, and the more affluent families—both black as well as white—and separating them. That's not equal education."

Gradually, as the fight continued, Skyline High School changed. The process began with open enrollment, which allowed a select number of junior-high students to enroll in Skyline. It was not random selection, however, so the new students would more than likely be able to keep Skyline's standards high and its neighbors happy.

Then, on January 16, 1985, a citizen advisory group recommended changing Skyline's boundaries to include more students from the less affluent areas. The boundaries were changed in 1987, and white flight began in earnest. From 1989 to 1992, the percentage of white students at Skyline dropped from 41 percent to 19 percent.

During those three years, the Asian student population grew to 23 percent. White students comprise just 8 percent of the students in the Oakland Unified School District; 55 percent are black.

An official in the Oakland Unified School District said, "The boundary change was political, so Skyline will never be threatened by underenrollment when the number of school-aged kids in the hills decreases. There was a fair amount of controversy when the school was built. The boundaries were intentionally drawn to make sure Skyline had a white student body. It was an exclusive school to begin with.

"Now Skyline is the same as every other school. The other schools get much more negative publicity than Skyline. We have the idea that Skyline is one of the last safe places, and we're supposed to protect that idea. We don't want to scare off the remaining white students. There are a lot of problems up there. We go out of our way to protect Skyline and ignore the problems. Because of that, they've been allowed to fester. There's an inability of the staff to relate to the students. I know somebody who said they wanted to put together a workshop for Skyline on gender problems and racial problems and a whole bunch of other stuff. I told this to the person who does the workshops, and she said, 'Those people don't need an in-service day. They need a *retreat*.'

"People come in here and think Skyline is the last place you can go and be safe. I actually steer people away from there. All they seem to care about is getting all their scholarships and grants for the graduating class. They do send a lot of kids to college, but they ignore a lot of other kids."

Callers to a Skyline informational hotline in the fall of 1992 were invited to a meeting concerning enrollment in the school. The recording extended a special invitation to parents of students who were considering sending their children to a private school.

The buses that serve Oakland—called AC Transit—line up on Skyline Boulevard before school ends each afternoon. They line up in front of the $1.55 million house, sometimes blocking its circular driveway. When school ends, they begin the short procession through the school's gates and farther up the hill. The buses stop alongside the school, their flatland destinations flashing across the front like slogans on electronic foreheads. They wait for the Skyline

High students to board the appropriate bus that will take them down the hill to their homes.

Many of the children who grow up in the hills do not attend Skyline High School. They go to private schools such as Head Royce or Bishop O'Dowd, or to the excellent and white public schools in nearby Piedmont or over the hills in Orinda or Moraga.

A real-estate agent in the area said, "People are doing what they can to get out of sending their children there. They're either moving or they're sending their kids to the private schools. And they don't care about the cost; they'll pay whatever it takes."

Many of the wealthy who send their children to Skyline do so out of some sense of idealism and duty to the public-school system.

There are good teachers at Skyline, teachers who spend their own money and time to challenge and help their students. They are a big reason why many families in the flatlands, those who live outside Skyline's boundaries, use false addresses or the addresses of friends or family to maneuver their children into the school on the hill. There are also teachers who have become bitter as the school's demographics change their job description. (As one said, "They all want to become either basketball stars or rappers.") They are not qualified to be social workers or police officers or psychiatrists, yet their jobs have come to include many elements of those professions. They hold on, biding time until they qualify for the full pension, or they leave. Football players are warned to avoid a certain mathematics teacher with a proclivity for failing black athletes. Will Blackwell heeded the warning, but one of his friends didn't. The friend found himself ineligible for the second half of the season.

There is also the simple matter of resources. There are only six full-time counselors for Skyline's nearly 1,900 students. Students who falter or drop out are often forgotten. As in many of America's inner-city schools, the situation has become one of triage, where students who show little or no inclination toward improvement are discarded in favor of those with a fighting chance.

Skyline students say their school has become a magnet for drug dealers, who see the school on the hill as an easy market for their products.

"There's definitely more drugs here," said a student named Sean. "It's because dealers see Skyline as an easy mark. The administration isn't tough at all. They want to pretend it doesn't exist."

Another student said, "Weed's making a big comeback. Man, everybody smokin' weed. Hella kids be stoned in class."

Skyline is the melting-pot high school. The student body includes Hispanics, Cambodians, Thai, Laotians, Tongans, Samoans, American Indians, Chinese, Japanese, Koreans and Filipinos. Sometimes the pot boils.

A "Code Red" warning was issued on campus the day before the two-week Christmas break, less than a week after the basketball team defeated Hogan. All Pacific Islander and Asian students were asked to stay home. Word had spread that a series of violent incidents involving members of Tongan and Asian gangs would culminate on campus that afternoon. There were several unsettled scores, and the warning made it clear that nobody expected them to be settled diplomatically.

During lunch break four days earlier, a Tongan student insulted an Asian student. According to administration reports, there was a short argument. The Asian student then reached into his backpack, past the notebooks and textbooks, and produced a handgun. He pulled it out and trained it on the Tongan's chest.

"Go ahead and shoot me," the Tongan student said. "I ain't afraid to die."

Later that day, two Asian students were beaten up by two Tongans near the gymnasium. One of them left a trail of blood from the outside basketball courts, through the gym's entrance and into the coaches' office. Three days later, there were police cars all over the hill. The Tongans were supposed to be gathering below the school at Woodminster Park. They were armed and ready.

According to security personnel, two guns were confiscated from campus, the first time more than one gun was taken at Skyline in a single day. "There were hecka kids with hecka gats," one student said. Darren Albert walked into the bathroom at lunch just in time to see a student slip a .25-caliber revolver into his oversized pants.

"Was he a senior?" Albert was asked.

"No, just a kid playing OG," Albert said. ("OG"—a term popularized by rap artists—stands for "Original Gangsta." However, in Oakland OG sometimes stands for "Oakland Gangsta.")

Several students said Asian gang members were on campus that day. Their appearance and age—they wore trench coats, were heavily tattooed and obviously older than high-school age—gave them away. The efforts of the police and the security force changed whatever plans were in the works, and the campus remained quiet. Donlea arrived on campus around three in the afternoon, ready to run his teams through practice, but he found the campus deserted. Everyone had been sent home. One student said he heard the issue eventually was settled, but he didn't know where. The Asian student who flashed the gun at the Tongan did not return to the school.

Guns are as much a part of life in Oakland as basketball, and everyone seemed to know where to get one.

"I could take you to ten guys selling guns in the next fifteen minutes," said one Skyline basketball player who said he owned a handgun. "It ain't hard. It's as easy as walking into a store and buying candy. Maybe easier."

The player said the gun was for protection. "I don't really have to use my gun, but you never know when it might be five against two and you don't know who's got a gun," he said. "The chances are pretty good somebody does. It's not hard to get a gun. If you aren't afraid, you can get one. It's easy. I didn't have no problems. I've shot at people before, but I didn't hit nobody. At least I didn't think I did. You can get into a fight so easy. You can say the wrong thing, or maybe not even say anything. They might just say, 'Let's get that guy.' Then if somebody says, 'No, man, that's my partner,' you're all right. You have to watch the way you look at somebody. You can look like this—" he makes eye contact, then looks away. "But you can't look like this—" he makes eye contact and holds it. "You do that? They'll say, 'What the hell you lookin' at? What do you want?' and pretty soon it's a fight. Then something's happening. There's times when you have to have protection. Guns are everywhere. I wouldn't use it just in a fight, but if—like I said—five against two? Yeah, I might have to. I would never bring it up here to school because I don't need it here. I've got enough friends that I wouldn't need it up here. And if you don't have a gun, there's always a friend who does. I know there are guys who bring their guns to school, but that's not something I need to do."

Many Skyline teachers say they wouldn't send their own children to the school, and many of them mean it.

"I would never send my kids here," said one faculty member whose children attend private schools. "Five years ago? Maybe. Now? Never."

Oakland, with a population of 376,000, is one of the largest predominantly nonwhite cities in the United States. And Oakland, like most urban areas, is in trouble. The murder rate is one of the highest in the nation. Unemployment is high and getting higher. It has the most violent crimes per capita of any city in California, a decidedly violent state.

In 1992, Oakland's 175 murders set a record. Of the victims, nearly 80 percent were black males, and more than 50 percent of them didn't live to see their twenty-fifth birthday. Being a young black male in Oakland is a dangerous proposition.

Oakland's 175 murder victims were killed in drive-by shootings, in execution-style drug slayings and in domestic disturbances. Many were innocents. One man died in early 1993 when a stray bullet passed through his chest as he was standing in his kitchen, preparing dinner for his children.

Darren Albert, a member of the Skyline basketball team, is intimately familiar with the dangers of the streets. His family has been directly affected by violence. An introspective, bright young man, he is more likely than most to see the human side of the statistics.

"As it got close to breaking the murder record, I heard people saying, 'Yeah, we about to break the record, we about to break the record,'" Albert said. "It was like this was something to be proud of. They were talking about it like it was a good thing. I was like, 'Man, this is *life* we're talking about here. This is *death*.'"

Connie Lee Darden, a 24-year-old mother of two and a crack addict, was shot in the back as she stood on C Street in East Oakland, talking with a man in front of a house. It was November 29, a Sunday afternoon, a clear day typical of seven years of drought. Ordinarily, Connie Lee Darden would have warranted a two-paragraph brief in the back of *The Oakland Tribune*. If anyone had bothered to investigate, the obit might have mentioned that she was a straight-A student in junior high whose life veered off course when she fell in with the wrong crowd at Castlemont High School. There would have been the typical outcry for an end to the violence, followed by the grim, stark numbers of a record-breaking murder year.

But Connie Lee Darden was No. 166, *the* record-breaker. Her photograph made the next day's *San Francisco Chronicle*. In it, she is standing against a background of lights that appear to be part of a skyscraper. She looks healthy and neat, though her smile does seem a bit forced. Connie Lee Darden was, by all accounts, a harmless, lost soul. Police and relatives said the intended victim was the man with whom she was talking.

The three-year dropout rate for Oakland's public high schools hovers around 30 percent. There is easy—and big—money to be made on the streets, and many students find the rigors of education to be less than cost-effective.

"The educational system isn't delivering what it has in the past," says Patterson of the NAACP. "If we don't reduce the numbers in the streets, they will become the norm, and anything else will become the exception. I think that's what we have to guard against. We have to guard against the social conditions and economic conditions that foster the street life. We have to return to the biblical idea: The last shall be first and the first shall be last. We need to get some people off the bottom, or there becomes a certain hopelessness about everything we do."

Barry Krisberg, the executive director of the National Council on Crime and Delinquency, said, "For some, life on the streets *is* jail, or worse."

Moreover, the political, social and religious leaders who are striving to change Oakland's image find themselves battling an historic fascination with violence. Oakland is the birthplace of the Black Panthers and the Hell's Angels. The large, nationwide street gangs—the Crips and the Bloods—have been unable to establish a foothold in Oakland, because the local street-corner gangs are too strong.

"People talk about gangs, but in Oakland it's not Crips and

Bloods and everybody knows the difference," Will Blackwell said. "It's like this: I live on 104th. It goes for a long way. Somewhere on that street, somebody's sellin' drugs"—he's drawing with his finger on the floor of the Skyline gym, tracing an imaginary grid of East Oakland—"and they're sellin' 'em in this block, and in this block. You need to have people there who know you. They don't want somebody there they don't know. I can pretty much go anywhere, but it matters what time it is. Like, if I go walking through some neighborhood at midnight wearing blue like this, somebody's gonna come out and ask me what it is I want. If I mouth off, tell 'em it's none of their damned business, then it might start something. Then they'll get suspicious."

The independent neighborhood gangs have controlled the drug trade since Felix Mitchell, one of the most famous entrepreneurs in Oakland's history, started the 69th Avenue Mob, the city's first organized crime gang in the early 1970s. Mitchell dominated the East Bay's vast heroin trade from 1975 to 1983, accumulating obscene wealth in the process. Mitchell and most of his gang's leaders were arrested in 1983, and Mitchell was stabbed to death in the federal penitentiary in Leavenworth, Kansas, in the summer of 1986. The murder allegedly resulted when a $10 drug deal went bad.

Felix Mitchell saved his best for last. His funeral turned into an extravagant procession that shut the city down on August 19, 1986. It was a stroke of madness and genius, perfectly suited to a man who flaunted his lawlessness with an ostentatious boldness. It was also very much in keeping with Oakland tradition.

The motorcade—three white Rolls Royces, a fleet of new gray Cadillacs, countless stretch limousines—was headed by a black hearse carriage pulled by two dark horses. Inside the carriage, and visible from outside through spotless glass panels, was the ornate bronze coffin that held the body of Felix Mitchell.

Oakland city councilman Leo Bazile called the display "hero worship of a murdering thug." *The Oakland Tribune* railed against the procession. "What might Felix Mitchell have done with that extraordinary mind of his?" the *Tribune* editorialized. "Suppose he had stayed in school and become a lawyer, a real MBA or a physician. His opportunities could have been limitless. Think about that. Then look the other way."

Many Oakland residents, those on the outside of the power structure, considered Mitchell a local hero, a man who gave jobs to the downtrodden and provided a service no worse than the local liquor-shop owner. He was, during his reign, the city's most successful businessman.

The funeral procession began at the house of Eddie Mae Hester Mitchell—Felix's mother—on the 1600 block of Seminary in the heart of East Oakland. It traveled, at a slow-horse pace, eight miles on East 14th Street, Oakland's main east-west corridor and a top-producing section of the 69th Mob's expansive turf. Residents left their homes and businesses to stand in the street or on rooftops and view the magnificent spectacle. The city was utterly powerless to halt the proceedings; funeral processions do not require parade permits and therefore cannot be regulated. There was no city ordinance prohibiting horse-drawn carriages from meandering down city streets, no matter how slowly.

Felix Mitchell's funeral made *Time* magazine and the front page of *The Los Angeles Times*. Oakland had found an inglorious path to national headlines.

CHAPTER TWO

SHAWN DONLEA, SELF-DESCRIBED IDEALIST, STOOD IN THE PARKING LOT
outside the Skyline gymnasium and watched his team go through its
first practice. There were 105 players on the asphalt courts in the
parking lot, and each of them was convinced his name soon would
become an indispensable part of the local lore. Each believed his
name would be spoken on playgrounds from West Oakland to East
Oakland, and on every campus in the Oakland Athletic League.
Donlea's job, and his responsibility, was to decide which players
were right, and which were wrong. It was not something to be taken
lightly.

Basketball matters here, in Oakland and at Skyline. The game
has become a life-force in every inner city, its codes providing the
bylaws of a unique constitution. It is a game ruled by self-reliance,
in a place ruled by self-reliance. Basketball and music provide the
rhythm of the streets.

Donlea knew all of this, but only from a distance.

As he watched four full-court scrimmages, he was amazed and
slightly intimidated by the turnout. He had been hired less than two
weeks before, and what he knew about the players came almost by
accident. There was no written record of the previous season; just
an unreliable and ever-changing oral history.

He had three days. Three days to assess ability and cut two
teams down to manageable size. It was Thursday, and by Saturday
the tryout period would be complete. Donlea prided himself on his
ability to judge talent, but he was having trouble matching names
and faces. They were playing with six threadbare rubber basketballs, some of which bounced unevenly, some hysterically. He had to
judge them on the basis of their athletic ability alone, because there

is neither time nor resources for anything more involved than layup drills and a scrimmage. In three days, he will have to turn away more than seventy players.

"How do I organize this?" he wondered aloud.

It was a warm, indian-summer afternoon and the courts were a miasma of energetic bodies and intent faces. The first forty or so cuts would be easy, that much was clear from casual observation. The rest, as Donlea said, would be a bitch.

His eyes were suddenly drawn to the right, to the court nearest the football field. There was a breakaway in progress, and the reaction of the players watching from the sidelines, and the students leaning against the chain-link fence, caught Donlea's attention. The ball was stolen in the backcourt by a sinewy, shirtless young man wearing baggy red shorts. The volume went up steadily and evenly, an anticipatory ladder of noise, as the player advanced across half-court.

The player's left shoe was the last thing to leave the asphalt. He leaped high, pulling the ball back in his right hand. His mouth was wide open as he ripped the ball through the nylon cord. The pole rocked, the basket nodded back and forth violently; it appeared to be bowing out of respect.

The dunk was followed by the spontaneous sounds of the playground—staccato raps and chants emanating straight from the solar plexus. A dunk has occurred, and none of them go unnoticed.

The player ignored the reaction—he looked as if he was used to it—and headed back downcourt. Donlea, holding his clipboard, stopped him halfway.

"What's your name?" he asked.

They were skeptical of Donlea, and he knew that. He expected that. Here he was, a boyish white man who spoke in a decidedly suburban dialect, trying to teach them *their game*. He discussed lofty concepts, such as the practice-performance curve. His basketball knowledge was vast, but it was university-bred. To some of the players, Donlea's connect-the-dots approach might as well have been lacrosse. Donlea was a low-level assistant at the University of San Francisco the year before. Before that, while working toward his master's in sports psychology at the University of Iowa, he was a graduate assistant at tiny Cornell College. His only high school coaching experience came at Westside Preparatory, a small private school near Los Angeles.

Donlea had a vision, though, and it consumed him. He felt that athletes in inner-city high schools were sometimes cheated by low expectations. He thought players should be challenged to achieve at a high level, not simply allowed to rely on their athletic ability. The city game is flashy and free-wheeling, all dunks and blocked shots and trash talk, but Donlea's game was disciplined passes and precise angles. He believed he could merge the two philosophies: that his team could run and dunk *and* set screens and change defenses. His team could run an intricate offense without sacrificing athletic ability. That was the dream, the ideal, and Skyline High School would provide the laboratory for the experiment. He also knew one other important fact: It wouldn't be easy.

He didn't care about anything else, though, and he felt that would make it easier. He didn't care about money or status or else he wouldn't be here. He would coach both teams and make slightly more than $3,000. He drove his 1985 Volkswagen Golf back and forth every day from Mountain View, a 100-mile round trip. To pay his bills, he would work as a substitute teacher. Whether intentional or not, he had pared away all the excess layers of his life. He had no close friends in the area. He was left with basketball—two teams and a burning, defiant desire to make it all work.

"I don't want to teach," he said. "I just want to coach. It's the only thing I really want to do. Nobody in my family has ever questioned me. Nobody—my mom or my dad—has ever said, 'Shawn, why don't you get a real job?' "

"This is what he wants to do," said his father, Michael Donlea. "And we understand. He's lived on virtually nothing for a long time. He has not asked us for money, ever. I don't know how he lives."

Donlea interviewed at Skyline two weeks before the first practice, and the interview lasted less than 20 minutes. He walked into the coaches' office and met with the principal, athletic director Joe Panella and football coach John Beam. After a few cursory questions, Panella took Donlea out into the hallway and offered him the job.

It wasn't easy to find coaches in the Oakland Athletic League. Sometimes idealism gets lost in the practical realities of self-preservation. Donlea's predecessor lasted one year before leaving to coach in a suburban high school in a wealthy district. There are several former coaches on the faculty at Skyline; they left coaching because the danger and the low pay outweighed the satisfaction. They stayed on as teachers, though, and their presence on the faculty left no teaching openings, which only added to the difficulty of finding qualified coaches. It is a continuous and unfortunate cycle, and one that is not unique to Skyline High.

On the day of his interview, Donlea hung around and watched the outdoor pickup games in the physical education classes. He saw immediately that there was more talent in one gym class here than there had been in his entire high school.

Donlea's presence at Skyline was completely accidental. He didn't start out with the altruistic goal of coaching in an inner-city environment. He wanted to coach, pure and simple, and he went where the game took him.

"I never intended to go anyplace specifically, the inner city or whatever," he said. "I wanted to go somewhere I could teach basketball, and I was lucky I got to a place where there's so much talent. I also didn't want to go to a place where I had to hear, 'Coach, I've got to go to trombone practice, so I can't be there.' I've come to realize that if you want to coach, these kids right here, in the inner city, are the kids you've got to coach. It just happened right for me. Sometimes you end up where you should be through luck or by accident."

The last day of tryouts—Saturday, October 17—was an incredibly clear fall day. Below Skyline Boulevard, where the view of the San Francisco Bay Area drops out of a travel magazine, little kids and their parents piled out of the minivans and foreign sedans and into the Oakland Hills Tennis Club.

"Youth Tournament Parking," the sign said.

At the same time, the Skyline High School basketball team made its way farther up the hill, some in their own cars, some driven by their parents, most in city buses. It's not an easy trip, especially with the reduced Saturday bus schedule, but it's worth it. At the end, where the uphill climb ends, the chance to be part of Oakland's rich basketball heritage begins. In their minds, regardless of talent, they are the next Gary Payton, the next Bill Russell, the next Paul Silas.

They were inside the gym this time, and they worked out for more than two hours. It was like the outside practice, a ragged, harried tryout that looked more like a slightly organized free-for-all. Some of the 105 players had dropped out or failed to show up, but most were still around.

Donlea walked around the gym, making notations on a legal pad. He would occasionally stop a player and ask for information—name, year in school—and then either circle the name or cross it out. Afterward, he gathered his team at center court. They slouched and wandered, paying their coach the absolute minimum amount of attention. When Donlea dispensed with a few procedural formalities and began speaking of cutting the team, the wandering stopped. The circle around Donlea tightened and more than 80 pairs of eyes welded their gaze at the coach.

"One hundred and five kids tried out for this team. Thirty of you will make it, maybe thirty five. It's my job to decide which ones of you will be back on Monday. It's a hard job—real hard—and I'm anxious about it. Not all of you are going to make the team, and I'm sorry. I know how much this means to you, and I know some of you are going to be upset. I'm sorry; that's just the way it has to be."

Donlea went on to outline his attitude toward discipline and on-court behavior. There would be no taunting, no fighting, no arguing with officials. A basketball fundamentalist with a strong belief in the geometric precision of the game, Donlea's only exposure to the Skyline program was a videotape of one game from last season; he didn't like what he saw.

"I'm not going to put up with any of that wild-ass stuff," Donlea said. "I'm not going to tell you not to dunk, but if you think you're going to impress me with a dunk, you're wrong. How many of you guys can dunk? A lot, I know. We're going to respect our opponent, and we're not going to get in anybody's face. I looked at that tape from last year, and I couldn't believe it. You're not going to get away with that stuff this year. You're going to have to represent the school better."

Several of the players looked at each other and smirked. They had to look away, or up at the sheet-metal ceiling, to avoid the laughter that would come with further eye contact. After Donlea finished, one Skyline player looked to a friend and said, "Coach don't know Oakland."

He would learn, however, because there was no choice. He would learn a lot, and he would learn it in a hurry.

Donlea made out a three-by-five index card for each of the players. In many ways, the index cards had the final say. Donlea took them home and filed through them—back and forth, back and forth—making two piles, then three.

The index cards held information more vital than height, weight and vertical jump. In the middle of the card, near the top, was the student's name. Penciled in at the bottom left-hand corner was the student's grade-point average from the previous semester. Donlea's piles consisted of the eligible, the ineligible and the borderline cases. There are six grade checks over the course of a school year, and a GPA below 2.0 for any of the intervals would mean automatic ineligibility. Donlea would cut his team with one eye on the index cards.

"How do I do this?" he said. "I'm really uptight about it. I'm going to have to cut some kids who can really play. How do you look at these kids and say, 'Get your education, because you aren't going to make it?' I'm going to say that to them, over and over, but what reason do they have to believe it?

"I know I can judge talent, but I've got to cut over sixty kids in five days. I know how important basketball is to these kids. It's as important to them as football is to kids in Texas. We don't have 20,000 people in the stands; sometimes, we might not have any. But I always have to remember one thing: to these kids, it's everything."

The average GPA at Skyline for the 1991–92 school year was 2.44. For black male students, it was 1.91. The average black male student at Skyline was failing.

Donlea spent that Sunday going through the cards and reading the notations he had made during the tryout period. Some of the best players in the school had no chance of being academically eligible, but Donlea chose some of them anyway, knowing the first grade check was three days away. He chose thirty-five players to make up his varsity and junior varsity teams. After the grading period, twenty-three remained.

When Shawn Donlea was thirteen years old, he returned home from a weekend trip to his mother's house (his parents had divorced four years earlier) to find that his father had married a woman with three school-age daughters, all younger than Shawn. They were all there when he got home, in the house he and his father shared in Lompoc, California, a small town near Santa Barbara on the Pacific Coast.

His father's remarriage was a cataclysmic event, a drastic shift in the tectonic plates of his life. It formed him in a way that he is just beginning to understand. His father had been dating the woman for eight months; Shawn knew her but was provided with no advance warning about the marriage. He had gone before a judge when he was nine years old, at the time of the divorce, and had chosen to live with his father. Since then, it had been just the two of them.

"I suppose that was a big surprise for him," said Michael Donlea, chuckling. "He didn't expect that. He was used to it being just me and him. He used to be the only one here, and now he was just one-sixth of the whole thing."

Michael Donlea was the varsity basketball coach at Lompoc High School, and Shawn was a gym rat who grew up shooting around in the corner while his father ran practice.

But after his father remarried, Shawn rebelled. He began hanging around the rougher edges of the high school crowd, which meant dabbling in drugs—mostly marijuana—and taking a keen interest in petty crimes. Shawn was arrested for trespassing when he was thirteen. He and his friends broke into a house, and his friends were on their way out with some small items. Shawn said he never had the guts to steal anything; he was just along for the adventure.

He had to perform 200 hours of community service, and the division between him and his father grew. Shortly after his father's marriage they had it out physically, and Michael Donlea slapped a six-month detention on his son. His father took him to school and made him eat lunch in the wood-shop building, where Michael taught. They went home together and spent every waking hour together for six months.

"It got to the point where showering was enjoyable," Shawn said. "I took two or three showers a day, just because that was the only time I could be alone."

Academics and athletics were steady currents in Shawn's life, even when he was walking toward the edge. He was a 3.7 student and a starter on the basketball and baseball teams. Whatever their differences, he and his father retained the bond that was created on the hardwood floor of the Lompoc High gymnasium.

"My childhood isn't something I'm proud of, but it's made me a better, stronger human," Shawn said. "I'm better equipped to deal with the things I face now. I can relate somewhat to these kids. I went through some similar things, although in a different environment. I wouldn't be as effective as a teacher, advisor, mentor or counselor if it wasn't for that. I'm not happy about my past, but sometimes you just end up in a position you should be in, through no real planning. I think that's what happened with me. I've worked with psychiatric patients and substance abusers, and I think I can deal with their problems better after having had some myself."

Basketball as the father coached it at Lompoc High School was different from the basketball the son was coaching. Basketball in the father's world was two-handed chest passes with the thumbs-down follow through. It was layups off the backboard and structured offenses based on the age-old concept of pass and screen away.

Micheal Donlea was from Iowa, where farm boys played the game by an ordered set of rules. They were attentive and earnest and respectful. When he got to Lompoc High, it was filled with middle-class white kids whose parents worked in the Johns Manville lumber mill. But Lompoc changed. Black families moved into the area, along with Hispanic families and Asian families. Michael Donlea saw his game being played by a different set of rules. He had trouble relating to the new class of athlete at Lompoc High, so he gave up coaching.

He remembers the precise moment he decided to quit. His teams were disciplined and structured, and his practice schedule emphasized that point. They practiced at 6:30 every morning, before school, and again later in the afternoon. On Saturday, the team practiced from 7 A.M. to 9 A.M., so the players could have the rest of the day to themselves. Michael Donlea always stopped at a bakery on Saturday morning and brought doughnuts for his players to eat after practice.

"It was always, 'Thanks, coach,'" he said. "Then, in my last year, I passed out the doughnuts and a couple of kids asked, 'You mean I only get one doughnut?' That's when I said, 'No, thanks.' I didn't want to take their shit. I couldn't relate to them anymore. The kids' attitudes, the way they changed, I just didn't have the stomach for it."

Michael Donlea couldn't change with the game, and he didn't have the patience or the inclination to change the players who played it. The attitudes had changed, and Michael Donlea decided to let it change. Now his son was right there in the middle of it, taking some of his father's influence and some of his own.

"His values were rooted in Iowa, and when the game turned black, my father gave it up," Shawn said. "It's funny; I'm trying to do something he couldn't do."

At the beginning, he did it without a frame of reference or a clear sense of what pressures and distractions his players faced. During the second week of practice, several players arrived late for a Saturday morning practice. Some straggled in fifteen minutes late, some half an hour, and two were more than forty-five minutes late.

When they arrived, Donlea told them they would have to stay after practice and run sets of lines for every minute they were late. If a player was thirty minutes late, he would run for thirty minutes.

"I don't understand this," Donlea said as the players lined up to run. He set his stopwatch. "How can all of you be so late?"

Nobody answered. They kept running. About fifteen minutes into his thirty-five minutes of running, a junior varsity player named Kenneth Forward slowed as he neared Donlea.

"Coach, the bus was late. Saturdays, you never know. Sometimes they be on time, sometimes they be forty minutes late."

Donlea struggled to comprehend. Why didn't they tell him? He had yelled at them for being late. He had told them they would run as punishment. Still, nobody spoke up. Where Donlea came from, excuses are given almost by reflex. These guys had a great one— they were waiting for a bus, for heaven's sake—and yet they kept their mouths shut until asked.

Forward's words hit Donlea hard. Donlea stammered a bit and struggled to keep the players from noticing his surprise.

"Can't you guys get an earlier bus?" he asked. "Is it just a matter of getting up earlier?"

"I was out waitin' at 7:45," Jason Wright said. "That's forty-five minutes before practice. I only live ten minutes away."

Wright had arrived at practice at 9 A.M.. Donlea leaned against the gym wall. "It took him an hour and fifteen minutes to get to practice," he said as the players continued running. "What can I say to that? I've never taken a bus in my life. I've never had to."

He stopped them after about 20 minutes. He had made his point, and they had made theirs.

"Man," Donlea said later. "I thought I knew something about all this. I can see I'm going to learn a *lot* more."

Donlea was determined to do things differently at Skyline. He had heard about the problems of the previous year, when the team had essentially been run by two star players. Donlea wanted to make it perfectly clear that he was in charge of the team.

He prepared a four-page contract to be signed by each member of the team and a parent. The contract outlined the rules that would govern Skyline basketball, placing a heavy emphasis on representing your teammates and your school in a respectful, dignified manner.

Donlea didn't want to be perceived as soft. In his previous coaching experience, he had not been a screamer or a severe disciplinarian. But at Skyline, from the start, he wanted to make sure nobody took advantage of him.

Three days before Skyline's first game, Donlea grew enraged toward the end of a practice. He saw a lack of attentiveness from his team, and he made them line up against the wall. They would run until he blew the whistle, and then they would turn and run the other way. The only way a player could stop running was if he touched the wall before the whistle blew.

They ran and Donlea blew the whistle until one player remained—a player Donlea felt hadn't been hustling. The player would run to within three steps of the wall and the whistle would blow.

"Get going!" Donlea called out as the player dropped his head and turned.

When the player reached the baseline at the other end, Donlea blew the whistle again.

"Get going!"

Two or three other Skyline players took the court to run with their teammate. They urged him to continue, to be strong.

After three more whistles, the player stopped in the middle of the court and began to cry. Again Donlea blew the whisle.

"Get going!" he yelled. "Touch the wall!"

The player continued to the wall, where he collapsed. The other players looked at Donlea, surprised. Donlea ended practice quietly and walked to the office. He sat down and ran his hand through his hair. He had just begun to grow the Fu Manchu and goatee. The whiskers formed a faint dark frame around his mouth.

"Just last night I had a dream that I made some kid cry and I didn't care," Donlea said. "I just kept on him. He was crying and I was in his face, screaming at him. It didn't bother me at all. I've always been soft; I've always had to force myself to be tough. It's just not my nature to get in somebody's face. That dream, and then today this happens . . ."

Donlea stopped, his voice trailing off. He shook his head.

"This job's changing me," he said.

The bus was late arriving for the first real test of Shawn Donlea's social experiment. Donlea and the team boarded the yellow, straight-from-the-fifties bus in the early afternoon. The driver, a middle-aged black man wearing a baseball cap and a windbreaker, strode through the aisle, ignoring the frenetic chatter, and requested their attention.

"A-a-all right. Everybody listen up," the driver said. "You're going to hear this a lot over the next year. Everybody here know how to use the emergency exit? You lift up and push. Everybody here know how to operate a fire extinguisher? You aim it at the base of the fire and pull."

The bus whined its way down the hill, past downtown Oakland and across the San Francisco Bay Bridge. Donlea constantly checked his watch and shook his head in disgust. They would be lucky if they made it to San Francisco's Lowell High School by game time. This wasn't a great way to start. The bus weaved its way through city streets, past Golden Gate Park and into the parking lot of Lowell. Donlea rushed his players out of the bus and into the room that would serve as Skyline's locker room.

They sat in a skinny room with a comically tall ceiling, underneath a gymnasium in a school most of them couldn't have found on their own. The room was white, clinically white, like a fallout shelter in a sanitarium. After thirty-five practices and two organized scrimmages, the Skyline Titans were ready to play their first game. What would take place over the next two hours would say a lot about them, and what would take place over the next five months would define them. In high school, in Oakland, it was as simple as that. Being a Skyline Titan would become a big part of their identity.

The rankings of Northern California high school basketball teams came out that day, and four Oakland Athletic League teams were in the top twenty. McClymonds, Fremont, Castlemont and Oakland High were ranked. Skyline didn't earn so much as honorable mention. Donlea liked that, liked the feeling of being an underdog, and he used that as motivation as his team prepared for its first game.

"Nobody thinks we're going to do anything," Donlea said. He paused and paced for effect. He stopped and looked into their faces. "Except us," he said. "And that's all that matters."

Darren Albert sat steel-straight, looking directly into Donlea's eyes and nodding slightly. His eyes were fixed in a meditative stare, his mind racing to keep up with the flood of instruction. This was Albert's senior season, and it meant a lot to him because it almost didn't happen.

Eric Oakley sat transfixed, a look of growing disdain rising in his eyes. Oakley's demeanor gave the impression that the world was a joke that only he understood. That changed when it came to basketball. He played it with a fierce aggressiveness, as if every game stood a chance of being his last. The game brought to the surface everything that boiled within him. Oakley couldn't relax. He simply wouldn't allow it. On this day, minutes away from the first game of the season, his hands were balled into fists. He listened. He was ready.

Donlea's talk was simple, direct—and long. They were late to begin with—the Lowell High players were on the court when the Titans arrived—and now Donlea embarked on a treatise about defense: how it should be played, how important it was to their success.

"That's what we're all about here," Donlea said. "How we play defense will tell us how far we can go."

The squeaking of shoes and pounding of basketballs on the floor above echoed in the room. The buzzer sounded once, then again, as somebody upstairs tried to get the attention of the team in the room below. Still, Donlea talked. The players fidgeted.

Eric Govan stood and bent forward, shaking his hair out. Satisfied that the hair had reached its optimum dishevelment, he began jumping up and down, over and over. Donlea continued to talk, the nervousness tumbling through the words. He glanced at his notes occasionally and told them to run the Brown offense, stay in the Up press and work for the good shot. None of the words appeared to be sinking in.

"Gotta go, coach," said Govan, still jumping. "Gotta play."

Donlea looked at his watch, then called them together. They each extended a hand, one atop the other. On a count of three, they bellowed their school's name and lined up.

They began a rhythmic, staccato clapping. The atmosphere became intense, important. The noise got louder, still louder, bouncing violently off the white walls, closing them in. Beads of sweat appeared on Oakley's forehead. Bursts of invective filled the space between claps.

Jason Wright stepped out of line, his arms gyrating at his sides. The noise gradually subsided.

"Man, I've got to take a leak," Wright said.

The clapping stopped.

"Aw, man, J," Bryant Johnson said. "You messed the *feelin'* up. We had a *feelin'* going . . . Ain't no feelin' no mo'."

Wright left and returned seconds later, smiling sheepishly. They walked up the stairs and into the gym, their clapping back in rhythm, the *feelin'* back. No more than kids, they wore the looks of hard men—men about to conduct some serious business.

Some Lowell students had filed over from their lockers to get a look at the opponent. The students stood near the doorway, about ten of them, and moved away quickly when it became clear that the Titans wouldn't allow their path to be disturbed.

One of them looked out onto the floor, where the Lowell players were shooting around. Then he looked back at the Skyline players as they clapped and chanted and got in each others' faces.

The Lowell student turned to a man standing next to him.

"We're screwed," he said.

The first test for Donlea's grand experiment ended in an 18-point Skyline win. It wasn't flawless or smooth—frankly, Lowell was not a good team—but Donlea saw enough to be encouraged. He also saw a little of the reality he would face every time his team played somebody in a different-colored uniform. There was trash talk and a few high elbows. Oakley leveled a Lowell player who made the mistake of setting a screen on Oakley. The referees missed it, somehow, or else they were too stunned by the flagrant audacity to make the call.

"Eric, come on, be cool," Donlea said during a timeout. "Relax out there."

"I can't relax, coach. That ain't me."

"I admire your seriousness, but you've got to keep it together out there."

Oakley looked up at Donlea and wiped the sweat off his face with his warmup jersey. Donlea walked away, shaking his head and smiling to himself. As Donlea turned his back, Oakley rolled his eyes and laughed.

Skyline entered the second game of the St. Patrick's Tournament with three wins, no losses and a growing feeling of invincibility. It was the third day of December. They rode through the rain and the fog, over the Oakland hills, through the towns of Orinda and Lafayette and Walnut Creek and Concord, over the Benicia Bridge and into Vallejo. The players were crammed into four cars: one driven by Donlea, two driven by players and one driven by Maggie Wimberly, the mother of starting center Nick Wimberly.

Bus service is not provided for Oakland teams playing in tournaments. The trip is more than 30 miles each way. Donlea, who did not have automobile insurance, had four players in his two-door Volkswagen.

Skyline's opponent that night, Sonoma Valley High, pulled into the parking lot in a chartered tour bus, with high-back cushioned seats and air conditioning. The players wore white button-down shirts, ties, matching navy-blue blazers and dress shoes. They carried their uniforms, which included custom warmup suits, in gym bags emblazoned with the school's green-and-white logo.

The Skyline players wore blue jeans or sweat pants. Some traveled to the game in their uniforms. They carried their belongings in store-bought gym bags or paper grocery sacks.

Sonoma Valley's team had one black player, 6-foot-6 junior Bobby Alexander. Donlea had seen Sonoma Valley play in an earlier game, and he wasn't impressed.

"I think it's going to be a rout," he said. "I don't see how they can stay with us. I would never let the kids know I feel that way, though. I just can't see it being close. That big kid's way too soft."

As the players sat in the locker room, after they had finished lacing up their shoes and removing their jewelry, Donlea told them not to be overconfident.

"This is a good team you're playing," he said. He pointed to a sign above the lockers. "See that sign?" The players turned around. "That sign's true. If you believe something, it can happen. Don't give them reason to believe tonight. If you let them *believe* they can beat you, they will. They're a good team."

"Yeah, but they ain't never seen petrol," Bryant Johnson said.

"One more thing," Donlea said, lowering his voice and drawing the team closer together. "We won't get one call tonight. Not one. Don't ask me why, just trust me. Maybe after we get to know each other better, I'll tell you why. I don't have enough time to get into it now."

Some of the players nodded, others looked at Donlea with looks of puzzlement. Donlea had seen the two referees who would call the game, and they were both white.

"Just trust me on this," he told the team. "Keep your cool tonight."

During the pregame introductions, Sonoma's cheerleaders formed a tunnel for their players. The Sonoma rooting section was practically filled. The Skyline rooting section consisted of Maggie Wimberly and two junior varsity players who were there to tape the game for Donlea.

Bobby Alexander played like he had something to prove to the guys from Oakland. He was *amped*. He had six rebounds and eight points in the first quarter.

"I missed the boat on that kid," Donlea said. "He isn't playing soft tonight. If I was still at USF, I'd recruit that kid in a minute."

Sonoma played zone defense from the start, with Alexander at the point, and Skyline wasn't ready for it. Donlea didn't expect to see any zones in the OAL, so he had spent just one day—the day before the Sonoma game—working on a zone offense. It wasn't working.

David Strom sprained his ankle in the second half. He remained in the game, though, constantly pulling his shoe laces tighter. He limped through the rest of the game, and it was clear he was hurt. The injury would keep him out for four games.

"They're tired," the Sonoma coach told his team before the fourth quarter. "They're tired and we're not. We can win. We will win. But one thing: Respect. Respect those kids over there. They can come back. Every single one of you, respect."

Skyline stayed close, but Alexander finished it off with a thunderous baseline dunk in the final minute. It left Nick Wimberly on the floor.

"Oh, man, that dude ripped on Nick," Strom said. "I can't believe he ripped on Nick like that."

It was drop-dead quiet in the locker room afterward. The first loss is always the hardest, especially under these circumstances. Donlea was fuming when he came into the locker room after the game. He tossed his clipboard against the forest-green lockers.

"We lost, and that's OK," he said. "We're gonna lose games. Not many, but we'll lose. There won't be one team in the state that goes through the season undefeated. But that's not why I'm pissed off. What really pissed me off is what happened at the end of the game."

One of the Skyline players committed a foul near the Sonoma cheering section. There was a scramble for a loose ball, and the Skyline player landed on a Sonoma player. As the Skyline player got up, he reached out and flicked up the skirt of a Sonoma cheerleader.

"That's no class," Donlea said. "No class *at all!* If you guys have no class, and that's the way it's going to be around here, I won't be around. I won't put up with stuff like that. That's not what we're about on this team."

Donlea began walking out of the room, running his hands through his hair. He stopped and returned.

"They beat us tonight, but they not only beat you, they beat me. I simply did not prepare you to play this game. I also made some moves that were too late. But when you fail, you learn from it. I learned something tonight, I'll tell you that. I should have put Jason on the big guy earlier, and you should have been prepared to play against a zone defense. I didn't do it, and I apologize for that. They came out and played hard and took us out of everything we do. Hey, they beat us. That's all there is to it."

The players remained silent. Darren Albert and Strom were watching Donlea; most of the rest were looking down or pulling sweat pants over their uniforms. Donlea looked around the room, then turned his back and picked up his clipboard, rubbing off the frantic scribblings of the previous hour. He left the room to watch the beginning of the next game. The room was quiet, underground quiet, for a few seconds; then some of the players began talking about the game in a hushed tone. Somebody pulled out a tape and clicked it into a boom box that had been left in the corner. The music filled the empty space of the locker room, and most of the Skyline Titans began rapping along with Ice Cube's "It Was a Good Day."

The basketball team's roster is constantly subject to change. The grade checks create a transient population.

The second grade list of the basketball season came out the day of the Hogan game, eight games into the season. At Skyline, the school in Oakland everyone wants to attend, the school of the privileged elite, 731 of the school's 1,900 students came in with a grade-point average below 2.0. Sixty-seven students were at 0.00.

Two Skyline players, including Oakley, failed to make the cut. They were gone, their seasons finished, unless a grade change could be made in the next three days. Oakley tried on Friday but couldn't pull it off. He turned in his uniform the next day.

A junior named Phil, a talented player with a polished game and a white-hot desire to play, met Donlea on the court minutes after the Hogan game. He handed Donlea a grade card and waited for the reaction. Phil had made the team after the tryout—hands down, no contest, start him at shooting guard and let him play—but his grades weren't there. Now they were.

Donlea looked over the card, then back at Phil. "You made it Phil, but it's close. Real close." It was a problem without a solid answer. If Phil is allowed to play, will it prod him to work harder in the classroom? Donlea wandered around as Phil waited patiently, impassively, wearing a leather pilot's cap and baggy jeans. He was a tough kid, the perfect player to replace Oakley. Donlea had talked about Phil a lot, about how he would make working with him a priority next season. Phil wanted to play, wanted it more than anything, but as he stood and waited for Donlea it became clear that he was too proud to plead.

"I'll let you know, Phil," Donlea said. "Give me a few minutes."

Phil waited. Donlea put away the basketballs, walked to the coaches' office, took two or three more looks at the grade card. It was late, the air outside was filled with a near-frozen mist. Phil stood outside the gym's entrance, his breath puffing white clouds into the air.

"Man, I'd really like to have him, but I don't know," Donlea said. "This kid can really play, but I feel like I'd be sacrificing everything I'm trying to accomplish. And I don't want to bring him in, start relying on him and then be let down in the middle of the league if he's ineligible again. I don't know. I need to think about it."

Donlea thought about it for about ten more minutes. "I just can't do it," he said. "He's not flying through his classes. I don't think it's fair to him, either. . . . No, I'm not going to do it. I can't."

He told Phil he would get back to him the next day. Phil took his grade card, folded it in half and slipped it into the back pocket of his low-slung jeans. The next afternoon, after school was out, Phil went straight to the coaches' office. Donlea was prepared.

"Philip, I think you need to concentrate on school," he said. "It wouldn't be right for me to let you play with these grades. School's more important. I'd love to have you. Get the grades up and come back. I'll be around next year, too."

Phil nodded slightly, his shoulders hunching almost imperceptibly. He walked back onto the asphalt courts, ran down a ball and started firing up 20-footers. He bent at the waist, rose up and followed through with the perfect amen flick of the wrist. Another student began retrieving the ball for him. One after another, they arched perfectly into the air and fell softly through the net. Four, five, six, they all ripped the nylon. He went about the task quickly, with a sullen determination, as if purging his system.

Donlea watched through the window of the coaches' office.

"He hasn't missed yet, has he?"

CHAPTER THREE

ON THE DAY AFTER CHRISTMAS, A BUS CARRYING THE SKYLINE basketball team left the hill headed for San Francisco's McAteer High at about the same time as a bus carrying the McAteer team left San Francisco headed for Skyline. Another mistake on the schedule—the third of the year—and another source of embarrassment for Donlea. He had the growing suspicion that he was beginning to look foolish in front of his team—the coach's ultimate fear— and he had no control over any of it.

Donlea felt as if he was traversing uncharted territory, as if Skyline had just started a basketball program. Nothing from the year before carried over, and so far nothing had made sense.

The schedule had been a particular source of misery for Donlea, but this went beyond inconvenience or annoyance. This was an especially bleak scene. The players stood in McAteer's vast, dirty, cold gymnasium on a Saturday afternoon, the day after Christmas. The bleachers had been removed, and the tartan floor—the remnant of some ill-conceived notion of the late 1970s—was littered with shoe-grabbing soda spills, old newspapers and cometlike streaks of chewing gum that emanated from a central pink gob.

Darren Albert stood in the doorway and looked across the floor. "This reminds me of that movie *The Principal*," he said.

Donlea sat on a wooden bench near what would have been the home team's side. His elbows were on his knees and he held his downturned head with both hands, like a basketball. He was the only supervising adult for twenty-four high school basketball players looking to play a game that apparently wasn't going to happen. The bus sat empty in the parking lot.

"What the hell do I do now?" Donlea asked. "This is so incredibly typical. It's perfect. Our schedule's been wrong all season—this is the third time in eight games. Look at this shit."

Donlea left the gym with sophomore guard Rod Ponder. They walked to a pay phone, where Ponder tried to call home to tell a family member to drive to Skyline and inform the McAteer coach of the situation. There was no answer.

When Donlea returned, Will Blackwell asked him, "What are we gonna do, coach? We gonna play or what? 'Cause right now, this seems like a big waste of time."

"I don't know, I don't know," Donlea said. "We can't do much of anything now, so let's just wait it out."

McAteer's bus returned to the school about forty-five minutes later. The game had been scheduled to start at three o'clock, but it was already after four. Donlea and the McAteer coach huddled in the corner, with Donlea apologizing profusely without volunteering to take the blame. McAteer's coach went downstairs to his office. He wouldn't promise anything, but he thought he could find two referees who didn't have anything better to do on the day after Christmas.

About twenty minutes later, two elderly men wearing referees' uniforms walked in the door. One was tall and overweight, his stomach drooping like fluid over the belt of his too-tight pants. The other was fit and trim, but clearly much older. They were serious, all business, and they peeled off their standard-issue officials' jackets as soon as they entered the gym.

"Ten minutes, gentlemen," one of them said. "We'll get started in ten minutes."

As the teams met at center court for the tip, the older official bounced the ball twice, held it up to the light and then tucked it under his left arm. He stood slightly stooped and presented his ground rules in a terse rhythm, his rough, grainy voice echoing off the walls.

"If you plan on doin' any mouthing off, you got the wrong guy today," he said, turning from the center circle to meet each set of eyes. "I've been doing this for sixty years, and you can't show me anything I haven't already seen."

"Sixty years?" Govan asked him.

"Yes, sir—sixty years. I'm eighty-three years old, so don't give me any guff. I stopped takin' it a long time ago."

• • •

The first half wasn't a contest. Strom, playing at close to full speed for the first time in two weeks, met no resistance on his way to the basket. Blackwell and Albert ran the wings and ended up with easy baskets. Skyline led by 10 at halftime.

Donlea thought he was watching his team waste its time. They were running down the court, getting easy baskets against a team that didn't play defense. He knew they could do that. Now he wanted to see if they could play a structured, evenly paced game. As he told them what he wanted, Strom silently rolled his eyes. Govan shook his head and laughed.

"Let's blow 'em out, coach," Blackwell said.

"We will. We will," Donlea said. "That's what I want, too. But I want you to run the offense. Blow 'em out with the offense."

Donlea provided the second-half soundtrack, repeating the same phrase over and over. Strom would dribble toward the free-throw line. *"Set it up."* Jason Wright would grab a rebound and look deep for Blackwell. *"Set it up."* Albert would drive toward the baseline. *"Set it up. Set it UP."*

During a timeout early in the fourth quarter, Blackwell dropped his body onto the bench and said under his breath, "This is Oakland, man. This ain't no setup kinda town."

It turned into a 46–44 loss. Jason Wright had two points. Nick Wimberly took two shots. They were out on the court running their offense instead of playing basketball. They were stagnant, their athletic ability reduced to a series of worthless passes and slow cuts to the basket. McAteer figured out the pattern and closed off the passing lanes. Skyline passed the ball on the perimeter, back and forth, side to side, as Donlea's frantic accompaniment bounced off the walls of the near-silent building.

Afterward, Strom could no longer contain his frustration. He felt shackled. He had lived for this season. This was his last chance to convince everybody that he could do it, that he could keep playing this game after high school. As a junior, he started at the point but was relegated to watching everybody else go one-on-one as the team concept disintegrated. He knew the junior season was the important one; now he was forced to make up for lost time. He wanted two things more than anything—to win and to keep playing. At this point, it was hard for him to see either happening.

"The last two years we beat that team by forty points," he said. "They aren't any better this year. I don't know about that offense we run. It just doesn't work. We should be runnin' and pressin', all game long."

They couldn't hide this or pretend it didn't happen. The next day the score would be in the *Tribune*—you could bet McAteer would call it in, because San Francisco schools relished every rare win over the Oakland schools. Every one of the Skyline players knew that the guys from Fremont High and Castlemont and Oakland High and McClymonds—especially McClymonds—would see the score and say the same three words: Skyline ain't shit.

Strom could hear those words as soon as the buzzer sounded. He slumped against a wall and shook his head, anger and confusion buzzing around in his head like runaway electrons. He'd worked so hard for this, and so long. Without basketball, he was just another smart white kid toting his books up the hill. With it, he was something different, a smart white kid who could hold his own. The difference was immeasurable. You could have the books; that was the easy part. For David Strom, the challenge came when he got the ball in his hands, a defender back and a teammate open on the wing.

Skyline ain't shit. They are the words every basketball player and coach in the flatlands loved to throw out. In the flatlands, they like nothing better than to see Skyline fall hard. In many ways, Skyline still pays for its past.

Donlea didn't know what to say after the game. He had challenged them beforehand, questioning whether they had the heart and the competitiveness to make it a good season. ("I wonder how much you guys want it," he had said. "Sometimes it seems that you really don't care as much as you should. That's one thing I wonder about when I look at each of you: How much do you want to compete? Do you want to compete or do you just want to score and play schoolyard basketball?") He stood in front of them now, partly exasperated, mostly embarrassed. And he still had a junior varsity game to coach.

"I don't know what to feel after that game," he said. "I don't believe we lost it—I still don't."

A heavy pause hung in the air. The players stared off into the distance. They had their own ideas as to why the game was lost, ideas they would share in private, but not now.

"Don't let this change anything," Donlea said. "We'll practice Monday and get it back together. Hang in there. We'll make it work."

There was nothing in Donlea's voice that made it seem as if he believed his own words. It was tired and reedy, and he spoke with his head turned away from his players. As he picked up his clipboard and walked back to the bench, Donlea stopped and looked at the junior varsity players. They were standing in a tight circle by the bench. Junior varsity player Mike Scates stood in the middle, urging his teammates to get it done.

"Poor JVs," Donlea said. "I've got nothing left for them, and look at that. They're always ready to play."

On the bus back to Oakland, Donlea stared out at the lights of San Francisco and asked himself the question he asked from the beginning: *What the hell am I doing here?* He felt as if he had suspended his entire life to pursue the idealist's dream, one that managed to merge his love for basketball and his social conscience, and now he was watching it slip through his fingers like dry sand. Was it worth it? Was he cut out for it?

The players congregated at the back of the bus, talking and laughing with only an occasional reference to the game. They felt they were blameless, and so did Donlea.

"Games like that make you doubt yourself," he said. "You wonder if you'll ever find the right profession. Am I taking away their talent? Why can't we come together? I'm here—" he spread his right hand far out to his side "—and they're way out there." He threw his left hand out to the side, like an umpire finishing a safe call. He pulled his hands together, meeting in the middle. "We need to be *here*. I don't know what to do except keep going. We can't learn something new now—they don't even know this offense, so how can I put in another one?"

It was Donlea's belief that he could have taken three people off the street and put them on the court with his two worst players and they still would have beaten McAteer.

"If we had no offense at all, if we just ran up and down the court and set a few screens here and there, we would have a better record than we have now. I've hindered them with that offense, but

I think we have to run it. We need something when we get to OAL. I just don't see the talent to say, 'OK, do it your way.' "

The next day at practice, Donlea held his first team meeting. Only six players arrived at the coaches' office on time, another troubling sign. Donlea sat before them, knowing he was opening himself up, making himself vulnerable before of a bunch of unforgiving teenagers. It didn't matter; it had reached that point.

Jason Wright, sitting in the corner, under the baseball section of the Wall of Fame, began the discussion. Extroverted and talkative on the court, Wright had followed along with Donlea quietly to this point. He was an unlikely spokesman, but he was also the team's most gifted player, and that made him the one most affected by Donlea's strictures.

"People be thinkin' that practice is like detention or something," Wright said. "It's like nobody wants to come because it's no fun. We need something to get us hyped up, to get goin'. It's just not as fun as we'd like it to be."

"You don't have fun playing basketball?"

"No, I have fun, coach. The games are fun, but the practices . . . I don't know."

"Yeah, we need to scrimmage for the last ten minutes of every practice," Eric Govan said. "The loser does some runnin'. We need to make it competitive. You lose? Put your head against the wall and get ready to run."

"We scrimmaged for fifty minutes the other day," Donlea said.

"Yeah," Govan said. "We whupped you around a little bit, too."

"No, nobody did anything to me. I hadn't played in years, and I was getting shots off. Nobody put a body on me, nobody knocked me around."

"Hey, guys want to play, coach," Wright said. "What if Darren gave you an elbow? You might bench him or somethin'."

"Look, I'm really worried about our emotion," Donlea said. "Why don't we get fired up before games? Why does it always feel dead? We don't seem to get going before a game like I think we should. Darren, what do you think?"

Albert, pacing around the room carrying a baseball bat, shrugged.

"You're a senior, Darren. Tell me what you think. And put that bat down. You're making me nervous—especially if you're mad at me."

Albert put the bat down. He riffled through a calendar from the Oakland Unified School District.

"I think you talk too much before the game," he said. "It's like studying for a big test: You prepare for it for so long, then you sit down and cram for hours the night before the test. Then you get in the test and you're not comfortable because there's too much going around your head. You talk so much before the game about running the offense, and what we should do. You stress it so much that we get out there and we don't take shots. Sometimes I'll take a shot and you'll be like, 'Why are we shooting so fast?' That's why I didn't shoot the whole third quarter the other day. I was just passing the ball. The last two games, I could have taken the man who was on me to the hole every time. Every time. But I didn't because you want us to run the offense."

The other players looked down at their feet, some nodding slightly. It was something they had wanted to say for weeks, and now that Albert had come out with it, they awaited the reaction.

Donlea, sitting on a desk, nodded and looked down. He started to say something, then stopped. He stared down at his feet as they swung in front of him.

"OK, I can take that," he said. "I'll take that into consideration. I think you might be right."

He looked back up, focusing his eyes on the entryway outside the office.

"You know, I was thinking this weekend: Am I taking away your athletic ability? And I think I have been. I just want it to come together—my philosophy and your ability."

"I'd like to say something," Govan said. "At halftime, I think you talk too much. We don't get enough shooting in. We don't warm up. We just go out there and it's time to go to the bench."

"Jason, what's your strength?" Donlea asked Wright.

"I don't know—help defense?"

There were a few muffled, grunting chuckles.

"I mean on offense," Donlea said.

"When I get warm, when I get in a groove, I can shoot. I don't think I shoot enough before games. I try to do as much shooting as I can, to get warm, but we never have enough time. Now I don't even think about shooting anymore."

David Strom, quiet throughout, raised his head.

"Hey, I tell all y'all to shoot the ball. Whenever you're open, shoot the ball."

Donlea shut his eyes and rubbed his forehead with his left hand, as if trying to massage away the whole scene. Nearly two months into the season, and they still didn't see him as an ally. To them, a structured offense was a noose gradually tightening around their necks. To him, it was the lifeblood of the game. At practice the week before, Nick Wimberly had passed up a two-foot turnaround. When Donlea asked him why he passed instead of shooting, Wimberly said, "I wasn't sure if that shot was in our offense."

"We're obviously not communicating very well, and that's my fault," Donlea said. "I want you guys to shoot the ball. I don't have a problem with Nick Wimberly shooting a seventeen-footer; that's no problem at all. I just see too much slippage here. Guys aren't showing up, guys are late, guys are going skiing. I just wonder how much we want it. Instead of coming together, like we have to, we seem to be fragmenting.

"There's too much giggling and joking around when I'm talking. I'm not teaching this because it makes me feel good. I'm doing it because it's what I think we need to do to compete."

There were no conclusions reached, no tidy ending in the aftermath of one of Skyline's most embarrassing losses ever. They didn't meet at center court as coach and kids and vow to bring it together, whatever the cost. They simply slipped out of the coaches' office and onto the court for another humorless practice.

But Donlea made a promise to himself. Before the next game, he wouldn't give them any instruction. He would take an emotional, purely visceral approach. He would fire them up, pump them full of energy and adrenaline and maybe a little anger. He would get in their faces, tell them some things they wanted to hear and some things they wouldn't. He would appeal to the Oakland in them.

"There's only one problem," Donlea said. "I'm not very good at that kind of thing."

"I think I've got something that'll fire them up. It's a complete lie, but I think it'll work."

It was three days after the McAteer debacle. Donlea and the players stood in the cold and rain waiting for the bus to take them to Moreau High School in Hayward. The bus never came, forcing twenty one players and Donlea—still without auto insurance—to pile into the five available cars and make the thirty-minute drive on their own.

Moreau is a Catholic high school located at the base of the Hayward hills. The campus is flanked on one side by a dairy ranch, where a group of Holsteins were grazing less than ten feet from the school's parking lot.

"Man, they got cows at they school," junior varsity center Kenneth Forward said.

Once inside the gymnasium, Darren Albert said, "It just feels so *clean* in here."

Two of Moreau's coaches scouted Skyline at McAteer. Donlea had noticed them at the time, figuring they wouldn't be too impressed with Skyline's performance. When he gathered the team before the game, he held to his promise not to overload his players with instruction. He spoke in a hushed, halting tone, as if the words were fighting to stay inside.

"Listen, I was in taking a piss after the McAteer game, and the Moreau coach was in there. He didn't see me, but he was talking to his buddy. He said, 'Too bad Skyline isn't any good this year. They're weak. They've only got one guy who can play, and I don't know if we'll schedule them next year.' This guy over there thinks you guys suck. I say we need to teach him something today."

The players came closer, first trying to hear the words, then trying to fathom them. They backed away in disbelief, their faces knotted, tight, grimacing. This was disrespect of the highest order, the kind that called for immediate and stern retribution. Only Strom seemed unperturbed; he sat on a bench, holding a ball and staring down at his feet. Will Blackwell stood up quickly.

"He said that?" Blackwell asked. "He said that about *us*?"

"We gotta serve," Nelson Burns said. "*Serve.*"

Afterward, after his players took the floor with a renewed sense of purpose, Donlea asked, "Do you think they bought it? I wasn't very convincing, was I?"

Donlea's only fear was that his players would confront Moreau's coach. And if they did? "Hey, welcome to the big city," Donlea answered.

The pregame inspiration simply gave an added edge to the Titans' message: they were out to prove something to Donlea more than anybody. They had been crying out for more freedom, and now they had a chance to show it was warranted. They were given license to go to the basket, to push the ball up the court and to talk a little shit. Darren Albert blew past his man to the basket the first three times he touched the ball. Jason Wright squared up and drilled three long jumpers. David Strom made fast breaks where none previously existed.

Moreau called a quick timeout barely three minutes into the game. Donlea, out of habit, reached under his seat and grabbed his clipboard and pen. Then, remembering his pregame pledge, he dropped the clipboard and kicked it back under the chair.

"No, I'm not gonna do it. It's gonna stay right there."

Skyline led by eleven at halftime. Blackwell picked up his fourth foul halfway through the third quarter. The Moreau coach called one of his players over to the sideline. Blackwell followed.

"He's got four," the coach said. "Take it to him."

Blackwell got in the player's face as he ran downcourt. The player backed away, stuttered his steps, nearly fell. Blackwell stayed in his face, his cadence of the court flowing with each step.

"You want some? You want some? No, you don't want none. You don't want none of what I got. You can't handle what I got."

In the last minute of the game, with Skyline safely ahead, Wright finished Moreau off with a two-handed breakaway slam that sent the Skyline bench into an impromptu dance session. It was the season's most genuine display of emotion. They had played their game, and it had worked. The Moreau coach glared at the Skyline players, and after the game, as the players shook hands, he approached Wright and told him, in Wright's words, "to grow up."

Donlea erupted.

"It hurts to lose! Yeah, it hurts!" he yelled across the floor. "If you don't want to play Oakland, don't schedule Oakland. You schedule an OAL team, you know what you're getting into. Don't come to my players and tell them how to act. That's bullshit. What is he— afraid for his little white boys?"

And thus began the transformation of Shawn Donlea.

In the locker room after the game, he stood before his players, his hair disheveled, and said, "I think we showed that coach a different team."

Donlea was buoyant. They were on their way. That anticipated meeting of his philosophy and the players' talent appeared to be gathering focus. Cohesion, a concept that was a blip on the radar screen just a week earlier, was nearing reality.

"This is what it's all about," he said. "That was a pretty big win for us. I see progress. Now we need to build on that. It might sound stupid, but I think we can win this thing. I really do."

He gave the players New Year's Eve and New Year's Day off. They would practice Saturday, a solid three-hour run to shake the holiday sluggishness and begin earnest preparation for the OAL season. Donlea left the locker room at Moreau with the impression that he had just seen his team's breakthrough game.

Donlea arrived at Skyline early on Saturday morning. He went for a run through the hills and spent an hour sitting in the office outlining his practice schedule. There was a lot he wanted to accomplish, and he wondered if he could squeeze it all into one session. Saturdays were typically days to cram; it was the only day that the varsity and junior varsity each had the gym to themselves.

The practice schedule was broken up into ten-minute segments. He wanted to implement a new zone offense, one that would allow for more creativity and take advantage of Govan's outside shooting. He wanted to put in a trapping zone press, one that would utilize Blackwell's quickness and incredibly quick hands. Donlea didn't like the idea of giving the players two days off, but he felt they deserved it. Now they would go back to work.

Just four varsity players, all guards, showed up—David Strom, Darren Albert, Rod Ponder and Nelson Burns. They spent the morning working on shooting drills and trying to stay busy. Donlea left his practice schedule on the bleachers, folded in half.

"It's unbelievable. It's supposed to be getting easier. Everything supposed to get better—practices, games, dealing with the kids. This is so discouraging. How does this happen?"

• • •

On Monday, Donlea held another team meeting, the second in a week. Again, he expressed doubts about whether his team would ever come together well enough to accomplish anything even resembling his goals. The final preseason game of the season was two days away, against Riordan of San Francisco, the fourth-ranked team in Northern California. "I'm tired of being jacked around," he said. He was ready to take a stand.

As the players slouched in the coaches' office, most of them oozing disinterest, Donlea went over his player contract, a four-page document that listed punishments and transgressions and also defined how he expected the players to represent their team and their school. Missing practice meant an automatic drop in status: a starter to the second team, a second teamer to the third team.

"Can anybody identify with the way I feel right now?" Donlea asked them. "Can you understand how I feel?"

"I understand you got a big drive up here," Blackwell said.

"Yeah, but even if I lived right down the street and I walked here. Still, I plan and work on things for you to get better. And that's how you get better: You practice. You prepare. You don't learn much in games. You really don't. You may think you can, and there are certain things you can learn in games and certain things I can learn about you in games, but I don't teach you anything in games. Practice is where it's done, and you may hate practice, tell me it's boring or it's not exciting, but you still got to do it. You've still got to practice."

Donlea held up the contract. "Are these rules unreasonable? You tell me."

Blackwell, who had missed Saturday's practice because he didn't have a ride, repeatedly stated that he hadn't signed the contract. In fact, because he came out late after football, he had never even seen it. Blackwell said he didn't have any problem with sitting out the game, but he didn't want to be held to the letter of some law he'd never read.

"Some people got to work, too," Blackwell said, referring to Damon Gardner and Nick Wimberly.

"If you have to work, if you have to work to support your family, then you have to make a decision," Donlea said. "If you can't do both, you're not doing yourself justice to one or the other. Is it possible for you to work and play basketball? If it isn't, and you try anyway, you're just going to hurt yourself and the team. And your employer. At some point, unless you can juggle it—and I know at your age juggling is not an easy thing to do—then you have to decide. I don't believe in special privileges."

The excuses ranged from work to a history project to a skiing trip ("Who would have thought I'd have to deal with a kid going skiing in a situation like this," Donlea said. "That's almost unbelievable.") Eric Govan was absent from the meeting because he was in court attempting to clear his name. Somebody, possibly a Skyline student, had been pulled over for driving erratically. The driver didn't have any identification, so he gave Govan's name. Govan had been in court twice attempting to get it straightened out. Everybody agreed that this was a legitimate excuse.

"All I want from you guys is to listen to how I feel, and how I'm sure David, Nelson, Rod and Darren feel. I think they feel a little abandoned. I mean, going skiing? That's not a legitimate excuse. That's a very questionable decision."

"Hey, my dad said we was going skiing, so we went skiing," the player said.

"Did you discuss it with him?" Donlea asked.

"Hey, he takin' me skiing, I appreciate it. He's doin' somethin' for me? I don't argue."

"Aren't you happy playing basketball? Doesn't that mean something to you?"

"Yes, but my family mean somethin' to me, too. All I know is, my dad say we goin' skiing, we goin' skiing."

"So there was no way you could get out of it? You couldn't say, 'Dad, look at the contract'?"

"Look, he wants to take me skiing, I'm going and I'm happy. That's all there is. He don't care about the contract. Basketball's more important than skiing, but my father's more important than basketball."

Donlea let it drop. He dismissed the players who had missed practice, leaving Strom, Albert, Ponder and Burns.

"We're looking at four players right now, and maybe a couple JV guys, if I don't at least discuss it with you guys," Donlea told them. "David, what do you think?"

Donlea couldn't figure Strom. He knew how much he loved basketball, and how much he played, but Donlea sensed something mildly, and quietly, subversive in Strom's attitude. Donlea wanted Strom's respect—in fact, he needed it—but he wasn't convinced he would ever get it. There were times when he felt threatened and intimidated by Strom's cerebral silence.

"I think that you have to realize that you're dealing with a group of inner-city kids who have never had any structure in their life," Strom said. "They've never been on a team with a coach who said, 'You have to be at practice now or you're not gonna play.' They've never had any discipline in their life. Then again, you had some chances early on, and once you didn't discipline them early on, that shook the confidence everyone had in you. They didn't think anything was going to happen to them. You know, I don't think there's no excuse. There's no excuse for showing up even five minutes late, ten minutes late—let alone missing practice. I think it might be too late for this year, because us seniors have had three coaches and we've had to adjust every year. I think for next year you need to try to be more consistent."

"I could argue that," Donlea said, "but I want to hear what you guys have to say."

"I ain't gonna say who should play," Darren Albert said. "That's your job; I'm not management, I'm just a player. But I will say this: I came to practice, and these guys came to practice. I don't see why the other guys should play."

Throughout the preseason, Donlea thought he was being tough, thought he was pushing them about as far as he could. He was constantly wary of pushing too far, of coming down too hard and losing them all at once. He found out they wanted to be pushed harder, much harder. If they wanted discipline and order, he'd accommodate them.

Donlea made his choice: the four players who practiced Saturday would play against state-ranked Riordan. It didn't matter that the four were guards. It didn't matter that the starting lineup would amount to a concession speech. Those four showed up, those four would play. Sophomore guard Mike Scates would come up from the junior varsity to complete the starting lineup.

The decision ran contrary to everything Donlea felt. He had complained about the team's weak preseason schedule and had looked at the Riordan game as the perfect test going into the OAL season. He knew his players would be sky-high to play the game; they had a history with Riordan. They also responded to challenges like the one presented by Jaha Wilson, Riordan's 6-foot-8 center. Wilson had committed to play at the University of Southern California, and he had received the kind of widespread media attention that made no-name kids from Oakland want to take him on.

"I've got to do this," Donlea said. "I've got to take a stand. They probably don't believe I'll do it. They're thinking, 'Oh, he's just bluffing. He might start those guys, but we'll be in after a minute or two.' I can tell by looking at them that that's what they expect me to do, but that's not going to happen. I'm going to go with those kids who showed up. Maybe this will get their attention, and they'll know I mean business."

It was just another test for the new guy. Donlea stood at the chalkboard in the visiting locker room and silently diagrammed his strategy for breaking Riordan's full-court press. His back was to the players, who sat waiting to see whether he would back down.

"Mike Scates, you're on Jaha to start," Donlea began, and the suspense was gone. The players looked at each other with raised eyebrows. Strom, standing against a side wall, smiled and nodded. Somebody yelled, "Stick 'im, Mike." Donlea continued without waiting for a response, as if it was perfectly normal for Mike Scates to come up from the junior varsity and guard an all-state player. Scates, intense and serious, sat looking at the chalkboard, not at all intimidated by the challenge ahead. Scates would be giving up eight inches and at least a hundred pounds to Wilson, but in his mind he wasn't giving up a thing. Donlea loved Mike Scates, because Mike Scates did what he had to do and asked no questions. By the time he got out on the floor, Scates would have himself fully convinced that he was the best player out there. *To hell with Jaha Wilson, I'm Mike Scates.* It was that attitude that had Donlea convinced that Mike Scates, with a better jump shot and some more muscle, could go a long way.

• • •

"That's a good move by coach," Will Blackwell said as he sat down on the bench. "But I want to repeat: I didn't sign no contract."

"It's like we playing in the six-foot and under league," Jason Wright said as Scates stood toe to toe with Wilson for the tip.

Wilson got the tip and set up on the left wing. He looked at Scates and immediately began clapping his hands, asking for the ball. He took a pass and headed for the middle like a pass-rushing defensive end. Scates got there first, though, and that startled Wilson. He tried to pick up his dribble, made contact with Scates and traveled.

Darren Albert took the ball to the basket, right at Wilson. He took off from the right side of the basket, with Wilson coming at him hard, and hung in the air long enough to switch hands and lay it in with the left. The Skyline bench erupted, the press was on, and Strom intercepted a pass and tossed in an eighteen-footer.

The players looked at each other on the bench. This just might happen. Riordan was confused, out of sorts. Wilson took the ball on the wing and Scates stuck like a barnacle on a rock. "Stick him, Mike! Stick him!" Jason Wright yelled from the bench. Wilson drove across the key and threw it away.

Blackwell stood up off the bench, turned toward the crowd and raised his hands high over his head in the universal pose of disbelief. "Is this happenin'? This is happenin'. Those little men are stickin' with those guys."

Donlea stood up and walked down the bench, clapping and exhorting his team. They responded, for perhaps the first time. "They're fired up to play this game," he said. "It kills me that I had to do this."

It was tied 9–9 when Nelson Burns drilled a three-pointer from the top of the key. Skyline led 12–9, and Riordan called time out. The Titans met their teammates halfway to midcourt. Wilson watched the Skyline team out of the corner of his eye. He appeared disinterested and bemused, as if this was all some silly joke. In the huddle, Donlea told them to keep the pressure on and keep firing. He told Albert to drive at Wilson. He told them they could do it.

After the team took the court, Donlea said, "This is going just like I thought. It'll be close for a while, then they'll wear us down."

After the time out, Wilson took over. He posted up or backed his way in, and Skyline couldn't stop him. Scates bounced off Wilson's broad body and kept bouncing back. Wilson would miss a two-footer, then get his own rebound and drop it in. Strom, Burns, Albert, Scates, Ponder—they all tired simultaneously. Skyline scored just two points in the second quarter and went to halftime trailing by twenty.

"Do you think they've got the message?" Donlea asked as he stood outside the visitor's locker room. "I don't want to lose them. I can't. I think we've got to go out there with our best guys and try to get some momentum for the league season."

He took a deep breath.

"Damn, this is a hard job," he said before opening the door to the locker room, where his team waited. He charged in and tossed his clipboard on the cement floor.

"Now do you guys think I'm serious? Do you think I'm fucking serious when I say I want you to come to practice? Damn right I'm serious. You think I wouldn't do it again—even in league? I would, I would in a second.

"If I didn't care about this team—if I thought this season was shot and it wasn't worth the trouble—I wouldn't do this. I wouldn't bother. I'd say, 'Screw it, let 'em play.' I'd say, 'Shit, I don't want this job anymore, so let's just play out the season.' But I don't feel that way. I think we've got something here, and I think you guys do, too. We need to get it together. I divided the team tonight, and now we've got to bring it together."

The clapping began. Donlea stuck out his hand and ten more piled on immediately. They were with him. They would end up losing by thirty to Riordan, but Donlea went after respect, and as Will Blackwell said, "He got some. He might not get any more, but he got some."

Donlea stopped Eric Govan before he got to the door. He held out his hand and they shook.

"E, don't lose me, man," Donlea said.

"You won't. You won't. You got me right here, coach."

Blackwell's left foot had been hurting more than he would volunteer. He strained ligaments in the ankle and his Achilles tendon during the fifth game of the football season, and it hadn't healed as quickly as expected. He could no longer drive to the basket and slam down a dunk. He had to jump off his right foot and he felt his lateral movement slipping. Privately, he was frightened that it would never heal, that he would never get his speed or agility back to where it was.

After a visit to a doctor, Blackwell decided to stop playing basketball. He enjoyed the game, even more than football, but he was staring at a full-ride scholarship for catching passes, not playing basketball. He walked into the coaches' office two days after the Riordan game and turned in his uniform.

"I understand, Will," Donlea told him. "I'd do the same thing if I was you."

"Can't mess with my future, coach," Blackwell said.

The OAL season was next, and Donlea didn't think they were prepared even with Blackwell, one of just three experienced seniors. Now he knew they weren't ready. After Blackwell left the room, Donlea shook his head and closed his eyes tightly. A pained smile crossed his face.

"What else could happen? What else?" He opened his eyes. "You know what? We may not win a game."

CHAPTER FOUR

THERE ARE NO NETS ON THE FOUR HOOPS AT ALLENDALE PARK, JUST red metal backboards and rims with no give. Each of the rims is bent from the dunking and hanging. It is a small neighborhood park on a narrow street lined with trees and California bungalow homes. It is mostly quiet. There is a broken-down dryer on the lawn of the house directly across the street, its door laid open like a tongue. As always, there is a game in progress.

The game is black. The people driving past in their cars are black. The people eating lunch on the lawn are black.

The music is black.

The talk is black.

The players are black. All except one.

David Strom is white. As obvious as the sun.

David Strom knows his place here. He keeps his mouth shut and plays. He plays hard and he plays to win. He doesn't give in. To give in is to show weakness. He knows where that can lead.

David Strom is about 5 feet 11 inches tall, with a crewcut and a long, skinny neck that seems to extend when he has the basketball. He does not look street-hip, and he doesn't try to. He has a thin blond mustache that is visible only at close range. He looks like something out of a Clair Bee novel, white even among white people.

He has something of a reputation here at the park. He kept coming back, for one thing. That meant a lot. He played here and at Brookdale and at the Oakland YMCA, and pretty soon he became one of the regulars. But not one of the guys.

Not everybody here likes him. He knows that. Not everybody wants him around. He knows that, too, because they tell him so.

He plays here because this is where the game is. The game isn't in the suburbs or the tony hills; not the game the way he wants to play it.

He is aware that he is different, but that feeling fades when the games start. Then he is the same. Everybody is the same when the ball's in play.

His legs bear the sinewy signs of hard work, of running up hills and down streets and—more than anything—back and forth on basketball courts. There is muscle and bone and not much more.

He is like something out of a movie, a skinny, left-handed white kid too stubborn to give in and too enamored of the game to give it up.

He doesn't see any great sociological meaning behind his presence on this court. This is his neighborhood. This is his game. He loves the game. It attached itself to him when he was in the eighth grade, and he attached back.

He used to show up here or at Brookdale with his ball and stand by himself, dribbling between his legs and behind his back, waiting. He'd see the looks on their faces. He'd ask the eternal question of the playground—"Anybody got winners?"—and he'd see the looks intensify.

"I could go on to a court without shooting and just stand there — and I could feel it," he says. "I would ask if someone had winners, and I could just feel that already they just *knew* I couldn't play. The way they'd look at me. I just loved to play and show them."

He likes it here, despite everything. He likes it here because it's real.

Brookdale was more intense, and the games were better. On the backrest of a green metal bench on the sideline at Brookdale, somebody had spray-painted "FUCK MC HAMMER" in perfect block letters, as if it were an advertisement. Hammer is from Oakland, but his music doesn't reach the boys at the park. To them, Hammer sold out, went white to make money.

There are fights on the playground, fights over issues as simple as the score. Strom has seen fights start over one disputed point. Big fights, too. He claims he has never been involved in a fight on the basketball court, and he is proud of that. It is difficult to believe, but he swears it's true, that he has always been able to walk away. He speaks of the problems he's experienced with a calm placidity, the lack of emotion serving as part of his armor.

He loves basketball, but he doesn't think it's worth fighting over.

"If I saw it was heading that way, I would just let it go. I never

understood how it could be that worthwhile to fight over a basketball game. All I want to do is play basketball."

Nothing has ever happened to him, so he is not afraid. It's mostly
overcoming perceptions. He lives only a couple of blocks away, so
to be afraid here would mean he would always be afraid.

"A couple of times, when it seemed like people were getting out
of hand and saying some things that had to make you wonder, I got
kind of worried," he said. "Mostly it was just talk. You can tell
who's all talk."

He has to watch himself. That's just the way it is. He lives here
and he plays here, but he doesn't totally belong here. He used to
talk some on the court, because that's what everybody was doing.
He stopped that. He wasn't like everybody.

The talk is constant. It is serious or it is fun, and sometimes it
takes a second to decide which. The talk is as much a part of the
game here as the ball. Some guys can't play without talking, as if
their mouths serve as the ignition for the rest of their bodies.

"I learned that I play better when I'm worried about myself,
when I don't have time to talk to the other team. Really, when you
play at certain playgrounds, you know not to talk. Unless you have
a lot of friends with you, you know not to talk. You'll get hurt. You
will get hurt."

He won't play just anywhere. He sometimes drives around in his
beat-up red hatchback Toyota for two hours, looking for a game.
The car lists a bit to the left, and the body has some dents, but he is
proud of it. He bought it with his own money and pays for the insurance with his own money. He has been working since ninth grade.
He keeps a baseball bat in the back seat, within reach.

He looks for good games, competitive games. He'll go south to
San Leandro or north to Berkeley. He has even gone to the suburbs, looking. Mostly, he stays in Oakland. He won't go into the
housing projects and play, because that would be stupid. That is
something that has nothing to do with color.

"Some of the projects, there's places I would never go," he said.
"It's bad enough if you're black and they don't know you."

He is the only white player in the Oakland Athletic League. He
will graduate from Skyline this year. It is nearly a certainty that
there will be no white players in the league next year.

He puts up with a lot in the OAL—taunts, elbows, curses—but mostly he is accepted. After three years, players from other teams know him and respect him. What he faces in the OAL is nothing compared with what he sees here, on the playground.

"I've played at some pretty bad playgrounds," he said. "I was always able to stay out of trouble. There were pushing matches and many, many threats. Threats of what's gonna happen if a certain person gets fouled again, what they're going to do to me."

Everything they did and said was based on his color, his appearance. He is sure of that. He is also glad for that. They weren't criticizing his game.

"I don't think I *play* white," he says.

Slowly, the trips to the playground got easier. As he kept coming back, they found that he could play. He plays tough defense and can handle the rock. He likes to pass more than score, and that helped him gain acceptance. On the playground, there is no better way.

He has friends here—Jason Wright, Nelson Burns, other players from the OAL. He is not alone out here, at least not always. His friends are black, not that he would really notice. It's been that way his whole life.

His friends sometimes run interference, telling the doubters that he's OK, that the white kid can play. Then sometimes he'll find himself among new players, players he hasn't played with before. He'll stand there, dribbling. They'll look at him, doubting. The cycle repeats itself.

"Every time I went there, if it wasn't someone I played with before, it was always the same thing," he says. "If there's different people at different parks, it's always the same thing."

He kept coming back because he loved the game, but there was more. He could have loved the game somewhere safer, somewhere easier. He kept coming back because most people in his situation wouldn't. Part of it was the challenge.

"A lot of it, actually," he says.

David Strom has seen a lot, but not as much as some of his friends. He has lived in Oakland since he was four years old, at the same house on a side street that runs parallel to 35th Avenue. He lives with both of his parents, an older brother and a younger sister. His father is a postal-service employee and his mother works for the county as a budget analyst. Their neighborhood is not the hills. It is in Fremont High's district, not Skyline's.

David's mother always saw to it that her children went to school in the hills. David isn't sure how she did it; she just did.

She didn't want any of her three children to go to Calvin Simmons Junior High, even though it's just down the street. Calvin Simmons is considered rough among rough schools. David, his brother and his sister went to Montera Junior High, in the hills. His brother also went to Skyline. He dropped out in the eleventh grade.

David hated Montera. To him, it was a school ruled by money and status, two things he has no time for. He saw it as a place where the children of the wealthy stayed for a year or two before moving on to a private high school.

"I couldn't relate to a lot of people there. Everything was about money, and it was a fashion show just about every day. They were real different. Skyline—most of the people who go here don't live in this district. Anyone who lives in this district has enough money to send their kids to private schools, to Head Royce or Bishop O'Dowd."

When David and his family moved to Oakland from San Francisco in the early 1980s, the neighborhood was far more ethnically diverse than it is now. Now it is black families and a few Hispanic families and the Stroms.

There used to be some bikers—Hell's Angels—living next door. Funny as it sounds, they were something of a comfort. "We knew nothing would happen on that side of the house," David says, "Nobody would mess with them."

Then one night David heard arguing and gunfire next door. The next day he woke up and saw the bullet hole in the passenger door of his parents' car.

There are drug dealers on 35th, in plain sight. Houses on the Stroms' street turn into drug houses every so often. David can tell because the street is normally quiet at night. If the traffic picks up, with cars pulling in slowly off 35th and then leaving quickly, that's a sure sign.

"You hear gunfire every now and then," he said. "It's mellow, though. I just go home and go in my house. I don't know anyone on my street, except for the next-door neighbor who's been there for about fifty years."

Most of the white people who lived in the neighborhood have since moved out. The Stroms stay.

"My mom wants to get out of there very badly," David said. "We just can't afford to move."

David's sister, who is fourteen, goes to Bishop O'Dowd, a Catholic high school. His mother borrowed money from her mother to help pay for the tuition. David didn't want to go to O'Dowd, but he thinks it's a good idea for his sister.

"I think the public schools are getting ridiculous," he said. "It's a joke."

A former Skyline basketball coach calls Strom "The Enigma." He doesn't divulge much and volunteers little. It is part of his defense, his armor. Basketball provided Strom with an identity at Skyline, a social status that protected him and earned him some respect. Still, it doesn't make him feel completely safe.

After four Los Angeles Police Officers were acquitted of the Rodney King beating in late April of 1992, there were problems at Skyline. Oakland itself was remarkably calm, but black students at Skyline were jumping and beating white students. At least one ambulance had to be called up the hill.

Strom went home.

"I haven't gotten into any fights up here, but I had a few problems during the Rodney King. White people were getting jumped and getting beaten and ambulances were having to take them to the hospital. I left. I just left. No way I was going to stay."

Strom is smart, one of the finest students at Skyline. He possesses a natural depth of thought, as if he has another set of eyes to see beneath the surface of things. There is a cynical, sad edge there, too. He likes Oakland, but he doesn't see much hope for the city. Or for the children it is raising.

"The economic system keeps the poor people poor," he said, his eyes and voice far away. There is a sadness in his voice, nearly tangible.

"Especially these black kids, they're living in poverty. Some of them are running around with one parent, who's strung out on crack. Everything they learn is from what they see and what music they listen to. 'Bitch this' and 'bitch that'—that's how they view women now and that's how they treat women. When they grow up, they'll view them as objects. They don't even know what they're saying yet, and it's already things I would never have my child say. Everything they learn is from what they see and what they hear. It's not their fault. And these schools—there's not enough money in these schools and the classes are too big. I can just see how that keeps it in the cycle. It's incredibly hard to break out of it. Good teachers leave; they're not getting paid anything. They have to serve as psychiatrists and mothers and fathers as well as being educators. There's not a lot of hope you can see, especially with the kids in elementary schools. That's where it starts, and the problems just get bigger and bigger as you get from junior high school to high school."

Some of Strom's good friends go to McClymonds High in West Oakland, the poorest and most depressed section of the city. They are his friends because they are basketball players, *serious* players. McClymonds is a heavy favorite to win the OAL championship. They could win the state.

"You worry about what's going to happen to McClymonds," Strom said. "If they win the state championship—what then? Next year they're not going to be that good, there's not going to be all this attention and it'll go back to the way it was. And not just basketball; the situation in general is not going to get any better. You don't really see it getting any better; not right now. I don't know . . . I don't know. My brother earlier this year got stabbed in his back near my house, at this burger place, by a Mexican guy. My brother's not a conservative, but when we argue he's conservative, when he's around me. He says, 'That's a bad person.' I say, 'You have to look at what he's been through. Even though he did a terrible thing, what made him do that? What would make anyone do something like that?' It's just not that easy."

Montera Junior High did one thing for David Strom: it was there that he discovered basketball. He was in eighth grade, and things were happening at home that he wanted desperately to avoid. He needed some way to lose himself, an outlet to help ease the pain and confusion.

There were fights at home, he says, and a lot of arguing. The situation has calmed since. "It's more mellow, more stable," David says. But at the time, he needed something. He found basketball. From the start, it seemed like a harmonic, almost celestial, convergence. Before long, he was bringing a basketball to school. He would dribble off the bus in the morning and bring the ball right into class. He'd dribble between classes, whenever he could. He would spend the lunch break on the basketball court, shooting and working on moves to use on the playground. He'd rather play than eat.

If there were problems at home, he would grab his ball. It was always there, and it carried him away. Far away.

"I don't want to give the wrong impression; I didn't grow up in a housing project. I'm very fortunate that I have two parents in my household. I see a lot of my friends who grew up in terrible situations, and it's a miracle they're still alive. When I look at them, there's no way I can feel sorry for myself. I did have my share of problems when I grew up, and basketball has been the escape. I could always go play basketball. It was like, basketball was always there. You could always depend on basketball. Don't have to worry about it yelling at you . . . or whatever."

Whatever. The word hangs there.

"It was bad sometimes, but it's better now," he said. "Yeah, it's much better."

He worked on his game for a year before he felt confident enough to venture to the playgrounds. He worked on his ball-handling until there was no difference between his left and his right hands. He worked on his speed and his strength and began taping games from the television. He would watch Kenny Anderson while he was playing for Georgia Tech. He chose to learn from him, especially the way he passed the ball in the open floor.

He shot and shot and shot, free throws and three-pointers and pull-up jumpers in the lane. His form was unconventional, sort of a shot-put release that started at his left hip. It was the weakest part of his game, and remained that way into his senior year at Skyline, so he worked at it harder and longer.

He needed the challenge he got from the game. School wasn't giving it to him; he doesn't get anything lower than a B. He had a 3.6 grade-point average at Skyline and scored 1280 on the Scholastic Aptitude Test. His mother dictated that. "She's the one who stayed on me about my grades," he said. "I was real fortunate to have her. It's not acceptable to have anything below a B."

Basketball was an escape, but it was more than that. Basketball became the only thing that was truly his. It represented what he fiercely sought: independence.

"Basketball is the thing that's not related to my family," he said, "and I kind of like it that way."

Strom plays the game he loves with a dour, joyless determination, a stern and almost implacable demeanor. He plays as if the game is the only thing in his world. He doesn't smile much, and when he does it's only for a short time.

He plays defense with his eyes fixed on the opponent's midsection. That is where all movements on the basketball court start. The temptation is to watch a player's eyes, to predict movement by line of sight. Strom stays low, his quick hands jabbing at the ball, his feet moving as quickly as the ball-handler's, maybe quicker. He is excellent at predicting movement. It is one of his strengths. His voice barks out, keeping time with his feet and his hands, *"Hah! Hah! Hah!"* with each dribble and each jab. He doesn't get beat very often.

Skyline is playing in a lifeless preseason game before a mostly white crowd in a half-filled gym, and Strom is dribbling the ball hard up the middle of the court. He has Eric Govan on one side and Darren Albert on the other. There are two defenders back, and they are both shading toward the wings. Strom senses this, so he takes it straight to the basket, his left-handed dribble low to the floor, his body leaning forward. He picks up his dribble in mid-stride and whips the ball around his back, as if preparing to pass to Albert on his right. Then he pulls the ball back around 360 degrees into his left hand and flips a reverse layup off the board. It spins off the glass and into the basket.

The people in the stands gasp reflexively, as if inhaling all the air in the building. There is a certain appreciation that isn't there for Jason Wright or Will Blackwell or any of his teammates.

It is like that every time. They react to him because they don't expect it from him. Just like the guys at the playground.

"I kind of notice that," David said. "There's a showboat inside of me, a little bit. I like to make the fancy pass. I like to surprise people."

Darren Albert has played basketball with Strom for three years at Skyline. They are both seniors, and Darren sat on the bench while Strom started in the backcourt the year before. Darren is perceptive and introspective, in some ways just like Strom.

"I don't look at David as a white person," Darren said. "You know, he's another player as far as I'm concerned. But then, I see different people who aren't like me, who might be racist, who can't relate to that. They say, 'Why that white dude in there startin'? You should be startin' over him' and all that. But if you ever practice with him or see him play, you'll say, 'Yeah, he's good.' In the OAL, you're going to see the crowd be even more amazed when he does something good than if a black person who's playing just as good as him does something. They're going to be like 'Oh, wow, he can do that?' When there's just one white person playing, they're going to think he's the weakest in the league, when he might really be the best. He's very strong in the mind."

Nelson Burns: "Nobody be sayin' nothin' directly to me, but I know they be saying racial stuff. I'm sure of it. It's not hard having a white friend, though. I think we the same, other than he's white and I'm black. We got almost the same wants. To get good grades and play good basketball. I think guys say things under their breath. I hear people say he's the best white player they've ever seen. So if they're saying that, I know they're saying negative things, too."

Donlea didn't think Strom could be a scorer, and Strom knew it. Donlea's offense wasn't devised for a point guard to score, and he didn't see enough from Strom to change that.

As a junior, Strom passed. He brought the ball upcourt, if he was lucky, and passed it off. He didn't get it back, and he didn't expect it back. He played defense and passed. And he accepted that.

Until now.

He was a senior, and he had big ideas. He had been the good soldier, had sacrificed himself for the team. Now he had ascended the totem pole. It was his turn.

"All I know is, I can score," he said. "That was never a question."

Donlea didn't agree. He thought Strom's problem was talent. He saw the determination, and he knew how much the game meant to him. He just didn't see the talent. He thought his shot was flat and inaccurate, and he didn't think Strom was quick enough to take a defender off the dribble and to the basket. To Donlea, Strom had reached his talent level, and he was best at what he was being asked to do: play tough defense, run the offense and—above all—play smart.

Donlea couldn't reach Strom. There were too many layers to pass through, too much history to overcome. Strom had been a varsity basketball player since his sophomore season, and Donlea was his third coach in three years. Strom had structured his life around the prospects for his senior season. He had three goals: Average 17 points and seven assists a game; win the OAL and state championships; get a Division I scholarship.

He thought the third goal would follow logically after the first two. He understood some of the doubts about his foot speed and his jump shot, but how could anyone look at his situation and possibly doubt him? He was a pale, skinny, scrawny white kid with a Marine haircut who held his own—more than held his own—in the Oakland Athletic League.

He would work on his speed and his quickness. He would shoot more. He would do whatever anyone wanted him to do, just so he could keep playing. That's all that mattered.

What else could a college coach or scout possibly want? He felt he could answer every question. Toughness? Spend an afternoon at Allendale. Attitude? Watch him in practice. Desire? That's an easy one—who else goes to the YMCA at night to play pickup games *after* a three-hour practice?

The thought came to Strom early on: It wasn't going to happen.

"I knew from the start he didn't want me to shoot. Guys would tell me what he was saying on the bench. I knew everything that was going on. I realized from the very start of the season that if I missed, it was a bad shot. If I made it, it was a good shot. I knew he just wanted me to pass the ball."

Donlea admitted to being slightly intimidated by Strom, by the extreme seriousness and the quietly cerebral way he approached the game. When he talked to his team, Donlea could feel Strom's eyes bearing down on him, penetrating his thoughts. It was almost as if Strom could read Donlea's mind and didn't like what he saw.

Strom never said anything about it, which only made it worse, more unnerving, for Donlea.

"I don't have that good of a read on him," Donlea said. "I don't know if he likes what we're doing or if he hates it. I have a pretty good idea he hates it, but what am I going to do? I like him, and I think he can play, but I can't build an offense around him. We'd never score."

Strom wanted to be a basketball coach someday. He watched Donlea closely, dissecting every practice, every drill. He had an idea what practice should be, and what the philosophy should be. He idolized Don Lippi, who coached Skyline during Strom's sophomore year. Under Lippi, Skyline ran teams ragged and pressed full-court and turned the game into an organized blur. Lippi's teams were wildly successful (Skyline finished second in the state in 1989) and everybody came to practice; Lippi made sure of it. He said he made it so that "missing practice was like missing a meal." Nobody missed. Strom held Donlea up a high standard—Lippi's standard—and he thought he fell short.

"I don't think he's ready for coaching a high school in Oakland," he said. "I don't think he's ready for the discipline problems. I think he thought that he was just going to come in and everyone was going to come to practice every day and stand at attention and do whatever he told us to do. Maybe it's like that at private schools or out in the suburbs. But here, the first thing you have to do before you even think about basketball is deal with the personality problems, the discipline problems. That's the hardest thing about coaching in Oakland. You have to know that coming in."

Strom knew he couldn't count on a basketball scholarship. His earnest work ethic and complete devotion to the game wouldn't carry him. He hadn't received one letter or one phone call from a college coach. He had heard that a couple of small-school coaches had inquired about him, but he was less than enthusiastic about the prospect of playing for San Francisco State or Cal State-Hayward. Besides, that was secondhand information.

"I've gotten no letters. Nothing. Not a thing."

He was accepted at the University of Oregon, and he decided that's where he would go. He had been out of California just twice, once to visit his grandmother in Chicago and once to play youth soccer in Japan. He looked forward to seeing something different, and to meeting different people, but he wasn't trying to escape Oakland. In fact, he had ambivalent feelings about the prospect of leaving.

"I like Oakland because it's real," he said. "There are problems, I know, but ... I don't know. I don't know how to explain it, but it's just real to me."

He also knew he couldn't go to Oregon without significant financial assistance. He applied for every scholarship possible and was a finalist for the National Merit Scholarship. He applied for direct financial aid and was disappointed when it informed him that his family could pay for most of his education. He knew that wasn't true, so he began to make alternate plans. If Oregon fell through— and he estimated he was $4,000 short—then he would go to a junior college in the Oakland area and go from there.

Of course, basketball played a large role in Strom's desire to go to Oregon. He liked their system and thought he would have a chance of making the team as a walk-on. The Ducks were the worst team in the Pac-10 the past two seasons, and Strom watched their games and envisioned himself fitting in well.

"This isn't one of those stories you read about," he said. "I'll be OK without basketball. I'm not basing my life on it. If I have to go to a junior college, that's OK. You take general-education classes the first two years anyway, and I'll be able to work and save some money. And I know I can play at a JC."

David refused to think of himself as the underdog, claiming that anyone who had seen him play outside knew he could do more than he showed at Skyline. On the playground, he was an improvisational scorer, an adequate shooter who knew the game well enough to score without overwhelming talent.

"I have moves I don't even use in the games," he said. "I've got a whole bunch of moves coach has never seen. I just don't get a chance to use them in our system. Coach thinks I just want to score, that I'm selfish. That's not it. We have to have some balance. We can't beat McClymonds or Fremont with two guys doing all the scoring. If you know a guy's only going to pass off, that he'll never shoot, it's pretty easy to guard him."

• • •

If he went to Oregon, he would play. If he went to a junior college, he would play. It wasn't even an issue. He would play because he *had* to play. He took school seriously, but he was a basketball player.

"If I don't make it my freshman year, I'll try the next year. Then the next year. Then the next year . . . I'm going to play. I don't worry about that."

Above all else, he thought he would play because he had beaten tougher odds before. He would always come back.

CHAPTER FIVE

THE HENRY J. KAISER CONVENTION CENTER SITS NEAR THE SOUTHERN tip of Lake Merritt in downtown Oakland. On the morning of Saturday, January 10, 1993, ten Oakland Police squad cars were parked in front of the building, and fifteen uniformed officers were inside. Five of them worked the building's entrance, where spectators bought tickets and passed through one of two metal detectors before being allowed into the second tier of the cavernous building. There was at least one officer in each aisle, and they talked intermittently on their radios. The security was airtight, officers on the scene and backups at the ready.

The Jamboree is unique to the Oakland Athletic League. On the Saturday before the start of the league season, all six of the teams get together to give the city, and each other, a look at what lies ahead. Each team plays two quarters against two different opponents. The Jamboree was an idea proposed by the players in the late 1970s, and its purpose is only marginally tied to basketball. It's really a debutante's ball for the baggy-shorts and tank-top set, and the action spills over the boundaries of the court. It has elements of a block party, a dance, a revival meeting, even a family reunion. It is a rocking, rapping, raucous place to be.

After this day, they would play for one reason: to return to what they call "The Henry J." The top three teams make the Oakland Athletic League playoffs, and only the winner advances to compete for the state championship. Although three Oakland teams—McClymonds, Fremont and Skyline—thought they had a legitimate chance to contend in the regional playoffs, only one would get the opportunity.

• • •

The bus carrying the Skyline basketball team ("Bus No. 5—Skyline," read a sign on the side) pulled up to the curb near a side entrance to the convention center. The players left the bus, ducked under a building-long strip of yellow police tape and waited at a locked door. Once the team was assembled, the door opened and a uniformed officer spoke to Shawn Donlea.

"All right, coach, identify each of your players as they come in."

Donlea stood off to the side, checking off the players as the officer watched closely. It was 11:30 on Saturday morning, and the Kaiser Center seemed to be the safest place in town.

Inside, an air of anticipation—generated by the Jamboree's recent history of violence and the massive police presence—permeated the building. An officer standing guard near the participants' entrance on the floor level heard a commotion in the rotunda. He sprinted out and came to a textbook jump stop, his head on a swivel and his hands hovering over his hips. He looked to the left, where three or four of the Castlemont High players were laughing and wrestling. The officer walked back to his post, slightly embarrassed.

"Isn't this sad?" the officer said. "We have twenty officers assigned to this. It's a shame, but we've got to do it because they've had shootings and fights at this in the past. When I was in high school, we didn't need that. These kids shouldn't, either. We've got metal detectors for the doors and officers at every corner. It shouldn't have to be this way."

The music pumped through the speaker system, the full force of its rugged beat nearing the decibel level of a busy tarmac. The players from the six Oakland public high schools, mixed together in a collage of uniforms, circled the floor and slapped hands and went through layup drills together. In three days, they would try to intimidate and talk trash and move each other out of the key with a speeding elbow. For now, they were one, just a bunch of kids doing something they love. Those who could dunk did and those who couldn't tried to make up for it with fancy dribbling or no-look finger rolls or loud slaps of the backboard. Everyone, it seemed, could do something to distinguish himself. Certainly everyone tried. The music ground its way out of the enormous speakers, Ice-T and

Wreckx N Effect and Dr. Dre and Sir Mix-a-lot and whoever else was considered hot enough for the occasion. The fans, nearly five thousand of them, clapped in rhythm, dancing back and forth with the hip-hop hip thrusts and synchronized arm movements that simulated midair push-ups. From the floor, the stands seemed to come to life as one weaving, smiling, singing organism. Parents, students, young mothers holding babies, people from West Oakland and East Oakland—they all stood together in a vibrant, exuberant communal celebration. The city's kids—*their* kids—were on the floor below, and that was reason enough. Besides, they could play.

The spectators were no longer bill-paying, bus-riding citizens. They weren't worried about their next check or about bolting their doors or protecting their children. What took place inside the auditorium went beyond that. People were brought together by a bunch of teenagers—children, really—and a game. The city around them might be rough and cold, every corner a danger, but inside it was warm. Still, it took just one look around the auditorium, at the police officers guarding every entrance and exit, to bring back a semblance of reality. This was a fragile peace. The Jamboree can also be dangerous—especially for a player wearing the black and red of Skyline High.

Anyone who questioned the level of security had only to ask Eric Govan. It was dark when the Skyline players left the Kaiser after the Jamboree in 1991, Govan's sophomore year. Each school was assigned its own exit door, but the Skyline door led out to a ledge that was about five feet above street level. Several of the players, coach Don Lippi and some cheerleaders jumped down, but the school's principal felt it was too steep. He led the rest of the team—unescorted by the police on duty—to the main entrance and directly into a group all too happy to see some easy Skyline targets.

They were on Govan right away. There was no time for him to move or yell or plead for reason. Their fists knocked him back, then down. He was buried under a pile of angry bodies, his face unprotected. He didn't know who they were or what they wanted. He knew only that he was from Skyline, and that, apparently, was the only requirement.

"We walked out that door and right into half of Oakland," Govan said. "They just wanted a piece of Skyline."

Another Skyline player was on the ground, taking punches from all sides. When Lippi heard the commotion, he ran around to the front of the building and began hitting the assailants with a gym bag filled with clipboards and rolls of tape. Without that, witnesses said, the player would have gotten his next ride in an ambulance.

The players were in their uniforms, or as Govan put it, "I didn't have nothin' on me, just this little number-five jersey. That made me pretty obvious."

Govan blacked out after reaching the bus and regained consciousness back at the school. A cut on his mouth required stitches. The other victim suffered a broken nose and had nightmares for three months. Besides being from Skyline, he and Govan were said to be singled out because they were the lightest-skinned players on the team.

On the first day of Skyline's practice, when Donlea stood before his players and said, "Hey, I'm new around here, but I hear nobody likes us," there was a quick burst of laughter from the players.

"You got that right," Govan said.

There is animosity toward Skyline, perceived as the privileged school on the hill. Any excuse to show that animosity is good enough.

The year after the attack on the Skyline players, the Jamboree was moved from the Kaiser to Merritt Community College, located below Skyline in the hills. The return to the Kaiser was a second chance for everyone—fans, participants, law-enforcement officers—to get it right. They didn't want to go back to Merritt; it lent a false air of pretense to the occasion, as if it was trying to be something it wasn't. The Jamboree is a downtown, flatland event. And moving it to the hills? They might as well not have it at all.

The players walked and talked and went to the basket to the beat of the heavy bass thrusts. The music is rough and raunchy, filled with misogyny and violence, rude and crude—but to them, it's real. To a kid from the projects of West Oakland or The Jungle of East Oakland, nothing documents his life like a good rap. It's what Woody Guthrie was to the Dust Bowl migrants, what Dylan was to the hippies.

Nobody would play particularly hard on this day, and none of the coaches was about to show anything he might use later. In fact, Donlea put Skyline through a two-and-a-half hour practice beforehand. But there was no mistaking the feeling coming off the court: if necessary, they were ready to play.

The Jamboree is all about style and show, and the showcase team came from the heart of West Oakland, a depressed but tightly knit community that considers high school basketball a proud slice of its history.

The demographic composition of McClymonds High School (known simply as "Mack" in Oakland) provides a concise synopsis of Oakland's history. In 1938, 648 of the school's 863 students were white. Six years later, after the first influx of black workers arrived in Oakland's shipyards and factories, blacks were a majority at McClymonds. In 1948, after the white exodus from West Oakland, just fifty white students remained at the campus on Myrtle Street. In 1992–93, just six of the school's 627 students were white, and 91 percent were black.

The people in West Oakland remember better times and see signs of their return. They are proud of the community's history and intent upon reviving what once was the bustling hub of black Oakland, back before the implementation of social programs designed to rid the neighborhood of government-perceived "blight." Beginning in 1962, acres of residential neighborhoods were razed to make way for the bureaucratic solution—housing projects such as Acorn and Peralta Villa and Oak Center. The residents were given something they didn't want.

They were uprooted from their homes. Commercial buildings were torn down, along with churches and community centers. Rows of "Captain's Houses," old mansions so named because they were built by ship captains before the turn of the century, were bulldozed. In their place, utilitarian blocks of compartmentalized stucco and cinderblock were erected to house the displaced. This, their government told them, was progress.

The community lost a big chunk of its heart. People who grew up in West Oakland before the 1960s remember leaving their doors unlocked at night. They remember walking the streets without worrying about time or crime. One longtime resident said the West Oakland of the 1950s was how he would picture a small town in

Iowa. The homes and buildings were deteriorating, but the projects—especially the Acorn—turned West Oakland into a many-fronted war zone. Nearly nine thousand residents were forced to relocate, and the housing projects had an ironic, cruel twist: they created a shortage of low-income housing that exists to this day.

West Oakland was also bisected and divided by freeways, I-980 from downtown and I-880 from the south and north. A neighborhood that fought to stay together now found too many obstacles. Many of the black residents of West Oakland moved to houses in East Oakland, which became available to blacks when the whites in East Oakland scattered to the suburbs. White flight started in West Oakland and spread to the east.

McClymonds High has come close to extinction more than once. Its enrollment is by far the lowest of Oakland's six public high schools, and the school has survived repeated threats to turn it into a vocational or trade school. After all, there's history to consider. Bill Russell went to McClymonds (bookish and awkward, he didn't play until his senior season), as did Paul Silas, Frank Robinson and Vada Pinson.

And this year's basketball team—The Mack Attack—started the season by staking a claim to a piece of the legend.

"It's all about making your own spot in history," Mack coach Willie Hearnton constantly reminded his players. "The history is nice, but we feel a lot better about making our own history."

When the McClymonds Warriors arrived for the Jamboree, children sitting in the balcony seats hung their heads over the rail to get a look at the hottest basketball team in the state. "There's Mack," the talk began as they entered, wearing their orange and black warmup suits. Those who hadn't seen The Mack Attack in person had at least heard all about it.

Darrnaryl Stamps led the way into the auditorium. A 6-foot-8 center with a shooting guard's touch and a point guard's court awareness, Stamps was the main attraction. He had gone a long way toward cementing his reputation in Mack's last game, a convincing win over Sacramento's Kennedy High, a team that figured to compete for the state title. Against Kennedy, Stamps had outplayed 6-foot-11 center Michael "Yogi" Stewart, who was considered one of the nation's best big players by college coaches. Stamps committed early to San Jose State, and there were some who felt he could have chosen a bigger-name school had he waited until the returns were in from his senior season.

Stamps walked past the Skyline team and silently extended his hand to David Strom, Darren Albert and Govan. Over the next hour, as the girls Jamboree concluded, Stamps and Kelton Runnels and Anthony Byrd and Louis Jackson—each a Division I prospect, each wearing a sweatshirt that read "Warrior Basketball: We Play Above the Rim"—filed back and forth in front of the Skyline team, with no destination apparent.

"Look how much bigger they are than everybody else," Donlea said. "Man, I'm already tired of seeing them. But I guess when you're fourteen and oh, you can walk around in front of everybody as much as you want. They've pretty much earned that."

Mack's standing as the unquestioned owners of city bragging rights was strikingly evident during the player introductions. They announced Fremont and Castlemont and Skyline—and then Mack. The tone of the crowd changed, the volume level inching upward. Runnels and Byrd and Jackson and Stamps, one by one they heard their names and walked through the human tunnel formed by each school's cheerleaders. Runnels advanced toward midcourt with his hands upraised, his head sweeping from one side of the seats to the other, his walk achingly slow. Everything about him commanded attention. He was living a powerful rush brought on by a small slice of fame. Five thousand people watching you, hearing *your* name, *knowing* your name.

The players all know each other, mostly from a park somewhere, Allendale or Mosswood or Brookdale. They've met in middle school or CYO or summer leagues. They broadcast each other's weaknesses and grudgingly concede their strengths. There are no secrets in the Oakland Athletic League. From enormously talented Mack to the perennially undermanned Oakland Tech, there is a respect in the OAL. They come from similar backgrounds and face similar challenges. It is the same type of respect shared by fraternity pledges or war buddies, the feeling of enduring something together. Basketball is their game, Oakland's game, the eternal city game.

It's the city game because it allows uninhibited freedom of expression and places a heavy emphasis on self-reliance. By its very nature, its ball-and-hoop simplicity, it is the only game that encourages such qualities. The rhythm of the music is in the game, sunk deep into the beat of a ball on the asphalt or the hardwood, deep into the swish of a net, nylon or chain. Even in a quiet playground—one player, one ball—the music can be felt in the up-and-down, back-and-forth movement. The music, in its evolution from Marvin Gaye to Dr. Dre, is embedded in the game.

Donlea was amused by the spectacle of The Jamboree. He had been warned by some of the other coaches at Skyline to prepare himself for a major culture shock. He had no intentions of coaching on this day, and his instructions to the team were simple.

"Get all your schoolyard shit out today. This is the last time I want to see it. Let's see your fifteen-foot finger rolls. Go ahead and cherry-pick and grab rebounds with one hand and dribble like hell."

"All right, coach, now you'll see what I been talkin' about," Jason Wright said. "I'm a playground legend. I've got my own court at Allendale Park. If someone's playing and I show up, everybody leaves."

"Yeah, right," Donlea said. "So if you go up there, everybody stops and says, 'Ooh, there's Jason Wright'?"

"That's right, coach. That's what they do. You laugh; I'm serious."

The Jamboree traditionally becomes a slam-dunk contest as soon as everyone gets loose. The OAL's history is filled with stories of dunks and dunkers, from Demetrius "Hook" Mitchell to Nate Williams to Joe "The Hanger" Tolliver, the only athlete in the Oakland Sports Hall of Fame strictly on the basis of his high school career. Without the dunk, there probably wouldn't be a Jamboree.

Stamps tried to get it started with a windmill swoop in the first quarter, but he crushed the ball against the back of the rim and sent it halfway to the ceiling. He was booed roundly, and the fans from Skyline and Castlemont and Fremont high-fived and laughed and rained epithets down on Stamps. The way the season figured to unfold, it might be their only chance.

They were fueled by the crowd and the music, but tempered by the camaraderie. They might have been ready to bust it back and forth like it meant something, but this was neither the time nor the place. But come Tuesday, when the league shifted to the small, cold gyms on the school campuses, when the stands might be half-filled and the crowd more intimidating than accommodating, all bets were off.

Toby Harris was the starting point guard for Oakland Tech. His transfer from Skyline had become a persistent annoyance to Donlea. A tenth grader, Harris had made the team at Skyline, and stood a chance of playing on the varsity, but he was academically ineligible after the first grading period. Harris met with Donlea the day the grades came out and asked the coach whether he would still be on the team if his grades rose above a 2.0 after the next grade check.

"I don't operate that way," Donlea said. "I want you to go to class and work on your schoolwork. I'd love to have you out here, but I don't think it's fair to you or these other guys to let you come back in the middle of the season."

Harris showed no outward emotion, but said simply, "Then I'll transfer" and walked slowly out of the room.

Now he had transferred, and he was playing. Each coach had his own rules, and Donlea understood Harris's decision. He also acknowledged that his own policy was subject to change, but he felt it was better to start strict and then ease off, rather than attempting to pick up a hammer after being too soft. Donlea watched as Harris, surrounded for the most part by inferior teammates, ran his team's offense.

"I hope he gets his lunch eaten, but he's a pretty good player. I really hate that—a kid becomes ineligible so he transfers schools. He got a new address, but his brother still goes to Skyline. Figure that out."

After the Jamboree, Donlea called Harris over and shook his hand.

"Toby, why didn't you stick around at Skyline?"

"I'm eligible now, coach. My grades came up. When you told me I couldn't play the whole season, I had to transfer."

"Yeah, but you've got to be a student, too. You can't just transfer every time something goes wrong."

"I am a student, coach. That school's just too tough for me. When I knew I couldn't play, I had to get out. I'm impatient."

• • •

They all know Fremont's Kareem Davis, a slight point guard with electrical quickness and a jump shot that always, always, appears to be going in. They know Castlemont's Michael Franklin, the league's most potent scorer. They know Stamps and Byrd and Jackson and Runnels and everyone else at Mack, because they're Mack. They know Will Blackwell. They know Oakland High's Robert Sasser, possibly the best athlete in the league. As a senior, Sasser played football for the first time in his life and ended up with college recruiters at his door. In baseball, he had a chance to be a high draft choice. In basketball, he could do about anything he wanted on the court.

Jason Wright wanted desperately to be included in the roll call of Oakland basketball. He wanted to be there with the players everybody in town knew, the players that eight- and ten-year-olds emulated on the playgrounds. The Jamboree was on his mind the entire week before, and in the unlikely event that he would forget about it, somebody was sure to remind him. His girlfriend, his neighborhood friends, guys he played against at Allendale or Brookdale—they all had something to say.

"J Wright, you gonna get a dunk for me?"

"There gonna be hella people there, J Wright. Best show 'em what you can do."

"It was getting to the point where I wasn't even thinking about doin' it for me," Jason said. "I did it for other people."

David Strom thought the Jamboree was a waste of time. Donlea would have rather used the time to practice or watch film. Jason Wright thought it was the best way—and the best place—to deliver a message.

"I want to have *me* a little name around the OAL," Jason said.

After Stamps missed his first dunk, he tossed down two or three more, but they were unspectacular. Mack's Armando Lewis had a two-handed breakaway, but it was all brute force and not much style. Jason Wright expected the competition to be a bit tougher.

The Jamboree is broken down into two teams (West and East) and six quarters; each West team (Oakland, Skyline, McClymonds) plays two quarters against an East team (Fremont, Oakland Tech, Castlemont). They keep score, but no one pays attention.

Skyline played the third quarter against Castlemont. Two minutes into the quarter, Jason put himself in position for a breakaway. He loped along with a high dribble to the free-throw line, then flipped the ball up toward the basket with his right hand. As the ball neared the rim, Jason elevated to the basket, elbows even with the rim, grabbed the ball with both hands and crashed it through the hoop.

He hung on the rim just long enough to accentuate his point, and the crowd responded with a reflexive grunt, followed by a tremendous ovation that filled every silent space in the huge building. This was what they came to see, and this was what Jason came to do. He ran downcourt yelling at the top of his lungs, his mouth wide open but no sound audible amid the roar. He ran with his arms tucked close to his chest, like a funny imitation of a chicken trot. He would back it up later with two more acrobatic slams—his change, they would say—but the first was the best. That one was for him, nobody else. Instantly, the Jamboree was Jason's show.

"Other people was dunkin', but I just made the one I did so somebody could remember that one. And remember me."

On Monday, the first school day following the Jamboree, Donlea was substituting in an auto shop class at Fremont. The topic early in the day was basketball, and a couple of the students recreated Wright's dunk to those who missed it.

"That boy's got hops," one said. "He *threw* it down."

Jason had accomplished his goal. Everybody knew him now.

CHAPTER SIX

JASON WRIGHT COULD HAVE BEEN SITTING AT HOME ON THE AFTERNOON of the Jamboree, hunched over the kitchen table with a pen in his hand, trying to form concise and legible sentences. His mother had come painfully close to mandating as much the day before, when she met with Donlea to tell him that Jason would be leaving the team to concentrate on his schoolwork.

They met in the coaches' office on Friday afternoon: Jason, Elaine Feemster and Donlea. Feemster was straightforward, saying that she was upset with the direction her son's grades had taken since the start of the basketball season. She wasn't blaming basketball, but she wasn't averse to using it to get the desired result. She wanted improvement, and she wanted it immediately.

Donlea didn't like to trot out that shopworn fable of the inner city, basketball as a way out, because he didn't believe it was either fair or real. But in Wright's case, Donlea had seen enough to believe there was an opening there, that Jason was good enough—with a lot of work—to use the game to get an education. He told Feemster that, and he told her to give Jason two weeks to work on managing his time better.

Feemster agreed. For Donlea, a crisis had been averted.

"I honestly don't think it would have helped him to quit the team," Donlea said. "That removes some of the motivation to work at school. Jason lives for basketball. Can you imagine him without it?"

Feemster could, because she was the one who saw the D in Spanish on his mid-semester grade check. She was the one who stayed up with him past midnight while he struggled to understand the lofty writing in his honors-level history textbook. She agreed to accept Donlea's plan, but she said the coach didn't make the decision. More than anything, she wanted to tell Jason—and Donlea— where she stood. This was a meeting they both could file away for future reference.

"The coach probably thought he changed my mind, but he didn't. He made some good points, but he struck me as a typical coach; he just wanted Jason to play. I guess I can understand that, but I've got to do what I think is right."

Elaine Feemster wasn't against basketball; in fact, she prayed that it would send Jason to college. For a single black mother working hard to get out of Oakland, that was a goal worth praying for. But she had seen young black men operate without a safety net, all sports and no school, and she had worked too hard to see her son fall into that dangerous trap.

Feemster is an attractive, slim forty-year-old with reddish-brown hair and shocking emerald-green eyes, their gaze studious and piercing. Strong-willed and defiantly independent, she moved to Oakland from Reno, Nevada, at nineteen, because she didn't think Reno was a happening place for a young black woman. She worked as an administrative secretary for the East Bay Regional Parks, but aspired to something better and more important. She began attending college part-time soon after arriving in Oakland, and she had continued taking classes ever since. Feemster had a degree in business from California State University at Hayward, a degree she earned while working and taking care of Jason. She took night courses in real-estate management, with the thought of someday buying and selling property for a living.

The week after her meeting with Donlea, Feemster met with some of Jason's teachers at Skyline. She discussed Jason's work with his Spanish teacher and asked that Jason get some extra tutoring. The teacher told Feemster that Jason didn't need any extra help in the class.

"Yes, he does," Feemster said. "He's got a D right there, so he's not getting it. Something's not sinking in."

She worked out a plan: she would receive progress reports on Jason from his teachers every two weeks. If his work slipped any further, basketball would be the casualty. And next time, she wouldn't bother to consult Donlea.

Jason did his schoolwork; it just took him forever. The honors history course was the bane of his existence. The course load called for reading two chapters a week from the textbook. Jason called the book a "big, fat, gigantic, sophomore-in-college book about history." He would pore over every word, the complexity of the parts making it impossible for him to grasp the meaning of the whole.

"We're supposed to read two chapters a week, and each chapter's like forty pages," Jason said. "Even if I had the time, I probably wouldn't be able to understand it. The book has big, gigantic words that some people ain't even heard in their life. There's words in there that doctors don't even use. That book—I don't know if I can stay with it."

Two nights before the Jamboree, Jason sat at the kitchen table until two in the morning. His mother demanded that he rewrite his history homework until the sentences were complete and comprehensible. The writing was the important part, she said. She had heard stories about illiterate high school graduates—and had known a few as well—and Jason wasn't going to be one of them. He was going to rid his work of the slang and the street language that kept turning up. He was simply writing as he spoke, in the same quick, run-on dialect of the streets. His mother would have none of it. If it came down to basketball or literacy, Jason would give up the game he loved.

"My mom, she treats my C's like F's," Jason said. "I don't think to the day I die she'll ever know how much basketball means to me. Even if I make it to the NBA, she'll always be thinkin' I could be doing something better with my time. That one night, I guess she was just fed up with it. I mean, I was doing it, it was just I was up till like two o'clock."

Jason was asked what would have happened if his mother had followed through on her threat to pull him off the team. He is sitting on the bottom row of the bleachers in the Skyline gym, and the question forces him abruptly to his feet, as if the wooden bench had suddenly become electrified. He paces and looks out onto the empty court, a half-smile, half-wince crossing his face.

"I don't even want to think about that. That's scary," he says, his eyes dreamy and distant. He pauses, then glances back. The smile is gone. "If she said I couldn't play, I'd go to the playground every day after school and play anyway."

Jason didn't think his mother would ever comprehend the importance of basketball in his life. When told that, Elaine Feemster laughed. She understood, she said, she just didn't want Jason to know. She saw the attention he paid to the game, the way he spent every spare second at the playground or watching basketball on the 52-inch projection television screen in the living room. She saw how meticulous he was about his appearance on the court, the way he made sure he got the ludicrously big shorts with the 38-inch waist to conform to the style of the moment. She definitely knew how important the game was to her son, and that was part of her reasoning behind pushing him in his schoolwork. She wanted to impart one piece of knowledge to Jason: in his position, growing up as a young black man in the inner city, nothing comes easy.

"I want him to get an education," she said. "I know how much he likes basketball, but I just happen to think schoolwork is more important. He'll get to college, one way or another—I did—and he knows I wouldn't be afraid to pull him off the team if I thought his grades were suffering too much."

Jason speaks with severe speed, the words running together in a seamless, commaless flow. Each word rounds off into the next. His hair rises about two inches above his tiny ears and levels off into a flattop plateau. He has a thin mustache and an even thinner goatee that tries, but fails, to be menacing. His body is a recruiter's dream, a raw, built-for-basketball body ready to sprout. He has long, gasoline-hose arms and size 13 feet. He refers to himself as "J Wright" and encourages others to do the same. He prides himself on his street smarts, on being able to walk onto any playground court in Oakland without worrying. He's quick to draw a distinction between being tough and being street-wise, saying part of being tough is being smart enough to stay out of trouble.

"I got street smarts, but I ain't stupid," he said. "You can have all the street smarts in the world and still get shot. I've been going to the park and playing basketball by myself since eight years old. I got a good judgment on good people and bad people, so I'm not afraid to go to the heart of East Oakland or the heart of West Oakland and just go ball. Once you get a reputation and people know you ball, there's a certain respect you get. People respect you and leave you alone just so's you don't try something stupid."

There was an inherent flaw in Jason's attempts to come across as a hard-bitten street youth: even when he tried, he couldn't look serious for long; there was always a smile hiding just below the scowl.

A year before, he was a 5-foot-10 sophomore point guard on the Skyline junior varsity. He was good, perhaps the best player on the team, able to dunk and consistently hit his left-handed jump shot from beyond the three-point line. But the growth spurt sent his basketball hopes flying in a new direction. He had added five inches in a year, making him a small forward or a big guard. He couldn't wait for the season to start. The possibilities seemed limitless.

Early in the season, it was clear that his coordination hadn't fully caught up with the weedlike growth. He had trouble dunking in the preseason, only able to throw down a few one-handed slams on wide-open breakaways. At six-three, he had imagined himself tossing down reverse slams in traffic, but the legs—the hops—just weren't there.

Donlea stopped practice one day before the first game and screamed at Wright after he missed three dunks in a row during a layup drill.

"I've seen enough goddamned missed dunks, Jason Wright," Donlea yelled from across the court. "You're not that good at it. Lay the ball in. Score the points and forget the dunks."

Jason couldn't, though. He worked on his dunks every chance he got—before practice, after practice. He would show his coach. Donlea didn't know him, hadn't seen him the year before. Jason knew it was inside him, so he kept working.

Even in this transition state, Jason was not clumsy. On the court, his liquid movements and loping running style exuded grace, and when he was interested there was an earnest intensity about his work.

He got the dunks down. His legs began responding shortly after Donlea's eruption, and from then on he worked on fine-tuning. He looked at the Jamboree as his chance to show everybody in town.

"I don't really trip off a dunk no more, 'cause I know I can do it and people know I can do it," he said. "If it happens, it happens. But at the Jamboree? I wanted that one. I just want to get the word out about J Wright."

Schoolyard. Playground. Street ball. Ghetto ball. Jungle ball. There is a vast and colorful lexicon to describe the game as it's played on the asphalt courts of the inner city. To a basketball technician like Donlea, the elements that rule the street game are impediments, bad habits that need to be exorcised. But to the players who play it, the street game is something to be revered, a staple of the culture.

At Allendale and Brookdale and Mosswood and the other parks in Oakland, players play to survive, to win and to embarrass the other guys. The emphasis is on the individual. It is ruthless, but it meshes nicely—and not coincidentally—with the rest of inner-city life.

"I'm a playground player," Jason said. "I'm a crowd player."

He thought people who criticized flashy play did so because they couldn't do it themselves. If you could, why not? That, to Jason Wright, was what basketball was all about. He saw nothing wrong with trying to dunk at every opportunity, and he saw nothing wrong with letting his opponent know, in no uncertain terms, that he had been beaten and beaten badly. He expected the same in return. Even when Donlea told him, as he did repeatedly, that he was in a gym and not on the street, Jason would roll his eyes heavenward and wonder how he was going to make it through the season.

"Some of what coach says is true," Jason said. "Sometimes I get carried away. But that's just a part of me. If I'm on the court, that's me."

To Jason, there was little difference between the street and the gym. His game, like so many others in the OAL, was formed on the hard asphalt courts of East and West Oakland. When you played there, you played to keep playing. It was basketball survival at its most basic. You lose, you sit. On a busy day, the sitting might last ten times longer than the playing. The object was to play and keep playing.

Donlea spent the preseason wondering if Jason was strong enough, in both body and mind, to compete at a high level in the Oakland Athletic League. Jason hadn't completely grasped Donlea's concepts early in the season, and he had difficulty pumping himself up to play against nowhere teams in nowhere gyms. He told Donlea he would be all right once OAL started. He said it because he knew that the pace of the games would be dictated by the players and the crowd—and not so much by Donlea—once Skyline started playing the Oakland teams.

Jason thought Donlea's worries about his competitiveness were ridiculous. He didn't want to be judged on his play in a slow-down game played before a crowd of four or five people with nothing else to do. Jason thought Donlea might get a better idea of his ability if he spent a Sunday afternoon at Allendale Park, watching Jason play like he meant it, at his pace on his terms, where bums and drunks line the outside of the court and drug transactions go on unnoticed.

"At the playground, don't nobody care about you," Jason said. "Nobody care. I had to get a root canal 'cause I got a tooth knocked out. Ain't nobody care. I was bleedin', ain't nobody care. I stayed and balled, too. Before every game, I just think this ain't nothin' but a big Allendale to me. And the people in the stands just got winners. That's how I picture it—a big playground. Every day in the OAL we play with people I know, so pretty much every day I got to prove something."

Jason knew that to get up and dunk—the more imaginatively, the better—was the best way to become known. He was a true connoisseur of dunks. He talked about them like an art collector discussing Van Gogh. He talked about playground legends in Oakland, players such as Demetrius "Hook" Mitchell and Brian Wortham, who had spread their name through town by getting off the ground. He knew their dunks in detail. He knew the history, and he wanted to be part of the history.

"Anybody who has tremendous ups—if you can jump and dunk—people gonna know you. Brian Wortham 360'd over a drop-top 5.0 Mustang. I'll never forget that."

The dunk was an all-purpose weapon: it energized the crowd, drew attention to the dunker and belittled the opponent. It was a tidy microcosm of the city game and the city attitude. And from the time Jason heard that first crowd reaction, that first "Oooh" following a dunk, it was all over. Jason Wright was gone, in another world. From that point on, he needed that reaction, craving it like a man staggering through the desert craves water.

"I'm like a crowd player. I've been playing basketball ever since third grade—organized basketball. I played ever since I could start walking. My whole family's got athletes, basketball athletes. I was always above the average, and the crowds would always go 'Ooh' and 'Aah.' So ever since then, I like to hear crowds. I'm a playground player. I'm a crowd player. I like playing on playgrounds when there's a lot of people trying to pick up winners. I just like the feelin' of somethin' like that. When I'm around a lot of people, I can't even describe it, I just get butterflies because I'm excited. When I get around a lot of people, I just hang. Maybe I just like attention. I can't even describe it; I just like to hear the crowds go crazy. And then when I know it's for me, that makes me feel even better. I try to do this every game: By the time I leave the gym, I want somebody to remember me. That's what I try to do every game. Just like at the Jamboree. Doing all that, the yellin' and screamin'—all of it. I don't know the reasons behind it. I'm an only child, so I get enough attention. I don't know why I feed off it so much, but I just really get into it. Every game day I wake up and think about the game, the game, the game. I have the same mentality as Jordan or Patrick Ewing: I'm gonna dominate, ain't nobody can guard me. That's just how I feel."

Jason said basketball was "second to God," his life. He also said it was "a close second. *Real* close." It seemed he could go either way.

He began attending the Evergreen Baptist Church in West Oakland during the summer between his sophomore and junior years at Skyline. He decided to go on his own, which struck his mother as an unusual—but highly commendable—move for a 16-year-old to make.

"I'm starting to get more involved," Jason said. "I guess I'm starting to become pretty religious. I still got a little more to learn. I still got doubts. Everybody got doubts."

He felt that God had given him the ability and the inclination to play basketball, and Jason believed he owed something in return. Jason was wise enough to what happens on the other side of the playground cheers. He knew how easy it was *not* to make it.

He talked, as all of the Skyline players did, of Ty Woodward, who would have been Skyline's starting center if he had been allowed to enroll in the school. Woodward was a force as a sophomore at

Oakland Tech, leading the OAL by averaging 28 points and fifteen rebounds per game. He was about 6-foot-5, he was strong and tough and mean. Woodward was academically ineligible as a junior; later that year, some gangsters from West Oakland showed up on the Oakland Tech campus. For reasons that are mostly unclear, they took two shots at Woodward and missed. Woodward tried to enroll at Skyline this season, but the administration deemed that his presence on campus would have endangered the other Skyline students.

"He's been good ever since he touched the rock," Jason said. "He got into a little fight with some people from West Oakland, and they shot at him and threatened his life. Then he started lagging. He gained about forty pounds, he's like six-five and three hundred. Ain't nobody was able to stop him. Nobody, nobody. He could post up and before he gained all that weight he could jump. He could come off the block and dunk with ease. He would definitely been the OAL player of the year."

Instead, Woodward wanders the streets of East Oakland, his body bloated and soft. He used to be a regular on the playground circuit, but nobody sees him there anymore. Jason talks about Woodward in quiet, almost reverent tones. The line is tenuous; people like Jason Wright need people like Ty Woodward, for perspective.

Elaine Feemster and Jason Wright had gradually moved from the flatlands to slightly higher ground. They had lived in East Oakland and near Lake Merritt, and now they lived in an older, three-bedroom stucco house on a side street running perpendicular to the bustle and noise of 35th Avenue. The houses were built close to the street, each house different from the one next door. The street was narrow, and trees that had overgrown their yards covered the street like a tunnel. The houses had been built in the 1940s, when it seems most of Oakland was built. Feemster had bought the house—her first—three years earlier. It was a transition neighborhood, represented by every possible nationality, but dominated by blacks. It is just barely inside the Skyline boundaries. Six blocks down, where David Strom lives, is inside the Fremont High district.

"This is a pretty good neighborhood," Feemster said. "I don't think we ever lived in a really bad neighborhood. Some were worse than others, but this is probably the best. One time last year Jason left to watch a basketball tournament somewhere, and he left the front door wide open. He was all excited about going to it, and the door stayed open for six hours. Nothing happened, so I guess it's a pretty good neighborhood. There's stuff that happens out on 35th, but that happens everywhere in Oakland."

At the start of the school year, Feemster began looking to move out of Oakland. She looked over the hill in the Contra Costa County town of Pittsburg and found an affordable home in a new development. Jason could still go to Skyline, because his mother could drop him off on her way to work. Feemster said she wasn't on a mission to leave Oakland, but acknowledges that the dangers of the streets provided her with some motivation. Jason talked about his mother expressing a desire to move after a man who lived on the same street was stuffed into the trunk of his car and later found dead in a wooded area of the Oakland hills.

Jason felt the sacrifices his mother made to save money for the new house. He might not get to go out as much as he wanted, and he didn't always get the clothes he wanted when he wanted them.

"I know the meaning of sacrifice," Feemster said. "I just want Jason to know, too. He never really had to want for anything. He might not get a pair of basketball shoes when he wants, but he'll have a pair of basketball shoes to wear."

There is a 1972 Jaguar in the driveway outside Jason and Elaine's house. Elaine bought it several years ago, a style-driven purchase. She hasn't driven it much since, and she has considered giving it to Jason when he gets his license.

"I should probably put a Chevy engine in it and give it to him, but it would be too much of a flashy car," she said. "I don't want him in there. It could cause problems."

Jason says of his mother: "She count every nickel. She knows what comes in and what goes out."

The playground at the elementary school Jason Wright attended is surrounded by a cyclone fence that is there as much to keep people out as to keep the children in. Jason Wright started his education here, in the heart of the "Rollin' 20s", where the streets would be practically empty were it not for the drug dealers and the drugged and the kids on the playground.

There may be a degree of embellishment involved, but Jason says he got out of this neighborhood just in time. He started getting into trouble in the third grade, and although it was small-time, schoolroom-bully stuff, Jason looks back on it now and sees that it could have been the genesis for something more.

"If I hadn't got out of there, I don't know what would have happened," he said. "I was doing some stuff I shouldn't have done. I knew right from wrong, because my mom taught me that. But . . . I don't know. I saw how easy it is to go the wrong way. The way I look at it now, with violence and everything, I try to think of myself as being higher than that. I just don't even try to think about it. I do, though, like every day I go home from practice. I think about what's goin' on out there. I think of it at school, too. When people think of violence in the school, people think Castlemont or Fremont or McClymonds that Skyline is better than all of them. Tell you the truth, I think there's more fights up here. But down at Castlemont, when they fight it's a little more serious. There's a whole reputation thing."

His mother discovered a lot about him through his schoolwork. One day his English class was told to write a paper on what makes them angry. Jason wrote about his mother.

"I said, 'I'm the only thing that makes you mad?'" she said. "'You mean you couldn't have written about your friends or anything? *They* don't make you mad, huh? Just me?' I understood, though, when I thought about it. You can't really be angry at something you don't expect, and you can't miss something you don't have. He was saying I have to be there for him. I said, 'Wait a minute. I have to provide a roof and some food, and that's about it.' People said I shouldn't look at it negatively, because he's saying he counts on me a lot."

Jason Wright's father left before his son was born. He lived in Bakersfield, and Jason saw him sometimes during the summer. Mostly he went down there and stayed with his grandmother. He didn't talk to his father much. Neither of them seemed to have much of anything to say.

Jason had played the scene out a million times in his head:

His father would come home from work, sit down in his living room and click on the television. He would go through the channels, past the news and the sitcom reruns and the game shows. He would find a basketball game on ESPN, and he would hear the announcer talking about a kid from Oakland named Jason Wright. Jason imagined this a hundred different ways, wearing a hundred different uniforms. Mostly he thought of Syracuse or Georgetown, or maybe an NBA team. Maybe the Portland Trailblazers. That would work, the Trailblazers. It could be a live game or taped highlights. In fact, taped highlights might work better. There Jason would be, winding up in the open court, prepping for a windmill dunk. The announcer is practically screaming, the crowd is beginning to stand as one—and his father just happens to be watching.

"That's the dream," Jason says. "I don't think he cares, but I look at it this way: I don't care, either. Let's put it this way: when he sees me on ESPN, he'll know I play hoop. He knows I play basketball, but he don't know I'm good or anything. At least I think I'm good."

"I can understand how he might feel abandoned," his mother said. "It's been kind of hard on him. He'll never really understand it."

For another English class assignment, Jason was told to write a poem about his family. His began:

> Dad is a one-syllable word
> that means nothing

CHAPTER SEVEN

THE PREPARATION BEGAN ONE HOUR BEFORE THE GAME, WHILE SCHOOL
was still in session. It rained hard and snowed briefly in the Oakland
hills on the first day of the OAL season. The weather created a stir
on campus, and it agitated Donlea because he knew every gym class
would be forced inside for the day. He knew the students had little
or no regard for the condition of the floor, and why should they? The
district didn't seem to care, the administration didn't fight to
improve it, so why should the students, especially those not on the
basketball team, think enough to walk around the baselines in their
street shoes?

Donlea looked out onto the floor. It was coated by a visible layer
of grime. He kicked his shoe across the floor near midcourt, and it
slid about two feet, as if on ice. If anything was going to get done,
Donlea knew he had to do it himself. Students from sixth-period
physical education were sitting in the stands. The girls track team
was going through striding drills under one basket. Three students
were setting up the speaker system for the game. The place was a
frantic rush of activity.

"Time to get the Sand Pit ready," Donlea said. "This ought to be
fun. Look at this floor. I got here this morning and some guys were
lifting weights in here, dropping the dumbbells right on the middle
of the floor."

He wrapped wet towels around a mop and shoved it along the
floor. After three round trips, the towels, once white, were nearly
black. Donlea unwrapped the towels, rinsed them and started over.
By the time he finished, it was thirty minutes before game time.

Govan, Wimberly and Johnson were shooting at the basket closest to the coaches' office.

"Govan, how's the floor?" Donlea asked.

Govan shrugged. "Same as always," he said.

Students were standing around anxiously in the gym's foyer, waiting for the doors to open. The girls were girlfriends or girls who wanted to be girlfriends. There wasn't a student in the school who wasn't aware that the OAL season was starting.

Some of the spectators had more at stake than a friend's performance or school spirit. They were the ones in the gold chains and hoop earrings and designer clothes. For some, showing school pride had a price. They would get together with rivals from the other schools and put some money on the game. They would bet on just about anything: first basket, first dunk, quarter scores, halftime scores, individual scoring, blocked shots. One Skyline teacher said he had been at games where a minimum of $1,000 changed hands before halftime.

The students were waiting in the foyer because nobody from the administration had arrived to sell tickets. Athletic Director Joe Panella and a member of the school's security force stood inside the gym, keeping the students from entering. Students were charged four dollars, two dollars with a student identification card. This angered many students; they felt the school shouldn't charge students to go to their own games. Some of the players felt it discouraged attendance.

"Some cats can't miss the bus and pay two bucks for a game," Nelson Burns said. "They got to pay to get home after, too."

Donlea fought his way through the crowd and into the coaches' office. He changed into a sport coat and tie, set up the scorer's table, made sure the clock was working and found some extra warmup tops in the back room. When he finally got around to addressing the team, game time was fifteen minutes away.

The schedule was kind: Oakland Tech, then Castlemont. Those were the only two teams Skyline was expected to beat. Mack was down the line, the fifth and tenth games of the ten-game league season. Still, Donlea was nervous. He had heard so much about the OAL and talked so much about it that he wasn't sure how to react now that it was here. He had the feeling everyone would be watching him—the new white coach in his first league game. It didn't matter that the opponent was the vastly inferior Tech. It didn't matter that he felt he had prepared his team as well as he could, despite the almost constant interruptions and obstacles. He had talked with enough people to know that nothing in Oakland counted like the OAL. You could go undefeated in the preseason and it still wouldn't impress anybody as much as one OAL win. He felt it from the players, too. The day before the OAL opener, everyone was dressed for practice on time. They went about their stretching without prodding, and the conversation was at a minimum. It was as if some inner alarm had gone off; playtime was over.

"Look at this," Donlea said. "Look at this turnout. Everybody's here. The day before OAL starts and nobody's got any problems. Everybody's healthy, nobody's going to the doctor, nobody's got an excuse. It's like contract time for a pro athlete."

As Donlea stood before the team before the Oakland Tech game, ready to give a speech he had lost sleep preparing for, two students were running a makeshift barber shop out of a dark corner of the locker room. The wrestling team, the track team—everybody was using the room. More than fifty students stood outside the locker-room door, waiting to be allowed into the gym. They were loud and animated. The basketball players met in a center row of the room, noise and anticipation swirling around them. They couldn't sit still, and Donlea wasn't much better. He was frazzled, his thoughts a scattering of semi-related concepts. This was the start of ten games that would shape their lives. He truly believed it went that deep. If they came together and stayed together, this would be a source of pride for the rest of their lives. Sadly, some of them might never see better times.

Donlea wanted to talk about strategy, about getting back on defense or getting the ball into the post. Strategy talk was a safe haven, devoid of emotion or nervousness. Donlea could lose himself in strategy. But as he looked out at the players' faces, he saw that he would be preaching to the walls. They were restless and distracted, ready to play. Donlea had learned to read the situation. And, as always, he didn't have enough time.

"Look, let's keep it simple. This is it. This is what we've been waiting for. This is what we've been practicing for. You can say, 'Aw, it's just Tech,' but you've got to play. Tech's oh-and-oh, Skyline's oh-and-oh. If you don't come to play in this league, you'll lose. You know that better than I do."

Govan hit a three-pointer to start the game and everybody in the stands and on the bench raised their hands high overhead to commemorate the occasion. Everyone came to see a rout, and that was the best way to start it.

But something unexpected happened. Tech didn't comply. The Bulldogs grabbed a couple of offensive rebounds and guard Ali Brooks—the team's one true player—raised some eyebrows with a fancy penetration move that ended with a scoop shot off the board.

Skyline trailed by five points after four minutes. They looked sluggish and tentative, while Tech was free and easy.

Bryant Johnson got the ball in the open court, and an immediate and audible air of anticipation rose in the bleachers. Everybody knew what Bryant could do, and, more importantly, they knew his willingness to do it. Energized by the crowd, Johnson dribbled between his legs and behind his back, then threw a behind-the-head, no-look pass to Wright on the wing. It was right there, but Wright wasn't ready. He couldn't handle it, it went out of bounds and Donlea bolted out of his chair as if suddenly discovering it was on fire.

"Trying to do too much, Bryant!" he yelled. He turned to the bench. "We're trying to do too damned much."

Donlea was learning that the OAL was different. He wouldn't have the control he had during preseason games in quiet gyms against teams nobody knew. This was neighborhood competition, with bragging rights at stake and friends in the stands. A good no-look pass or a breakaway slam were worth a few high-fives the next day at school, and maybe a closer look from the girl in algebra. They knew what Donlea wanted, but they also had their own ideas about what mattered.

"They aren't ready to play," Donlea said. "How could they not be ready to play in this game? They just want to do their own stuff. I can't figure these guys out. I've been wrong the whole time, every step."

Skyline led by four at halftime. There was grumbling from the stands, the sounds of annoyance more than anything else. After all, this was Tech. As the half ended, the team went to the locker room and Donlea took his clipboard to the scorer's table. He took a look at the scorebook and added up his team's numbers from the free-throw line. They had made just six of twenty-two. He wrote it on the clipboard, which had a diagram of a basketball court printed on it. He wrote the numbers in thick felt-tip pen, and he wrote it from baseline to baseline: 6–22.

Donlea looked at Wright's line—two points. The most talented player on the floor was nowhere to be found. He got lost somewhere in a game that didn't conform to his flow.

"I wish I knew how to turn that kid's key," Donlea said. "I need to know, and I need to know now."

He walked into the locker room.

"I've got some numbers for you guys. I don't know what good it does to tell you this, but here it is"—Donlea held up his clipboard. "That's what we are from the free-throw line. Listen, we can't do anything about it now. If you'd made half your free throws, this game would be a blowout. What's wrong out there? Are you guys nervous at the line?"

"I was," Darren Albert said. "I ain't gonna lie to you."

"That's understandable. We're all a little nervous, I think. This is what we've been working toward all year. You can't help but be a little nervous. I know I am."

"We got to pick it up, fellas," Govan said. As always, he had carried them through a rough time, grabbing rebounds and scoring inside on double- and triple-pump post moves. He had earned the right to talk.

"Grab the rebounds with both hands. You gotta block out, 'cause they're crashing the boards."

"That's exactly right," Donlea said. "You guys aren't playing physical out there. You've got to be more physical. You're standing out there letting them push you around. You're playing like pussies, like you're afraid. That's ridiculous! You can't be soft like that. Get some toughness, goddammit. That's not the way we play."

Donlea walked out and the team followed.

"I don't know if that'll work, but I guess it's worth a try. Sometimes I think that's the way these kids are used to being talked to, and that's what they respond to. If they don't do something at home, I bet they get their ass chewed."

Frustrated by his team's lack of toughness, Donlea looked down the bench halfway through the third quarter—with Skyline trudging through a score-and-let-them-score stretch—and called on Damon Gardner and Calvin Wilson. "We're gonna go football here in a minute," he told them.

Gardner and Wilson were both Division I college football

prospects. Along with Blackwell and two other teammates, their winter schedule had been filled with weekend trips to colleges up and down the West Coast. Gardner was a muscular, 5-foot-7 halfback who was recruited mostly as a defensive back. Wilson, at six feet and 235 lbs., was a fullback/linebacker known for his crushing blocks. Academic problems had kept him from completing a season on the football team, but the recruiters came calling anyway.

When they entered the game, a roar went up from the Skyline cheering section. Football players are among the most ardent fans at the basketball games, and they had waited—too long, in their minds—to see their fall teammates get into the game.

Skyline led by six points when Gardner and Wilson jogged onto the floor. Four minutes later, they left with Skyline leading by eleven. Wilson changed the momentum of the game, not with a slam or a blocked shot but by diving on the floor for a loose ball in front of the Oakland Tech bench. While he was lying on the floor looking to pass the ball, a Tech player came from the front and tackled him. It was a vicious hit; Wilson's body folded backward onto the floor. The players on the Skyline bench leaped up and headed onto the court while Donlea tried beyond his capacity to keep them from starting something. The issue was defused considerably when Calvin got off the floor with a wide smile across his face.

"Calvin and Damon know what it is to compete," Donlea said. "They can teach these other guys something."

He took Wilson and Gardner out to start the fourth quarter. "You guys got us back in this game, now these guys have to take it the rest of the way," he said.

Skyline won the game, 66–56. It wasn't a rousing start, but it was one win out of the way. Donlea was concerned that they hadn't shown Tech any respect. He realized he was fighting a losing battle. He knew they played as hard as they needed to play, but it killed him to let them get away with the minimum effort. He was too respectful of the game.

"We can't go into a game soft and quiet," he said afterward. "That's not our personality. We need to get that football mentality those two showed you today. You need to throw some elbows and rough each other up. It takes a controlled nastiness to play this game."

•••

Donlea watched the tape of the Oakland Tech game over and over, and each time he was more impressed by Govan. He was as fundamentally sound as a high school player could be, a six-three kid who could play any position but point guard. He was Skyline's best perimeter shooter, but he was also the best rebounder and post player. Donlea always wondered if he was playing Govan in the right spot—regardless of where it was—but he knew for sure that Govan got the most out of what he had.

The only problem was that Govan didn't respond to Donlea. Govan was the son of a coach, and he was aloof and noncommittal when Donlea asked about his college plans. Govan had been contacted by some major colleges, but he didn't tell that to Donlea. He didn't respect the coach, and he made his disdain alarmingly apparent. Donlea saw it and was bothered by it, but he always fell back on the ancient coaching credo: *They don't have to like me, just play for me.* And Govan played. End of problem.

Besides, Govan didn't feel he needed Donlea's advice or direction. His father was a coach and a teacher, and he taught his son how to play the game with skill and toughness at an early age. His father was a counselor at Oakland High, and he set his son on the right course academically as well. Eric took most of his classes at Merritt Community College, and he was as prepared for college as anybody at Skyline. The family owned a nightclub in the Hispanic-dominated Fruitvale section of Oakland, and they had just moved from the Oakland hills to the wealthy town of Orinda. Govan sometimes drove the family's Mercedes to school, and he was getting his father's Corvette for graduation. He had just about everything he needed, and he played basketball because it was in his blood. His unspoken message to Donlea mirrored Donlea's message: *You don't have to like me, just let me play.*

On January 15, 1993, a Friday, the bus went east on MacArthur, past the Center of Hope Community Church, Jim's Liquor and the African People's Socialist Party. There were more storefront churches and Asian groceries and corner marts, known by the criminals as Stop-N-Robs. Coming from the hills to The 'Hood, the land-scape quickly recedes from gentility to danger. Wrought-iron bars appear on every window. Three men leaned against the wall of a liquor store, underneath a neon sign for Olde English 800. One of them slowly raised his middle finger as the bus whined past.

The side entrance was locked when the Skyline varsity, junior varsity and cheerleaders got off the bus. They walked around the back of the gym, through an empty parking lot. Castlemont is considered the toughest high school in Oakland, a place where drug dealers work the streets surrounding the school. As is the case with most of the Oakland high schools, the problems come mostly from outsiders. They talk of the time at Castlemont when a man ran across the football field in the middle of the morning, zigging and zagging through the grass in a desperate, and ultimately futile, attempt to dodge a hail of bullets coming from the street outside the stadium.

"We gonna have to walk all the way around?" one player asked. "We'll be lucky if we're not shot."

"I ain't worried," Bryant Johnson said. "I got folks here—family. They take care of me."

"You need that," Nick Wimberly said. "You need that everywhere."

"The Castle" was quiet, filled with the same after-school solitude found in suburbs and country towns. On this afternoon, the only noise came from a group of Castlemont students that stood near a row of classrooms.

"Who those niggahs?" one boy asked. "That Skyline? Skyline niggahs? Hey, this ain't Skyline. No way, this ain't Skyline in the hills. This is Castlemont."

As Donlea walked into the Castlemont gym and identified his players for the police officers, he thought this game would tell him all he needed to know about his players—whether they could play in a hostile environment, whether they could play strong, whether they could *compete*. That was his favorite word—*compete*—and he still had his doubts. He thought this was the biggest game of the season for his team; but then again, he thought that about every game.

Donlea didn't know if Nick Wimberly, the team's starting center, was the kind of player who could handle adversity. Donlea thought

Wimberly was soft and easily intimidated, a kid who could get thrown off by the emotion of the moment. Without Will Blackwell, Skyline needed someone to emerge as a rebounder and an emotional force. Donlea hadn't seen the desire or the attentiveness he wanted from Wimberly, and his worst fear was that Wimberly would come into the OAL and get talked and shoved right out of the building. If that happened, Donlea thought Skyline would go right out the door with him.

He looked at what surrounded Castlemont and worried that they were facing kids with rougher edges. He wondered if his players were good kids—too good. From what he'd seen, he didn't think you could win in the OAL with kids with rounded edges.

Donlea's pregame speech was buttressed by a cacophony of terse, clipped remarks from the players. They sounded like background singers, and their lyrics combined to produce a beat all its own.

"Every deflected ball, every loose ball—that's ours," Donlea said. "If the ball gets on the ground, dive to get it. We've got to be scrappy today—"

"Get dirty. Gotta get dirty."

"Down and dirty, that's us. Down and dirty."

"What's up, niggah? What's up?"

"You, J. That's you."

"—and no one in this league runs offense like we do, and you guys are good enough and athletic enough to make it work. You know it will work. If we get pressed, it's all in your head—whether or not you beat that press or you crumble to it—"

"Let's go, fellas. Let's go."

"This is it, time to serve."

"Time to SERVE."

"Come on, fellas. We about to get this win."

"—so talk to each other. Fire each other up. I want to hear it. I want to hear it on the bench."

They were ready to go. The restlessness had set in. Govan was jumping in the corner. Bryant Johnson couldn't stand still. Wimberly was pacing in the corner, talking to himself. Donlea had one more thing to say.

"Now listen, I sub in Oakland. I've been to Castlemont. No one knows who I am. No one knows who I am, right? So I go into these schools and I start asking about their basketball teams. I always do that. I want to find out what I can find out. We get to talking about the league and talking about the teams. Skyline comes up. This is at Castlemont. You see that guy I was talking to out there, that white guy? That's who I sub for. I was talking to his kids, and one of his kids is a player, the big guy. So I'm talking to him and you can just hear it in his voice—they don't have respect for you guys. They don't think you're shit, and I'm not kidding you. They really don't—they think we're weak. They don't have much respect for Skyline. They're not gonna really care. They think they're gonna kick our ass and push us around and muscle us out of this game and talk shit to you and take you out of your game. Hey, don't talk to them, talk to each other. *Fire each other up. FIRE each other UP.* I'm excited about this game because I know we're not soft and I know we're a tough team.

"No matter what happens out on that floor tonight, we are a team and we stay together as a team. Score a basket, I want to hear it on the bench. You get a steal, I want to hear it on the bench and see it on the floor. Show them you're not no pussies out there. Show them. Just because you're up at Skyline doesn't mean you're soft. You're just like them, just like them. You're hungry, you want to win and you know you can win. You can do anything you want."

Donlea walked out of the room and looked up at the crowd—nothing but black faces staring down at him. The Castlemont crowd was filled with students who lived in the same neighborhoods as the Skyline players. Many of them would have gone to Skyline, but they couldn't pull the right strings. There was a built-in animosity because of that, but Donlea had to remind himself that they were all kids. Just kids.

Castlemont had the distinct disadvantage of opening the league season against McClymonds, ranked third in the state. Castlemont lost, 128–98, and the players knew that the realities of the league meant an 0–2 start was deadly. Castlemont was ranked in Northern California to start the season, mainly because of junior Michael Franklin, who scored 40 points against Mack and could score 30 by accident.

Donlea told Wright he would guard Franklin. This was another chance for Jason to show some people—scouts, teammates, Donlea—that he could stand in the OAL's center circle with Franklin and Darrnaryl Stamps and Fremont's Kareem Davis. It was a place he desperately wanted to be.

"I ain't about to lose this game," Jason Wright said.

"You screwed up, Jason," Donlea said. "You showed me early in the season that you can play defense, so now I expect you to do it. I expect it out of you, and you can do it. You can stay with this guy, take him out of his game."

The challenge went beyond this one game. Jason knew Franklin from the playground. He knew Franklin's moves and he knew his temperament. He also remembered a time when Franklin would show up at Allendale and nobody would pick him up. He knew all that natural ability Franklin had shown was born of hard work, work that comes with being left out on the playground. In the city, there is no greater disillusionment. Wright and Franklin had played before, but not with this much on the line. You can concoct your own history on the playground, but now there would be witnesses. Now everybody would know, one way or the other, if Jason Wright could play for real.

"He built just like me and he play just like me," Jason said. "Anybody who can score 40 points play just like me. People been comparin' us like by face and by the way we built and by the way we play. We about the same size and same weight. He handle the rock more than me, but I say if I was in that same atmosphere and I got to handle the rock as much as he does, I'd be putting up 40-point games, too."

Donlea's main worry was that Wright would turn the game into a personal confrontation between the two best juniors in the OAL. He could envision Wright and Franklin going at it back and forth. Wright scores, Franklin goes for the payback. Franklin scores, Wright goes for the payback. He didn't want it to turn into a one-on-one with eight on-court bystanders. Then again, Donlea wouldn't let that happen, anyway. Wright would sit if he lost sight of the team game.

Skyline came out strong, stronger than even Donlea could have hoped. Strom broke the Castlemont press with ease, and Wimberly and Govan handled the inside. They ran the floor and showed that they were every bit as athletic as Castlemont. Donlea didn't think they could run in the OAL, but here they were, doing it with ease.

The game is played at a manic pace. Coaches and players fight a constant struggle to keep from getting caught by the tide and swept away. As it so often does in the OAL, this game turned on a dunk. Skyline led by 11 points halfway through the second quarter when Castlemont's Paul Rapier stole a pass and threw down a strong two-handed slam. Suddenly, Castlemont was alive. Fans were out of the stands. Some of them ran onto the court, holding their hands to the sky and recreating the dunk. One of the officials had to skip away from two Castlemont students who were showing their excitement by dancing on the court. Donlea looked down the court and shook his head; he started to plead with the officials and then stopped. He sat down and crossed his legs. It was out of his hands now.

"It's always a dunk or a blocked shot in the OAL," Will Blackwell said. "You can think you've got it going, everything's going your way, and all of a sudden somebody rips one and the momentum shifts like crazy. Especially when the home team does it. The team who dunks gets hyped and the guys who get dunked on get mad. People around here get off on dunks."

Rapier's dunk was followed by nine straight Castlemont points. By the time Skyline regained its bearings, its lead was down to three points. Skyline led by six at halftime.

"That's half a game, but they don't put that in the paper tomorrow," Donlea told them. "They only print the *final* score."

"On defense, don't pay no attention to their eyes, man," Govan said. "They're trying to shake you with their eyes."

Strom's face contorted into a compressed look of disgust. "No one looks at their eyes, man. That's stupid."

The father of a Castlemont player sat behind the Skyline bench and complained bitterly throughout the first half. He was disgusted with Castlemont's selfish play, and his monologue was constant and sometimes explosive. At halftime, he sat down next to Donlea on the Skyline bench. He wore a painter's cap with a plastic cover, and his beard was sprinkled with white spots, like flecks of snow. He wore a windbreaker with the insignia of a local union.

"I like the way you coach," he told Donlea. "I'm gonna send you a ballplayer—a great one."

Donlea shifted back on the bench, his mind temporarily away from the game.

"OK, I appreciate that," he said. "That would be great. We're always looking."

The man walked away to borrow a piece of paper and a pen from someone in the stands. Donlea stood up, amused by the scene, and said, "Man, I hope his son's Michael Franklin."

The man returned and gave Donlea his name, telephone number and address. He said he had a brother living in the Skyline district, so a transfer wouldn't be a problem. Donlea took the paper and said he would give him a call. It wasn't Michael Franklin's father, however. The man's name was Benjamin Hill, and his son was a freshman point guard.

"You coach one good half of basketball and you've got guys wanting to send their kids to the school," Donlea said. "That's what I love about this job. If I stay here, we can really build a program. We can get just about any kid in town to come up there. All the parents want their kids at Skyline."

Donlea kept an eye on young Ben Hill throughout the season, but he never made the call. He had heard stories about coaches actively recruiting in the OAL, and he also had been warned that administrators at other schools kept a vigilant eye on Skyline. Sean Colter, a star of the 1989 Skyline team that finished second in the state, transferred from Hayward High after his freshman year. He said he got at least one phone call a night from OAL coaches who wanted him to play at their school.

Darren Albert couldn't get it going. He started poorly and watched as it escalated to the point of complete frustration. He would get trapped in the backcourt and lose his grip on the ball. He would find himself open for a fifteen-foot jumper and he'd smack it hard off the back rim. He'd find himself with a free lane to the basket, only to see the opening close off when a defender stepped in to take a charge. It was Darren's worst game of the year, maybe the worst game of his life, and in the third quarter Donlea decided he couldn't let it happen any longer.

Albert missed horribly after pulling up at the free-throw line and Donlea called Bryant Johnson to replace him.

"No, Bryant, forget it," Donlea said. He walked away, running both hands through his hair. "I can't do it right after that. That'll kill his confidence."

At the next dead ball, Donlea replaced Darren Albert. Darren came to the bench and buried his head deep in his hands. Donlea walked over and crouched low, beneath Albert's buried head, and spoke upward into his covered face.

"You're our man, Darren. You're still our man. Don't get down. You're a tougher kid than that."

After the game, Donlea said, "Darren's such a great kid. I want him to play well so badly. It just kills me when that happens."

Skyline won, 78–77. Franklin hit a 35-footer at the buzzer for Castlemont to bring the final margin to one point. The score meant nothing to Donlea or the Skyline players. The team some thought would struggle to stay out of the OAL basement had started the league season with two wins and no defeats.

With thirty-one seconds remaining, the players on the Castlemont bench left the court. They rose as one and walked off, headed for the locker room. They were trailing by five points, and coach Ron Caesar had seen enough. He sent them off, leaving their five teammates on the floor.

"That's the OAL," Jason Wright said. "Nobody takes losin' easy."

The loss made Castlemont 0–2 in the OAL. They entered the season ranked in Northern California, and now they were a team divided. During the junior varsity game, Caesar pulled his players into a tight huddle behind one of the baskets. The game went on around them, but they paid it no attention. He was animated, his face bearing a look of deep concern. His players listened for close to ten minutes, then Caesar stopped speaking and went from one player to the next, hugging each one.

• • •

Jason Wright and Michael Franklin battled to a draw. Wright scored 22 points, Franklin 28, but Wright won the style points. He had five dunks, and one of them nearly unhinged the basket from the rafters. As important as anything, he had ample opportunity to unveil his new post-dunk celebration. He cupped his hand over his ear and leaned toward the crowd, like a first-grade teacher encouraging a shy student to speak up. He heard it, too, mostly jeers from the Castlemont students, one of whom ran down the sideline in front of the Skyline bench and yelled at one of the Castlemont players to "Take him out! Take him out! Don't let him do that to us!"

"He better watch himself," Donlea told the bench players. "He's such a ham, somebody might come after him."

Early in the second quarter, Wright stood near halfcourt while Govan shot a free throw. Wright looked up into the crowd and thought he saw some friends sitting in the tight cluster of Castlemont students. He looked up in the stands and nodded in the general direction of the group. A slight smile crossed his face.

One problem: these weren't his friends. He had just finished a dunk-and-celebration routine, and the gesture toward the stands wasn't appreciated. Showing off was one thing; rubbing it in was another.

"Yeah, J Wright, you do that again and we gonna *smoke* yo' ass after the game," somebody yelled.

Wright turned back to the court and put his head down while Govan shot his second free throw. The smile was gone. He wasn't sure if the threat was real, if the person actually cared enough about the game to pull a gun on him afterward, but in these parts it wasn't entirely unthinkable.

"I ain't never had that happen before," Wright said later. "I kind of shut my mouth the rest of the game. It didn't really scare me, though. It made me feel kinda good, tell you the truth. Because that showed I had a little respect. I pretty much know the serious people from the others. But in the second half, I kind of toned it down, just in case."

When he's on the court, Wright gives the impression he's not only playing but simultaneously watching the highlights. He's always aware of appearances, always trying something new. But it wasn't too far out of the realm of possibility that somebody could exact some retribution. Donlea thought about that, too, as he watched Wright's third dunk turn into a high-stepping, arm-wagging run downcourt. Jason was having a great time, meaning no harm, but there was a nagging feeling that in a more important game, in a similar setting, he might not get away with it.

After the game, in the aftermath of the nervous tension and the constant noise, Donlea closed the door to the visiting team room and unleashed a hoarse, cathartic monologue. The players were happy, but Donlea's reaction went somewhere else, to some previously unexplored realm of happiness.

"YEAH, GODDAMNIT, YEAH! WE AIN'T NO PUSSIES! WE'RE TWO AND OH AND TEN AND FIVE! THAT DOESN'T LOOK TOO BAD, DOES IT? WE SHOWED THEM SOMETHING. YEAH, NICK WIMBERLY! YEAH, CALVIN WILSON! WE DID IT! WE HUNG TOUGH! GODDAMN THAT WAS A BIG WIN FOR US!"

He went around the room, continuing at the top of his lungs. In another setting, maybe any other setting, it would have been the ravings of a madman. But here, in this small room, in front of his team, in light of the past three months, it seemed entirely appropriate.

"You're tough, Nick Wimberly! You're tough!" He slapped Wimberly's hand. Wimberly smiled sheepishly, not sure how to respond. The rest of the team laughed and slapped hands, watching their coach. They had never seen this kind of emotion from Donlea, and most of them stood transfixed by the spectacle. Slowly, they joined in. Govan began clapping.

"That's right, fellas," Bryant Johnson said. "That's right. Skyline."

They were interrupted by a police officer, who urged them to get moving. "Your bus is waiting, fellas. Got to get going."

They finished dressing and left, single file, with the officer as an escort. They had won, in unfriendly territory, and it was best to celebrate quickly.

"I don't think they've believed in anything yet," Donlea said. "I think they might believe now. That was big."

• • •

The next day in the *Tribune* the headline read: "Skyline tied for OAL lead." Donlea liked the look of that. Even better, he liked the visit from Will Blackwell later in the day.

"I'm comin' back," Will said. "My ankle's healing, and I can't stand to watch anymore."

Donlea's heartbeat quickened. He looked at his team and believed it was one player away from serious contention in the OAL. That one player was Blackwell. Still, he didn't want to appear too anxious. He didn't want to be blamed if Will reinjured his ankle and lost his football scholarship. He would have completely understood the situation had Blackwell decided to forget basketball and let it heal.

"I'd love to have you back, but I don't want you to rush back," he said. "It's up to you, but don't risk it."

Will had heard the talk on campus that day. Nobody had expected much from the team, and now basketball was again dominating conversations. There was no way he could let that happen without him. In his mind, Will Blackwell was Skyline football, and Skyline basketball. Besides, they needed him.

"I'm comin' back," he repeated. "I've never quit anything in my life."

CHAPTER EIGHT

STELLA BLACKWELL HAD GROWN ACCUSTOMED TO HAVING VISITORS FOR dinner. She had fed a lot of football coaches over the past six months, and they were all exceedingly polite. They complimented her on her food, on her decorations, on her clothes. And, of course, on her son. In the fall and winter of 1992–93, college football coaches could be broken down into two categories: those who had a chance at Will Blackwell, and those who didn't but wanted him anyway.

Two coaches from San Diego State visited on January 18. Letter of intent day was less than two weeks away, so nothing could be left unfinished. Sean Payton, the Aztecs' running backs coach and regional recruiter for Northern California, brought along Curtis Johnson, the receivers coach. Johnson needed to be there. If Blackwell chose San Diego State, he would answer to Johnson. Besides, Johnson was black and had a growing reputation as the kind of recruiter who could talk the Aztecs into the national rankings.

When these meetings take place, Skyline football coach John Beam is always there. A burly 34-year-old Korean with a wispy Fu Manchu mustache and a reputation for being able to walk into the toughest neighborhoods in Oakland and be greeted like family, Beam has been the liaison between recruiters and players countless times during his eleven years at Skyline. He's vocal and straightforward, not afraid to ask the questions he believes need to be asked. He's face-to-face and right up front, with street smarts. Most of his players are athletes first and students second, and many of them are the first in their families to attend college. They need Beam, and their families need him. He has sent players all over the country, at least two a year, and he tells them each to operate under one direct principle: Use them, because they're sure as hell going to use you.

Beam teaches his players how to order from a menu, how to speak to newspaper reporters and how to play football. Intensity surrounds him like a force field. ("For these kids, life is intense," he says. "If you want to turn them on, if you want to reach them, you have to have that intensity.") If one of his players was going on a recruiting trip, Beam tells him what to pack and how to behave. He makes sure the player has proper clothes in case he was taken to a restaurant. He has often lent his own clothes to players whose best piece of clothing was a T-shirt.

During the summer, Beam takes his players to weekend passing-league tournaments at universities such as Pacific and Nevada-Reno. At the end of each day, they go out to dinner at modest restaurants, and the long line of mostly black adolescents draws uncomfortable looks from the white clientele. Beam lives for those moments.

"I've gotten a few letters from people telling me how impressed they were with the way my players behaved," Beam said. "I get a little defensive about that, because I'm not sure it's a compliment. I want to ask them: What did you expect? Why did you expect something different?"

Before coming to Skyline, Beam taught at juvenile hall and at Havenscourt Junior High School, the toughest one around. He grew up in San Diego, but he knows Oakland from the inside. He can take you down 77th Avenue and identify members of three rival gangs (77th Bancroft; 77th Rudsdale; 77th Greenman) that work a half-mile stretch on either side of East 14th, near the Oakland Coliseum. He can do the same on Seminary Drive (Bromley, East 17th and Seminary). He's taken members of some of those gangs and turned them on to football, changed their lives by teaching them how to use their athletic ability.

"I don't care what they've done," he said. "I just care what they're gonna do. If you take a kid who's used to making twenty grand a week on the street, he's gonna give you everything he has. And you know why? That kid's given up something to play football, and he's gonna make it work."

Beam taught the successor to notorious Oakland drug lord Felix Mitchell. The successor took over on the streets of East Oakland when Mitchell was sent to federal prison. The new leader was running a multimillion-dollar drug operation by the time he was in ninth grade.

Beam would open the gym after school so the Havenscourt students could play basketball. He remembers a line of kids waiting to hold the dealer's clothes. One boy would be picked out to follow the dealer into the locker room. The dealer would methodically take off his street clothes and hand them to the student, who would hold them until Beam closed the gym.

The dealer was an important figure in Oakland. He was the heir to Felix Mitchell, the great heroin entrepreneur and possibly East Oakland's largest employer. Young and idealistic, Beam saw the clothes-holding scene play out one day and decided to end it.

"Get over here," he said to the dealer.

"Put that down," he told the student who was holding the clothes. Then he turned to the dealer and said: "Take your clothes; he's playin'." Beam's orders were followed. The kid played.

Beam quickly developed a reputation at Havenscourt. They called him "The Crazy Chinaman," but they respected him because he could relate. One day the dealer approached him.

"Hey, I like you, coach," he said. "I'm gonna kick you down fifty a week, 'cause you just good."

"No, man," Beam said. "Keep your damned money."

The living room in the Blackwells' home is dominated by a sparkling-clean glass shelf that holds nothing but Will's athletic awards—four layers of trophies, plaques and certificates presented to Will over the past three years; six feet of photographs, letters and medals. Certificates from *The Oakland Tribune*, basketball and football trophies from Skyline—it all sits in the center of the room, next to the television set. In a back room there was a box filled with letters from universities across the country: Notre Dame, Michigan, Miami, Penn State, Clemson, Texas. There were red, blue, yellow, green pages. Some were form letters, others personal. He had tried to keep them all, but it soon became impossible. The University of Pittsburgh was still sending letters, and still calling, even though Will hadn't expressed any interest at all, ever.

His first letter came early in his junior year at Skyline. It came from the San Diego State basketball coach. It was still there, too, buried under the piles of adulation-filled letters from panting football coaches. Will indicated that he would walk-on to the basketball team if he went to San Diego State.He said he would play Division I college basketball "in his leisure time."

Outside, on 104th Avenue in East Oakland, the sounds of the street dominated. Old cars revved and coughed and backfired as they passed the house. Sirens blared. Inside, it was quiet and calm. Serene, in a way. Two men in suits and ties were attempting to persuade a young man in blue jeans and a T-shirt to accept their offer of a football scholarship. There had been many before them and others after them. Everyone knew the routine: The men would stay until they felt confident they had left nothing unsaid.

Stella prepared an enormous amount of food—fried chicken, green salad, corn on the cob, homemade biscuits and "Arkansas potatoes." There was homemade punch to drink, apple pie and cake for dessert. The kitchen was overcome with food, enough to feed every recruiting coordinator who had ever sent Will a questionnaire. Curtis Johnson was from Louisiana, and Stella wanted to give him a Southern country meal worthy of her Arkansas roots.

"Ms. Blackwell, this is amazing," Payton said.

Johnson nodded vigorously.

"It sure is. I haven't had a downhome meal like this in a long time."

"Well, thank you," Stella said. "I'm glad you like it."

Payton told Stella he liked her outfit, a black blouse with a flowing red and-black skirt.

"Aztec colors," Payton said.

"Skyline colors," Beam said, and everybody laughed.

Payton and Johnson knew Will was leaning toward their school even before they arrived at the Blackwells' modest home. Then, when they saw the spread Stella laid out and the special gastronomic consideration she had shown Johnson, they felt even better. They had learned to keep track of such things.

This was the final home visit for San Diego State. It was their last opportunity to extol the virtues of their school, and their football program, before leaving the decision up to Will and Stella. After this, they would stay in touch, but not in control.

Beam had been running interference for the Blackwell family, ever since Will began attracting attention with his one-handed catches and his outright refusal to be tackled once he caught the ball. Beam followed it through, too; many of his former players still called him first when something went down and they needed somebody to listen. He knew that college was a paralyzing culture shock for most Oakland kids, no matter where they went. The people were different, the pace was different, the rules were different.

"A lot of our teaching with these athletes has to be social skills," Beam said. "When Will goes to college, a lot of things that were acceptable here in Oakland aren't gonna be acceptable anymore. You can't walk up to a girl and say, 'Hey, bitch, what you got?' You can't do those things, so we work on these things constantly. They've got to come to my house for dinner; they've got to be able to behave in *my* house."

Blackwell's athletic ability had made him a celebrity on the Skyline campus. Everyone knew he had it made—*Parade* All-America, constant coverage in The Tribune, recruiters begging for his attention—but Beam knew the other side. He knew that Will's college choice would be scrutinized just as closely. And he knew Will would have to live with it.

"The one thing I worry about is whether Will is strong enough to go out into Oakland and tell his homeys," Beam told Johnson and Payton. "They're gonna say, 'Will, where you goin'? Will, you're a Parade All American, you goin' to Miami? Michigan? Notre Dame?' When Will says, 'Nah, San Diego State,' those folks are gonna say, 'San Diego *who?*' Because in Oakland, those guys don't know San Diego State. They don't know what kind of football they play in the WAC. They just know the national schools, and they see that Will's a Parade All American. That might be tough for him."

There appeared to be a sense of immediacy to this evening, a certain casual intensity to the discussion. Neither Payton nor Johnson asked for a commitment, but each knew that Will was going to the University of Colorado for the weekend, the last of his five campus visits. The specter of Boulder, the Big Eight Conference and the likelihood of playing in an Orange Bowl weighed on their minds. Payton and Johnson felt they had done everything in their power to convince Blackwell that San Diego was the perfect place, but they also knew Colorado was a formidable opponent. The Buffaloes had more tradition, more recognition, more ammunition—and they had already shown that they wouldn't hesitate to flaunt it.

On December 2, Colorado coach Bill McCartney, along with assistant coach Greg Brown, the regional recruiter for Northern California, had chartered a Lear jet from Boulder to Oakland. They got off the plane and took a limousine up to Skyline, where they stood on the cold, concrete floor of the gym's entrance, waiting for the privilege of speaking with a teenager from East Oakland.

The most notable thing Payton did was beep Will's pager just before the basketball game against Moreau. Will seemed impressed when it happened, but he didn't return the call. He was accustomed to such intrusions.

The day McCartney showed up at Skyline was a busy day around the coaches' office. Payton was there, representatives from California, UCLA, USC, Arizona State, Notre Dame and Michigan were there, too. They all wanted a word with Will.

McCartney, as a head coach, was allowed one visit to a recruit's school, and he used it on the second day possible, for the sole purpose of convincing Will to visit Boulder. He wasn't looking for a commitment, just a visit. *Come on out and give us a look.* Clearly, the Buffaloes wanted Blackwell, wanted him *bad*. That scared the guys from San Diego State. They knew what they had on their side: Will hated the cold, he wanted to be close to home and he wanted to play right away. As they added up pros and cons in their mental ledger, they felt they were ahead. Still, they knew exactly what would happen when Blackwell arrived in Boulder on Friday night: McCartney, his coaches and his players would do everything in their power to change his mind.

Like car salesmen, they would open the door to their multimillion dollar weight room and watch Will gasp. They would show him the indoor practice facility. *See, don't worry about the cold.* They would walk him down the black-and-gold carpet of the football offices and show him the 1990 national championship trophy. *How'd you like to be a part of one of those?* They would put him in a suite in the best hotel, take him to the best restaurants, introduce him to the prettiest girls. *Look at this; there's more to life than California.* They would show him the depth chart and talk about their four-receiver formation. *If you work hard, there's room for you right away.*

The guys from San Diego State had been through this before with schools like Colorado, and they knew San Diego didn't always win.

They also knew they held a few cards of their own. Johnson was in town not only because he was the receivers coach, the one man Will would answer to for the next four or five years. He was also the best pitch man San Diego State had. He was well-spoken, intelligent and easygoing. There was passion in his voice, and his words took on the lilting, up-and-down tones of a preacher. He could work a room, and he was smart enough to direct his message as much to Stella as to Will.

Johnson was responsible for recruiting Marshall Faulk to San Diego State, and for that he was held in almost mythic regard. He had stolen the best running back in the nation from LSU and Florida State and Texas A&M and Miami. He had received hate mail from people in Louisiana and Florida and Texas, a distinction he claimed as the recruiting equivalent of the Congressional Medal of Honor.

"They don't like me down there," he said with a laugh.

"No, they don't," Payton said, "and they're not going to like me up here in Northern California before too long, either." That, of course, depended on Will.

"You should hear the things they've been saying about me down there after Marshall," Johnson said. "They say I paid Marshall. They say I bought Marshall's momma a house. She still lives in the projects, you know? I didn't know they were sellin' those houses. When did they start that?"

Johnson had been the one to see Faulk as a great running back when other schools were trying to decide whether he would play receiver or defensive back.

"He played everywhere in high school," Johnson said. "Nobody was really quite sure where he would play. Everyone knew he *could* play, but it was clear to me where he belonged." Now Johnson saw Will Blackwell as a potentially great receiver, one to build a passing offense around.

"There's a lot of untapped potential there, and we're going to bring it out."

"He doesn't like to return punts, but you've got to make him return punts," Beam said. "He has the ability to make that first guy miss, and that's what you want in a punt returner. If you can return punts, you can make a lot of money playing on Sundays—just by returning punts. And I think he's athletic enough to do that."

Johnson looked straight at Will, then Stella.

"From what I've seen on film, he's athletic enough to play receiver on Sundays. No doubt in my mind."

Johnson had developed a reputation among college and professional coaches as a fine teacher. He had turned some average athletes, players with far less ability than Will, into NFL players. The message was unspoken, but clear: *Just think what we could do with you.*

After one of his receivers, Patrick Rowe, was drafted in the second round by the Cleveland Browns, Johnson said he got a telephone call that began with Rowe asking a question: "Coach, how much money you want?"

"What you mean, Pat? I don't want no money from you."

"Man, the reason why I'm at where I am today is because of you. When I got here, I didn't know one thing, not one thing."

Johnson used that anecdote on Will, who sat stock-still and impassive. He was impervious. Johnson noted that Rowe signed a contract worth more than two million dollars. Still no reaction. A brash, animated young man—the big man on a big campus—Will was withdrawn, nearly mute. He listened to every word with rapt attention, but he contributed almost nothing. He would nod his head in response to questions, but that was the extent of his interaction. He wasn't being rude or coy. He had spoken with hundreds of recruiters and taken four campus visits, but he still didn't know enough to ask a question.

Will and Stella's reticence increased Beam's role. He was the mediator, the translator, the interrogator.

Beam ignored Payton and Johnson for a moment, turning his attention to Will and Stella. He didn't want them asking their questions after the coaches had left. He'd seen that happen too many times before.

"I've been through this a lot of times, and no matter what you say, you're not going to hurt these people's feelings. They're drilled on this stuff. You're looking at four, maybe five years of your future. We can set the stage for your *real* future, wherever that may be—whether it's academic, getting a job, or maybe a shot at playing on

Sundays. Whatever. So you need to ask these people right now. That's their job; that's why they get the big money. They do, too. You see they've got nice suits and ties. They're used to it. Anything and everything that crosses your mind. This is it."

Will and Stella nodded but stayed silent.

"Now, are you going to want him to have his car down there?" Beam asked Stella.

"Yeah, I guess. He wants to take it."

"You're not going to need a car," Johnson said. "You're going to be so busy, you won't need it."

If the recruiters were to be believed, Will's success on the football field was assured, a given. But in order to make it onto the field, Blackwell had to score a minimum of 700 on the Scholastic Aptitude Test. He had scored 610 and 690 in his first two tries, and Beam told the coaches that he expected Will to make it easily with his third try. His score of 690 was just one correct answer away.

"We want him anyway," Johnson said. "One way or another, we want him."

None of the recruiters—not San Diego State, Colorado or UCLA—seem overly concerned about his SAT scores. He'll make it, they said, no problem. But Blackwell, like many black student athletes, can't master the flat, status-quo language of standardized tests. He says he wouldn't have had to take the SAT a third time if it wasn't for a series of questions in the reading comprehension section centering on a regatta.

"There were questions in there using words about a boat show," Blackwell said. "I didn't understand what they were talking about. Black people don't go to boat shows."

Beam tries to focus his players' energies on the mathematics portion of the SAT. "They can't change that," he said. "Numbers can't be culturally biased." According to school district statistics from 1981–1992, students in the Oakland public schools averaged 354 out of a possible 800 on the verbal section of the SAT—nearly 70 points below the national average. In mathematics, Oakland students averaged 430—45 points below the national average.

After a brief discussion of Will's academics, Johnson and Payton repeated their original statement: They weren't worried about Will.

"I looked at his core curriculum grades, and I didn't see any problem," Payton said. "We aren't worried at all about that."

Beam wanted to know if the San Diego State coaches could get Will a job during the summer. He reminded Stella that the free trips would come to an end as soon as Will picked a college. After that, he was on his own.

A job was no problem, they said. Al Luginbill, the head coach, could arrange it. Faulk worked in a law office last summer. They had players working for water districts, utility companies, a limousine service, Coca-Cola. Johnson said Will would almost assuredly qualify for a Pell Grant, which gives up to $1,700 a semester for low-income students.

"Al can get you a job, but the only thing he'll tell you is that he just wants you to go there," Payton said. "It's not going to be a job where you don't show up and you get paid. It's going to pay you well, but you're going to work for it. You need to let us know how much money you want to make. That means how many hours you're willing to work, because some guys don't want to work a lot of hours."

Payton and Johnson flooded the room with talk of bowl games, NFL possibilities, the Canadian Football League, senior all-star games. Beam wanted to know if San Diego State would pay for Will to attend summer school or winter session. He wanted to know where he would eat, what dormitory he would live in, where he could go if he needed a tutor. He wanted to know how many starters were returning, and how closely Will's grades would be monitored.

Johnson performed as if the discussion had been scripted in advance. He leaned toward Will and looked at Stella.

"In school—and your mother may not want to hear this—but you're gonna have problems—"

"Oh, yes, I know that," Stella said.

"You're gonna have girl problems. There's gonna be some things you're gonna get into that you're gonna say, 'Gaw-lee, I don't have nobody to turn to.' Well, when you see the atmosphere with the players, you'll know all you got to do is come into my office and close the door. We'll sit down and talk about it. If I need to inform your mother, I'll call your mother. If I need to call Coach Beam, we'll do that. That's just how it is—the bottom line. We've got to set some rules for me to get you a degree. And that's the rules. And I don't know another coach or another school that's going to take that kind of time with a young man, and that's going to work like that. I'll tell you, every kid I've coached at San Diego State has had an opportunity to play in the NFL, but you know the most amazing thing about it? All those kids come back."

Johnson's voice rose, picked up speed. This was his territory, his *turf*. He had Stella's attention. Now was his chance to let a proud mother know that she would be turning her son over to a man she could trust.

"This is all because of the relationship, and they understand I help them. Merton Harris? Played for the Giants half a season? Came back. He's finishing up school and lives right around the corner from me. Uses my washer and dryer more than I do. But that's the kind of respect we have for each other. If I need anything from Merton, I ask. I asked Merton a couple times when I'm on the road, 'Hey, Merton, why don't you cut my grass for me, man?' The next day, my grass's cut. 'How much you want, Merton?' He say, 'Coach, you know me better than that.' *That's* the relationship. It's like a family."

The telephone rang. Johnson continued, his voice never breaking stride. Will's sister told the caller that Will was not home. There was a pause.

"No, he's not home . . . Yes, there are some men here, but I don't know what's going on . . . I'm sorry, I just got home. My brother will be home later."

The caller was Rick Neuheisel, a former UCLA quarterback who was in charge of Northern California recruiting for the Bruins. Will had visited UCLA the weekend before, and Neuheisel had been calling ever since. He told Will that if he was going to attend UCLA, he needed to tell them by Thursday. Will didn't plan on telling them anything.

"Nobody pressures me," he said.

Will had eliminated UCLA, but he hadn't told Neuheisel. With Beam's advice, he hadn't closed any doors. The recruiting wars are filled with stories of players who made commitments, only to have the schools pull the scholarship when another player chose the same school. That wasn't going to happen with Will—he was at the top of most lists—but Beam wasn't interested in taking chances.

UCLA was considered too difficult academically for Will. He planned on going to class and getting his degree, but he understood his limitations. He was about to take the Scholastic Aptitude Test for the third time, and this time he was sure he would get the required 700 to qualify for a scholarship. But the prospect of sitting in an auditorium filled with students, *real* students, frightened him.

"I ain't no studious person," he said.

"If he goes and sits down in class at UCLA, everybody's going to know right away that he's a special admit," Beam said. "It's just the way it is. School really isn't his thing. Now that might change, but there are more average students at San Diego State. He won't stick out as much there as he would at UCLA or Cal. I think that's going to make a big difference in how he does."

The San Diego State coaches had heard that Will was impressed with their passing game and their beaches. The Aztecs' game plan—five basic running plays and four wideouts—was receivers' nirvana. Now Johnson and Payton were ready to hear something more. They wanted Will to look out over the steaming platter of perfectly fried chicken and say, "You've got me. You've got the thirteenth-rated prospect in the nation. You've got a first-team Parade All-American. Go out, tell the other recruits that Will Blackwell will be catching passes for the Aztecs next season. Tell the coaches of the Pac-10 schools, and Colorado, and Notre Dame, that San Diego State beat them to one of the top three prospects on the West Coast."

Instead, Will played it cool.

"What you need to do is ask questions," Johnson said. "I need to know what you're thinking. I don't want a commitment from you. I'm not asking for that. I just want to feel good about *you*. I don't care where you go or where you decide to go to school, I just want to know how *you* are, what you thinking about."

"If I commit to the school, when do I come down," Will asked.

Johnson jumped at the question. The words had barely left Will's mouth when Johnson said, "When you want to come down?"

Will dropped his head and stared at the table. He sensed he was walking frightfully close to the edge. His question sounded a lot like a commitment, especially since it was the first one he had asked.

"Look," Beam said. "I can call Colorado tomorrow morning and cancel that trip. That's no problem. If you want to go there and eat their food and spend their money, that's OK, too."

"That's your fifth trip, your last trip?" Johnson asked rhetorically. "If I hear that from a guy, I know I'm not gonna get him. I just know. He's made up his mind and just wants to take another trip."

Again, no response. The muffled sounds from the television in the other room filled the void. Will continued to look down, his hands folded in his lap under the table and his eyes fixed straight down. Again, Beam asked Johnson a question. It was his way of throwing Will a lifeline.

"If you were Will or Will's parent, why wouldn't you send him to Colorado?"

Johnson was ready.

"One thing about schools like Colorado: Guys will stockpile talent. You're on more or less a rotating system. As a freshman you redshirt. You sit around and learn the game, so they really don't deal with you much as a freshman. The following year you start playing special teams. Your junior year you're probably a part-time starter. Senior year you start. In general, the competitive level is so high they stockpile talent.

"That's one. Two, those guys have a rotating program. See, they're going to get the guys they want. They're going to get the best in the state of Colorado. Miami will get the best guys in Miami. San Diego State, we won't necessarily get the best guys. So you're looking at a situation where you got to say, 'OK, we're going to play who we gotta play.' We're going to play the best talent we can play if we're gonna win. And that's why right now we're starting to win, we're starting to turn the program around. Another thing is the level of care—"

"That's the thing I was going to hit on," Payton interrupted. "I can guarantee you you're not gonna have the same relationship with the receiver coach at Colorado, USC or UCLA that you will have with CJ. Just as far as being able to hang out or ask questions. At Colorado, you'll have six other freshmen, two of whom are probably in-state kids, and it'll be different that way. You're Will Blackwell, the kid who was at Skyline High School. Do you remember him, coach? That'll be different."

"When you look at a Colorado or Nebraska or Miami, they're

going to sign five or six Parade All-Americans," Johnson said. "They gonna sign guys like that. They're gonna get the number-one recruits in the nation, and once they sign them, you probably won't hear about them for another two years. But you take a Marshall Faulk—T.C. Wright was the starting running back going into his senior year. Understand his situation. He rushed for more yards than anybody else against the University of Miami prior to when Marshall got there. He had a great game against the University of Miami. This kid—the scouts were coming in talking about T.C. and everything else. Well, Marshall flat-out beat him out. I mean, T.C. was hurt, but that was kind of camouflaged. Marshall was the better player. T.C. would start the games, Marshall would end up playing. We are into playing the best players. If you're better than a guy—I'm telling you—you're gonna play.

"I know you met with some other coaches, but how many of them talked about *your life?* Your life after football, or within football or whatever. To me, that's very important."

"That's right," Beam said. "You got to ask yourself, 'Who can I call to talk about other things?' You're still goin' to need that. Whether you have problems with a teacher, problems with a girl-friend, problems with a friend, a problem at a party. If you don't have anyone, how you gonna move on? You can call me all the time, but you're phone bill's gonna go up—and I can't help you because I'm not there."

Will had been presented with a neat, orderly set of guarantees. Everywhere he went, the list was the same: five years of college, paid; five years of room and board, paid; four years in the spotlight, paid. Will Blackwell, wherever he went, wouldn't be a normal student. He would stay in an athletic dormitory, sometimes with a kitchen in the room. His meal card would allow him to eat anywhere on campus, free. He could get a personal, one-on-one tutor for each of his classes, just by asking.

He would also get priority registration. California's state university system had been crushed by budget cutbacks. Classes were eliminated, fees raised, professors laid off. Some students waited as long as three years to get the classes they needed. It wasn't unusual for it to take six years to graduate, simply because the classes were so impacted. Will Blackwell wouldn't have to worry about any of that. He would go to college and play football in an athletic vacu-um. He would get something from them, and they would make money off him. Bought and sold. That's the system.

"You're gonna get what you want," Johnson said. "We've got 35,000 students at that university, and a lot of them won't get their classes. You're going to get your classes at your specific times, so you have enough time to get your classes, have time to study and then have football practice. You're not going to have a class that will conflict with any of that."

"Who's gonna make sure that his classes balance out like that?" Stella asked. "I don't want him too overwhelmed."

"We generally start them off pretty slowly—twelve to thirteen units. It's also part of the academic counselor's job—and I worry about this all the time: there are some professors whose name doesn't get in the paper for nothin'. They've been there twenty years and their name's never in the paper, right? Will gonna be a quality athlete; he's in the paper, he's on TV getting interviewed or whatever. So some professors, and I'm talking about at every uni-versity, have got it in for athletes who succeed. So part of the coor-dinator's job is not to get you in classes with those guys, and believe me, we know who they are."

"That's what I'm concerned about," Stella said.

"So we gonna get him into the classes with the right professors. If he goes on a trip, that professor's going to say, 'OK, Will's on a trip, so he's excused absent and we're going to help him make the work up.' He's not going to be in with guys who say, 'That's unexcusable.'"

"The nice thing is, of course, you have priority registration," Payton said. "You have the luxury of saying, 'Ba-bing, ba-bing, ba-bing—I want it here, here and here.'"

Stella asked, "He doesn't know what he's going to major in, so who's there to make sure he takes the right classes?"

"The first two years he has what's called general education classes, which are social sciences, math, English, the humanities—just the general requirements everybody has to take."

"If they have a game, and he's gone, how they do that?" Stella asked. "If they leave on a Thursday or something, what's he do?"

"He'll get a slip, and it'll say, 'Will Blackwell's going to be gone on such-and-such a day," Johnson explained. "They'll sign it off.

The coordinator will get with him, or get with that professor, on any work he has to make up. He meets once a week with his academic counselor. He's going to have a copy of all his syllabus. If there's a test, they'll reschedule it. 'When can you take it? When will you be ready for it?' They'll go through that process."

Stella said she understood. She turned to Will.

"Do you like CJ, sonny?"

Will looked down from his mother's gaze. He hesitated, then shrugged.

"Yeah, I guess."

Beam laughed. "What's he gonna say? Will's bold, but he ain't that bold."

"You know, he's sort of shy," Stella said. "He takes a while to open up. I kind of put him on the spot there, coach."

"You did, but that's OK," Beam said. "You're supposed to do that. You're gonna give him up, and you've got to feel comfortable. Like in the car situation, I don't think he needs a car at first. One reason is, if something goes bad, it could just be personal, but he's gonna want to get in the damned car and come back to Oakland. It's so close. This way he can't. Now he's got to go deal with this man and say what's bothering him, whether it's playing time or whatever."

"You're not always going to like me," Johnson told Will. "I'm just lettin' you know. One thing about me, I am demanding. I'm going to bring the best out of you. I'm going to make a better man out of you. After the first year, you're going to understand. 'Ah, I see why CJ did that.' You will understand a lot, but initially you're going to resist it. It's going to be tough. But you've expressed that you want to play early. Well, I'm coaching you like I'm getting you ready to play early. The guys who play for me usually go and play after school, after college is over. You've got to take that into consideration."

Beam needed to leave. Will and Stella had heard all they needed to hear. The decision had been made: Will was going to San Diego State. The Aztecs had passed their final exam, and they had Johnson to thank. It didn't matter to Will what his partners said when he went out into the neighborhood. What did they know, anyway? He was going to walk to class in the sunshine, catch passes every Saturday afternoon and still live close enough so Stella could occasionally see him play. Nobody's telling Marshall Faulk he made the wrong choice, right? Will was going to San Diego State.

But he didn't want to tell them. He felt reasonably confident with his choice, and he could tell the coaches knew. Still, he was going to visit Colorado—"I may never see the place if I don't," he said.

Beam was late. It was nearing ten o'clock and he needed to get home. Will appeared uneasy at the prospect of being left alone with Payton and Johnson. He liked them all right, but he needed the security—and the thoroughness—Beam provided. Each time Beam asked for the time (there was no clock in the kitchen), Will would fidget. Beam had been in similar circumstances before, so he gave what amounted to a closing speech.

"You can analyze it, put it into a computer, but it's still got to be here," he said, pointing to his heart. "It's how you feel about people. One thing, it is a business—for everybody. If they're not winning, they're not going to be there. At the same time, some coaches are more than just business. I've had kids play for other coaches; some were genuine, some weren't. It's got to come from here, and both of you ought to talk. If you guys feel comfortable, then you need to do it. If you don't want to go to Colorado, I'll just make the call tomorrow morning. That's no big deal. If you want to go and eat their food, that's fine, too. You know, we've talked about it—you hate cold. When you go out there, you may not even want to leave your hotel. It's cold, and it's *real* cold when you're not playin'. When you're number three on the depth chart out of four, it's about twenty-five degrees colder than when you're number one. The number-one guy's saying, 'What you mean, cold? I'm catchin' the ball, it ain't cold.' You can tell these guys now or tell them whenever, but just feel good about it. There's going to be some remorse, just like when you buy a car or buy a house or get into a marriage. But it all comes back to whether it felt good *in here*. Then it works out."

Beam got up to leave. The discussion had lasted more than two hours, and Will had spoken barely ten words. Will followed Beam to the door and asked him to wait outside.

"What you mean? I ain't going out there to wait on 104th," Beam said, laughing. "I'm a 55th Street guy. This is *east* East Oakland. There's probably all kinds of gunshots out there."

Will ran upstairs; he had something for Beam, a T-shirt from some recruiting trip. He flashed up the stairs two at a time and came back slowly. He and Beam walked outside together as a light mist filled the cold night air. They stood in the soft glow of the porch light as police sirens wailed in the background, one overlapping the other. A few blocks away, on MacArthur and 98th, whores and pimps and crackheads walked the night away. They strolled in front of the Starlite Motel and leaned against the cinderblock wall of Keeton's Liquor. Will Blackwell stood in front of his house, on the verge of making the biggest decision of his life, a decision that would take him away from all of this. Maybe forever.

"What do you think, coach? What should I do?"

"Everything's right there," Beam said, pushing his right index finger into Will's chest. "It's all right there, and sometimes deeper. It's up to you now. If I tell you what I think, then I should go play."

"Yeah, that's true."

"You know, I *really* can't shake tough coverage. But the things that I asked, those are things you got to ask. I mean, you came back with certain gut feelings. From the heart, from the heart. What did our team shirts say this year? 'From the Heart.' That's where your decisions are always gonna be made in life, once you get the logic taken care of. I can tell you, this is logical. That school's gonna throw. UCLA's gonna throw. USC—we got rid of them. Cal's gonna throw with three wideouts. Colorado's gonna throw with four wideouts. So that's the logical. Now you got to go *from here*. When you meet with Neuheisel tomorrow, ask him those same questions. What can he teach you? And you got to be able to go up to a guy. If you call me up and say you got your girlfriend pregnant, you can tell me that. We can talk about it. You know what I'm saying? Is there somebody you can do that to, somebody you can feel comfortable saying, 'Hey, you know, something's going on at home. Can I come over to your place and kick it for a while, maybe call my mother?' Those are the things you've got to feel comfortable with. I can't tell you what to do because you've got to *feel* that."

Will nodded and took a deep breath. He shook Beam's hand and walked back into the house. Payton and Johnson stood stiffly in the living room, making conversation with Stella. Will decided to tell them nothing. They were going to get some good news, some really good news, but they would have to wait.

CHAPTER NINE

JASON WRIGHT LIFTED HIS UNTUCKED HOME-WHITE JERSEY AND PULLED a folded half-piece of paper out from under the elastic band on the right side of his baggy shorts. He read it and nodded, as if the contents reaffirmed something he already knew. The game against Fremont was less than thirty minutes away, and Jason appeared to be cramming for a test.

"This my hit list," he said.

Across the top of the paper he had written, in pencil, "Fremont Hit List." Underneath, in the same even hand, he had written:

1. Frank Knight
2. Kevin Sweetwyne
3. Lester Parham

"This is who I'm gonna serve," Jason said by way of explanation. "I walk out on the court, I walk up to him"—he points to Knight's name—"and I say, 'Frank, I'm gonna bust your ass.' Then I walk up to him"—he points to Sweetwyne's name—"and I say, 'Kevin, I'm gonna bust *your* ass.' Then I find Lester, and I walk up to him and say, 'Lester, I'm gonna *bust* your ass, and there ain't nothin' you can do about it.'"

Game time: 5:30 P.M., following the varsity girls game. It was the first and only OAL game scheduled to start after the customary 3:45 tipoff time. The later start was an effort to bring more exposure to the girls, who traditionally get lost in the glare of their male schoolmates.

The later starts were a risk, though. When darkness fell, everything changed. The atmosphere was charged with an excitement
that doesn't exist earlier in the afternoon. More people show up at
night, and the darkness brings an unknown element into the mix,
changing its texture. Tensions rise and senses heighten. The parking lot outside Skyline's gym was unlit, and the blind-black of the
country atmosphere had its own intimidating, closed-in air. City
dark, with its street lights and traffic, doesn't have this depth. The
darkness takes any commotion, no matter how minor, and imbues it
with immediacy and importance.

The players felt it, and they loved it.

Some of the Skyline players, including David Strom, lived within
Fremont High's boundaries. Fremont's student population includes
many students who were unable to maneuver their way into
Skyline, and there is a natural resentment that serves as a catalyst
for the intense neighborhood rivalry. In this case, however, ancillary
circumstances weren't needed. The basketball stakes were enough.

Both teams were undefeated after two league games, but they
had taken vastly different paths. Fremont was confident and aggressive from the start; they were defending OAL champions, they
were ranked third in the Bay Area, and they were the only team
that had been given half a chance to beat McClymonds. Skyline, on
the other hand, had just begun to believe they might have something. Their confidence had ebbed and flowed endlessly; now it was
at high tide.

Lamont Brown and Darren Albert are best friends. Brown is a
starting guard for Fremont. They are both boxy, strong athletes
with wide, shelf-like shoulders. Brown and Albert went to grammar
school and junior high together before splitting in high school.
Brown, Albert and Will Blackwell went to Frick Junior High together, three of the best athletes in the school, and their plan had been
to stay together at Skyline. However, neither Brown nor Blackwell
lived in the Skyline district. Albert did. Blackwell bypassed the
problem by giving the Alberts' address as his own. Brown wanted

to do the same, but he didn't want to risk it when he discovered that Blackwell was using the address. In the end, Brown couldn't find a way to circumvent the boundaries, and he went to Fremont. The episode put a temporary strain on the friendship. This game meant a lot to both of them, on a number of levels, and the OAL standings gave it a much higher pitch.

"They *way* too confident," Darren said as he got dressed before the game. "I'm not going to let them talk shit to me. Lamont— what's he thinkin'? You know what he just said to me? He said, 'I'm not going to talk to you. We're not friends until the game's over.' Can you believe that? He saying he's gonna guard me. They way too cocky."

Govan was lost in his headphones. He was pacing through the locker room, into the never-used showers, back into the barber-shop territory, trailed by the cricket-like whirring of the escaping sounds. He looked down at his feet, pumping his head to the beat and occasionally rolling his shoulders back and forth in time with his head.

Bryant Johnson sat by himself, separated from his teammates by a row of lockers, pulling his omnipresent vinyl sweat pants over his legs—inside-out, always—and talking to nobody in particular.

"We gotta get *amped*, fellas. *Amped*. We got to come out amped and stay amped. It's the only way we win."

A student walked hitch-legged through the locker room, his feet repeating the same practiced rhythm. He dressed big for the event, wearing his cap sideways, gold in both ears and more gold around his neck, a leather jacket, baggy Girbaud jeans—a walking cliche of the urban black youth.

"Got to tell my boys something," he said. "I lost big money on the 49ers-Dallas game. If I lose on this, I'm bustin' some ass. Just got to tell my boys that."

Most of the players ignored him, but those who acknowledged it did so by laughing. The threat wasn't taken seriously.

•••

David Strom, as always, sat by himself, oblivious to the surroundings. He was thinking about the game, and only the game. He would be guarding Kareem Davis, one of the OAL's biggest scorers and possibly its best outside shooter. Yet another test for the skinny white kid, but not one he hadn't taken before. Strom knew Davis. Davis knew Strom. It was an old story.

Davis was one player Strom respected. Davis worked on his game continuously, and like Strom he had made himself a player by playing after practice and on weekends. There was no offseason for either of them, no time when basketball didn't come first.

Donlea and the Skyline junior varsity had returned to the locker room after winning at Fremont. One of the junior varsity players walked to his locker, laughing and joking, enervated by a post-win euphoria that bordered on hyperactivity. He looked around the room and saw Strom sitting barely five feet away.

"Dave, you the rawest white boy in Oakland," he said. "You know that, don't you?"

Strom never looked up.

Outside the locker room, a young man waited in line to buy a ticket. He wore a red sweatshirt. On the back, from just below the hood to the waist, was inscribed:

> RIP
> Big
> Brother
> Don't Give
> A-Dam
> 7
> Dog

Shawn Donlea hadn't had more than three hours of sleep for the past three nights. He lay awake thinking about ways to beat Fremont, just as he lay awake in the past weeks thinking about ways to beat Riordan or Oakland Tech or Castlemont. He talked into the microcassette recorder he kept on his nightstand and thought of ways to beat Fremont's press, or ways to keep Kareem Davis from shooting the Titans out of the gym. He watched and re-watched the film of the Castlemont game. The more he saw, that less he liked. Skyline had only nine assists in that game, partly because of Castlemont's nonexistent defense and partly because of selfishness Donlea detected in some players. That wouldn't work against Fremont.

The day before the game, he gave a speech about selflessness. The issue became primary when he learned that Strom was discouraged by his lack of participation in the offense.

"I know that's what Dave's thinking, but I don't know why he don't say something—a closed mouth don't get fed," Will Blackwell said. Blackwell had begun to watch practices and take a more active interest in the team. After this game, Blackwell would be back on the court.

Strom was embarrassed by Donlea's talk, knowing it was directed at him. He said Donlea misread the situation, that his complaints weren't based on selfishness.

"If we play like we did against Castlemont, we'll never beat Mack," Strom said. "We can't have just two guys scoring; that's too easy for them to defend. Everybody has to be involved, but that offense doesn't work that way. That's all I'm trying to say."

The night before the game, Donlea was jolted out of bed by a telephone call. It was an old girlfriend from Iowa, calling to tell him that Chris Street, the University of Iowa's standout junior forward, had been killed in an auto accident. Street had lost control of his vehicle on icy streets and hit a snowplow. Donlea was a graduate student at Iowa when Street was being recruited, and they met briefly during Street's recruiting visit. Street was Mr. Basketball in Iowa, a household name by the time he was 17 years old. Donlea didn't think he had any role in Street's decision to pick Iowa, but he was shaken nonetheless. Given his frazzled mental state at the time, it didn't take much.

"I didn't really know him—I mean, I just met him is all—but I was really shook up by that. It just did something to me."

It proved to be the start of a miserable day for Donlea. He had been riding a pretty good string of substitute-teaching gigs at Skyline. He walked into the main office before school the morning of the Fremont game and saw Calvin Wilson, who worked in the office during first period.

Wilson's demeanor was quiet and withdrawn, but once the veneer was cracked, he became open and good-natured. His life wasn't easy, but he was attempting to make it work. He lived in San Francisco at the time, and his trip to school included three forms of public transportation and more than an hour of travel each way.

Donlea saw something different in Wilson's eyes on this morning. He inquired and found that Wilson had spent most of the previous night in an intensive-care ward of a San Francisco hospital, where his mother was clinging to life. Wilson was wary about sharing some of the details of his life. This was one instance where he held back. He said his mother had almost died and left it at that.

Donlea tried to offer his help. No pain or fear or concern registered on Wilson's face, and he told Donlea he was all right.

"I was almost crying, and he was just sitting there," Donlea said. "He was at school. He lives in San Francisco, and he was at school."

In the afternoon, Donlea substituted in a class for students he described as "troubled and tough." It was his third day with the class that week, and he was getting accustomed to the needs of the students. Everything was calm until two girls in the back of the room got up and began fighting. It wasn't a hair-pulling, slapping fight. It was more of a full-headlock, short-punches-to-the-face fight. These girls weren't fooling around.

Donlea rushed back and attempted to break up the fight. At the same time, he tried to call school security on the phone that hung on the back wall. Another student reached over and hung up the phone before Donlea could complete the call. The student then dialed the office and told them to cancel the security call. The students wanted to see a fight, not a security guard.

"I was just thinking how lucky I'd been," Donlea said. "Everything had been going real smooth, no problems like I expected. Then in one day I get this massive introduction to Oakland. I don't even care about basketball."

Calvin Wilson sat in the stands during the girls game, waiting for the junior varsity to get back from Fremont. He couldn't get dressed with his teammates because he had forgotten to pack his uniform in the rush and confusion of the night before. Blackwell found a pair of shorts for him, but he still needed a jersey. When the girls game ended and neither Donlea or the junior varsity players had arrived, Wilson was convinced he was wasting his time. He left the gym and headed home.

The Skyline gym was packed by the time Strom led the team onto the court for warmup drills. Fremont was already on the court, and several of the players laughed and pointed at each other as they went through layup lines. Kareem Davis and Strom shook hands in passing, neither of them showing any outward sign of recognition. They understood each other; they both had business to take care of.

Davis had three turnovers in the first minute of the game, which isn't unusual given the hectic pace of most OAL games. Skyline led, 6–2, before Davis hit a 15-footer and a spinning jumper to tie it. Govan brought the crowd into the game with a baseline double-pump move that turned into a three-point play when he was hammered on the shot.

"Go-van's clin-ic," Nelson Burns yelled from the bench. "A post-up clinic, every time."

Will Blackwell, who just the night before sat silent at the dinner table with his hands folded in his lap while his possible future was laid out for him, stood in the corner with a microphone and provided a running commentary over the loudspeakers. This public-address, on-the-spot broadcasting was another unique trait of the Oakland Athletic League. Nobody seemed to care what was said, as long as it was within the broad bounds of good taste. It was considered just another element of the home-field advantage. Blackwell made up nicknames for players and yelled "He smoked it!" every time Fremont missed a free throw. At one point he addressed the crowd directly by saying, "Well, folks, you can't ask for more from a basketball game."

• • •

Donlea fought a constant and humorous struggle with Bryant Johnson. The junior guard's natural ability and his on-court flair were undeniable. He could take over a practice and turn it into his own highlight show. There must be some key, Donlea thought, to blending that ability into the team game. It only needed a slight turn before all that natural ability and tremendous court sense would pour out like a broken levee. The ball-handling, the shooting, the open-court decisions—they were all there. And if it happened? Well, then the other coaches in the OAL would lay awake at night thinking of ways to stop Bryant Johnson. It was a fragile balance; Bryant needed to be both harnessed and cut loose, as odd as that seems, and there was no clear line of distinction. One minute, Johnson would do something on the court that would have Donlea pulling his hair. Then, the next time down the court, he would do something that would create an indelible memory.

By the time Johnson was in eighth grade, the comparisons to Gary Payton had begun. He raced up and down the floor with extreme quickness, and his drives to the hoop were filled with a liquid genius. His practice and schoolyard flair were undeniable, but it had yet to translate into game competition. His best moments in practice came in a three-on-two, two-on-one fast-break drill. It started out as a three-on-two break at one end of the floor. After a shot was taken, the two defenders would fast-break the other way, defended by the player who had taken the first shot. Coming back down the floor, it was Johnson and a teammate against one defender. Bryant would take the ball right at him, then decide his course of action in midair. His specialty was to fake a driving layup with his left hand while passing the ball over his left shoulder with his right hand. It didn't appear fully possible, with the ball seeming to materialize out of Johnson's head and into his teammate's hands.

After the play, the talking would begin. With Johnson, the talk was as much a part of the game as the game itself. One without the other wasn't worth the trouble.

"Don't let me get loose now, just *don't* let me get loose. I'm gettin' loose, and if I get loose in the game? Uh-oh, I don't know what might happen. If I get loose in a game? Look out. But coach—coach don't want me to get loose in the game. He won't let me. But if I do? If I do? No tellin' what might happen. There's just no tellin'."

Of course, Donlea said he *did* want Johnson to get loose during the game; he just didn't know how to make it happen within the team concept. There it was again: philosophy versus reality.

At halftime of the Fremont game, with Skyline down by six, Donlea addressed Johnson.

"You're talkin' a good game, but you've got to *play* a good game. Don't bring anything back into this goddamn locker room. Leave it all out on the floor."

Fremont held its six-point lead at the end of the third quarter, and the fourth quarter started badly for Skyline. Fremont's inside players began leaping over the tired Skyline players, tipping in missed shots and keeping the ball alive for Davis, who found his touch after a rough first half. Skyline needed Wilson. Fremont led by nine with five minutes left. Donlea called timeout and struggled to find something to say. He was playing with six players, and they were starting to slow.

"Look, we've got to press," Donlea told them, the veins protruding from his forehead. "We've got to force them out of their game."

Strom picked Davis clean and Govan scored. Fremont had trouble getting the ball inbounds; the press seemed to invigorate Skyline, in direct opposition to what Donlea expected. It was a desperate move at the time; now he cursed himself for not trying it earlier. Govan scored again. Jason Wright hit a three-pointer. Strom again picked Davis.

Skyline took the lead, 51–50, with three minutes left. Blackwell was breaking records for overmodulation and the crowd was spilling onto the court. The press was working; Fremont couldn't get the ball upcourt. After Skyline took the lead, Fremont called a timeout and coach Clinton Williams knelt in front of his team's bench and scribbled a press-breaker on the floor. Donlea watched, trying to see what he would devise. He couldn't tell, but he knew one thing: Fremont was rattled.

"OK, they can't break the press," Donlea said. "We've got to keep it on. Get the ball inside to the post. Work on them inside and hit your free throws. We can win this game."

Donlea said it as if it was the first time this thought had occurred to him.

Fremont missed on its first possession after the timeout, and Wimberly grabbed the rebound. He brought it down to waist-level and had it stripped. Fremont's Lester Parham put it back in and Skyline's lead was gone for good. Govan picked up two fouls in thirty seconds—one a charging call and one on a rebound blockout—and he was gone. Donlea went berserk after both of the calls, especially the charge.

"He's got no position, *NO* goddamn position," he yelled at the official. "You're guessing out there, sir."

With Govan out, Fremont had free reign on the offensive boards. They ended up with thirteen offensive rebounds in the fourth quarter alone.

"We had 'em, though," Donlea said afterward. "That's the amazing thing—we had 'em. As bad as it seemed, and as much shit as happened today, we came back. We had 'em. Goddamn, we had 'em."

CHAPTER TEN

THE PRODUCT WOULD SELL ITSELF. IT ALWAYS DID. THE MOUNTAINS, THE campus, the facilities—there were few high school athletes who could turn it down. Besides, the Colorado Buffaloes had a history of taking high school football players out of the roughest neighborhoods in America and recruiting them to play at the base of the Flatirons, in the crisp Rocky Mountain air. They came from the Los Angeles area—Compton, Watts, Inglewood. They came from the flat, hot, angry streets of Houston and New Orleans. And, occasionally, they came from Oakland.

Kids accustomed to seeing the horizon stop at their front door gazed in wonderment at the immediacy of the mountains to the west, and the vastness of the plains to the east. Kids accustomed to breathing the gray-brown air of the city saw nothing but blue. Kids accustomed to locking up at night and sleeping with a gun within reach found freedom in the clean, friendly atmosphere.

Will Blackwell fit the profile of a Colorado Buffalo. He was fast, strong and confident. He was also a city kid.

He went to eat their food, spend their money, see a new part of the country. San Diego State was his place, but he wanted to use his final recruiting trip to see a little of the world. He ended up like so many others before him, standing in slack-jawed awe at the way they do business in the Colorado football program.

"It was awesome," he said. "I think I might go there now. I ain't never seen stuff like they got."

Now Will understood why the San Diego State coaches had been so persistent in the past week. Now he knew why Payton left six messages for him on the Monday he returned from Boulder. Now he knew why so many athletes from the inner city went to school in the middle of the Rocky Mountains.

Greg Brown, Blackwell's recruiter from Colorado, had been waiting for this night. He was prepared. The Buffaloes waited six
months to see this door open, and now it was up to Brown to walk
in and make himself at home. He arrived at the house on 104th the
day after Will returned from his trip to Boulder. He carried a sleek
leather briefcase filled with everything he needed to recruit Stella
Blackwell. After the weekend trip, he felt he had Will. Now he
needed the mom.

"I've been very anxious to come in here and talk with you,"
Brown told Stella. "I'm prepared. I've been thinking *a lot* today
about what I'm going to say."

Brown went about his work like a door-to-door salesman on a
bad run. This was his last shot; after tonight, Will would have six
days to make up his mind. Brown started the pitch with the first of
two videotapes. It sold the academic institution and the community.
There's a Nobel Prize winner teaching freshman physics. There's a
top-flight novelist in the English department. It was rated one of
the safest major university campuses in the country. And the football's not bad, either.

The voice on the tape was smooth and professional:

> *I want to welcome you to the University of Colorado and
> to Boulder, Colorado. Boulder is a unique place. I think
> you're going to find its energy and its vibrancy very capti-
> vating every time you visit. Boulder's a college town. It's
> not like a city campus or a rural campus stuck out on the
> prairie. There's an incredible energy here that only exists in
> a college town.*

Beam sat at the end of a plastic-slipcovered loveseat and scribbled
notes on the back of a paper plate. He could see the look in Will's
eye, and the look in Stella's: he thought they were hooked, and he
wanted to be sure they didn't jump into a marriage without the
proper engagement.

"If you have a chance," Beam said to Brown, "talk about why you
haven't been here—just to reaffirm to them—"

"Oh, yeah. Yeah, I'll tell you exactly why. Oh, yeah. First of all,
we were not Will's first choice, but Will is our first choice. We tried

to get him in, but in all honesty, as near as I could perceive it, it was UCLA. Am I correct?"

Nobody answered.

"Or maybe San Diego State. Anyway, he was our first choice even though we weren't his. But we decided the best way to do it was to lay back, hang back and not pressure the guy. And, you never know, that approach might work. I know he's getting hounded like you can't believe."

Stella laughed at that. The only peace they had experienced since the fall came in the first week of 1993. During that period, the telephone lines throughout East Oakland were dead after some people in the area celebrated the coming of the New Year by standing in the streets and firing their automatic weapons into the overhead lines.

"That phone's driving me crazy," Stella said.

Brown had charts, videotapes and a polished presentation. His tone was cozy and patient. Aside from McCartney's grand entrance on the Skyline campus, Colorado had taken an understated approach to recruiting Will Blackwell. They would sit back and wait, let everybody else speak their piece, then rush in at the end. Kids like Will Blackwell tend to change their mind every time they visit a school. Colorado was holding out hope that last impressions would be lasting impressions.

The television screen showed the Dal Ward Center, a $14 million facility that is the core of Colorado athletics. In the center, athletes can study, eat, train, attend meetings, play basketball, get medical treatment—everything but sleep and attend classes. The place even had its own book store. A football player would walk in with his class schedule the day before classes start. He would hand the schedule to somebody behind the counter and within minutes his books would be laid out before him. He would simply say thank you and move on. No long lines, no hassles, no wading through the aisles in search of that Psychology 101 text. Dinner would be catered by one of two restaurants in town, either an Italian place or a rib joint. Brown told Stella that the owner of the Italian restaurant—Pasta Jays—is a "big CU booster. He dresses up like coach for the games," Brown said. "Seriously. *Loves* it." This, maybe more than most places, would be an easy life.

Will sat on the floor in shorts and a T-shirt (just back from basketball practice, there wasn't time to shower or change; in fact, he was late because he didn't want to leave practice). There were two cordless telephones at his feet, and they interrupted Brown periodically. There are three lines to the Blackwell house: one for Stella, one for Will and one for Roshanda. "I don't know how it happens, but these people get every one of the numbers," Stella said. "Those phones be ringin' for nine months now."

Brown was here to sell academics first, football second. Stella's main concerns, just as with the San Diego State recruiters, were academics and balance. She hadn't attended college, but she knew enough to know it would be a shock to Will's system. She didn't want him overloaded.

One of the phones rang. Will spoke quietly and politely. "Yes," he said, "I'm considering it. I like it there . . . I'm having a home visit right now, so it's not a good time."

He put the phone down. "Some Colorado paper," he said.

"Those papers are amazing," Brown said. "They cover us like a professional team. There are two big things in the area: the Denver Broncos and Colorado Buffalo football."

Brown shook his head at the incredulity of it all. He told Stella that Will would handle the press fine. "He likes that stuff, I can just tell," then he reached into his briefcase for three photocopied pages that might convince Stella Blackwell to become the parent of a Colorado Buffalo. The pages were the rankings of Division I universities not in winning percentage, but in graduation percentage. The numbers were broken down into two categories: all football players and black football players. Stella Blackwell was highly interested in this information.

The San Diego State coaches hadn't provided this information on their home visit. Brown knew his competition, and he knew where to draw the battle lines.

Based on the recruiting classes that entered college in 1984–85, Colorado was ranked fifth in the nation, having graduated 66 percent of all football players. Notre Dame was first, followed by Virginia, Cal and Penn State.

"Now these aren't our statistics," Brown said. "The NCAA did this study, and they provided the statistics."

On the second page, the universities were ranked according to their ability to graduate the black football player. Again, Colorado was ranked fifth, although its percentage dropped slightly, to 62 percent.

"As you can see," Brown said, "that's still pretty high."

Brown then went for the jugular. He asked Stella to flip to the back page, where the universities that didn't make the top twenty-five were listed. Brown made no comment, but Stella, Will and Beam saw his message: San Diego State's graduation rate for all football players was 29 percent, and for black athletes it was 31 percent. That was not even half of Colorado's rate in both categories.

"This is your call," Brown said, "but in my opinion, what you want to be concerned with is, anytime you start to get below fifty, that would kind of cause a red flag in my mind. You can go ahead and look at any school you want—they're all on there."

Stella looked closely, her brow furrowing. Brown stopped talking and let the information sink in as the room fell sea-shell quiet. He looked closely at Stella as her eyes followed the list three-quarters of the way down the page, then stopped. She found San Diego State. Brown kept quiet. He could tell he had struck the right nerve. A few thick moments passed before Brown resumed.

"You know what? Why don't you hang onto that. Will can keep one and you keep one. You can look at those and see how they stack up."

Beam spoke up, outlining the special circumstances universities such as San Diego State face. "A lot of people transfer from those schools," he said. "Those figures might be a little bit misleading, because I would bet they're better than the general student population."

Brown nodded, then got back to business.

"Let's throw out football for a minute. Just for a minute, let's throw it out. I know, and we all know, that Will has tremendous athletic ability. It's taken him places already and it's going to take him further in the future. But let's just suppose for a minute he didn't have that ability or he got hurt and couldn't play anymore: that's where this becomes more important. Because football is awesome; it's a great experience. But it's not going to be your life no matter if you're the greatest pro in the world. Pretty soon, you're going to have to retire and go on to something else. School's got to service you because you're helping them. They've got to help you become something in life you want to do. You don't want to pump gas. You want to go the best place that's going to help you get that degree. You've just got to forget about football—for a little bit. You look at that, and then you say, 'OK, now let's add football back into it. What does that got to offer?'

"First of all, wherever he goes, he's going to work hard. Right now I'm talkin' football. It doesn't matter where, they're going to work your butt off. So the thing I look at—my opinion—you work hard, you got to look at somewhere it's gonna reward you, have some possible big payouts. If you're gonna work hard, you might as well shoot the moon. And one of the nice things about our place— and I'm obviously pushing us—is that you've got a chance to play for all the marbles. We've already won the national championship, we're always ranked right up in there. So that's one of the things our guys go for. They say, 'Hey, if I'm gonna work this hard, I might as well play somewhere where I've got a chance to win everything.' You've got a chance to get these rings and go to a great bowl."

The phone again. Will spoke a few clipped words, then hung up. He shook his head and laughed.

"Who was that?" Beam asked.

"Hundley," Will said. Hundley was UCLA. Beam looked disgusted.

"Man, why's he still calling?" Beam asked. "Doesn't he know he's out of it?"

"I think so," Will said. "I told him."

"Next time, just tell him not to call anymore—or tell him to call me at the school."

Beam glanced at his paper plate. He had crossed off all but one item. He looked at Brown, who was looking toward Will's trophies with a thousand-yard stare.

"Greg, do you want to talk a little about Coach McCartney?" Beam asked. "'Cause I know that's going to come up, and it's better that it comes from you than other coaches, or in another roundabout way."

Brown looked up at the painting of Jesus that hung directly above Stella's head. There were brass angel figurines on the wall and a small statue of Jesus near Will's trophies. Would he talk a little about Coach McCartney? Would he take the time to outline McCartney's on-the-sleeve Christianity? Would he discuss McCartney's strict fundamentalist views? Jesus looked down at him from above Stella's head. Of course he would.

"Oh, yeah. Oh, *yeah*. Coach McCartney has a reputation—well-deserved, it's true—as being a very outspoken Christian man. A lot of people know he's a great coach, but what a lot of people don't know is that in 1986 he was named Fellowship of Christian Athletes man of the year. He's written two books on the subject. Where his views come from is that whatever the Bible says—"

The phone rang. Another Colorado newspaper.

"Those guys just dig at it," Brown said. "I mean, I get a lot of my information from them. They get it from calling the kids like that. If I want to know how a particular kid's feeling, I can call the reporter and get more information than I can out of the kid. It's amazing."

Will answered the reporter's questions, quietly, then hung up. Brown pulled out two of his business cards and wrote his home number on the back. He told Will and Stella to call anytime, collect.

"And, by the way, too—Coach McCartney *dearly* wanted to be here to talk with you. Here's the deal: Because of NCAA rules, he's only allowed to talk off-campus one time in the prospect's city. Now he talked to Will, even though he didn't talk to you, so he kind of shot his one chance. Now the reason we felt we had to do it that way was just to try to see if we could get him in here. We'd been trying unsuccessfully to get him interested since spring. I was out here in the spring, dropping questionnaires off, writing notes, dropping questionnaires, and I couldn't. So Coach Mac said, 'Let's just take our shot now.' We were here, we met with Will, we tried to spark his interest. And that's why you can't see him. But he *dearly* would *love* to talk with you on the phone. In fact, I wanted to get a time. Preferably tomorrow. I would love to have him call you, be it at work or at home. You decide, give me a number and I'll have him call you."

"Getting back to Coach McCartney . . ." Beam began before Brown interrupted.

"Yes. In my opinion, his values are in the right place. If you're going to send your son away from home, where you can't put your thumb on him, then you better trust somebody who will, who does stand up to those values and beliefs. He's got a proven track record; what Coach McCartney stands for is simply what's in the Bible. That can turn some people off. But that's the man, and you've got to know that going in. Whatever the Bible says, he is very, very much in line with that."

"I have no problem with that," Stella said.

"Yeah, yeah, well, that's good. I think that's great."

"My dad was extremely strict on us," Stella said. "He's a preacher, and I was raised in the Pentecostal church."

"Well, that's great. I'm glad to hear that."

"Will's good," Beam said. "But Oakland's startin' to wear on him. He was a lot better in the tenth grade than he is in the twelfth. He still had that Arkansas bringin'-up in tenth. Now he's been in Oakland maybe a year or two too much. It's about time to get him back in the Christian fold."

"Get him headed in the right direction," Stella said.

Brown laughed politely, then shifted back. Will was losing interest in this discussion, and Brown sensed there was a fence to straddle here; he didn't want Will to get the idea he was off to become a missionary.

"Now, Coach McCartney never pushed religion on somebody, *but* he'll certainly encourage it and a great deal of our team, a great many of our young guys, are very much true believers. He's never once said to me as a coach—or any of our coaches—'Hey, I think you should do this.' He's not going to tell you how to run your life. *But* . . . he runs his life based on what he believes, and he is going to draw a line between right and wrong, but he's not going to say, 'Hey, I don't want you because you wear an earring or your hair is too long.' He let our guys do what they want as long as they don't become felons."

When McCartney first arrived at Colorado, his teams had trouble competing in the Big Eight, and many in Boulder felt it was because he was trying too hard to recruit players who fit his model for citizenry. "We've got enough choirboys, now let's get some football players," went the on-campus plea. Since then, he has.

"Coach does have some rules," Brown continued. "He's got a three-strike rule. The first strike means you got in trouble with the law; you're arrested, you're suspended for one game. You get in trouble with the law twice, you're suspended for a season. If you get in trouble three times with the law, you're gone. And the thing is, there are no ifs, ands or buts about that. When I say trouble, I'm not saying a kid got a speeding ticket. You got arrested for stealing or something wrong like that."

McCartney was working on the third year of a fifteen-year contract, the longest in the NCAA. Brown told Stella not to worry about McCartney leaving, because his wife loved Boulder so much that she would kill him at the mere suggestion.

"Longevity—if you looked that up in the dictionary, you'd see a picture of Coach McCartney. He would be there not only to watch Will graduate, but to watch Will come back and get his master's. It's a long-term proposition, where you know it's something stable."

Brown personalized McCartney's rules by telling the story of defensive back Eric Hamilton, an NFL prospect from Compton who arrived at Boulder with a bullet in his chest from a drive-by shooting. Hamilton was all-Big Eight as a junior and the Denver papers were all over him, letting everybody know what he'd overcome to get where he was—the usual football, human-interest hyperbole.

"I don't know if you remember him on my wall," Brown said to Will, "but he was number six."

Will didn't remember.

"Anyway, Eric just had a tremendous junior year. Those Denver papers were going every day with something about him. He has a hole right through here"—Brown pointed to the left side of his chest, just above the heart and below the shoulder—"where the bullet collapsed his lung."

"That was in L.A.," Beam told Stella.

"Yeah, good point," Brown said, laughing. "That was when he was back home in Compton. There are no drive-bys in Boulder. You might see a speeding ticket, but that's about it. It is the number-one safest campus. There's no place where you say, 'Don't go in that part of town.' Boulder, you can go anywhere you want.

"So, anyway, Eric had a great year but he got two DUIs in a row. He got one as a sophomore and Coach McCartney suspended him for the Orange Bowl. You know, that's a tough thing—for the national championship. Then he got a second one after his junior when he was all-Big Eight. Coach McCartney said, 'You're gone for your senior year. In effect, you're done.' That's a great player, and he's not gonna bend the rules. It's tough, yeah, but you know the rules going in. It's a fact of life with that man."

Stella nodded. Brown looked at his hands, shaking his head.

"But he got to stay there—" Beam started.

"Oh, yeah. Oh, *yeah*," Brown interrupted. "He got to stay there, we paid for his school—oh, no question. Right now he's three hours away from graduating, just three hours. He's a great kid. He's still one of my best friends. We're very close. I see him every day, he comes in . . . Nobody's more sick about it than me."

At Colorado, even the worst stories still have a happy ending.

A Colorado Buffalo gets full treatment when he goes to a bowl game. He gets the maximum legal amount of per-diem money to live on. He gets a passenger van at his disposal for trips to practice, restaurants, night clubs. He gets sweats and T-shirts and rings and shorts. Brown said, "We always tell our equipment manager, 'Whatever the maximum is, give the maximum amount of gifts. Give 'em sweats, shirts, shorts.' And we always give them a winter jacket every year so they can always have a new winter jacket."

The competition for playing time would be rigorous, Brown said, but there were two or three receivers who might switch to defensive back if Will Blackwell decided to attend Colorado. That would increase the probability of playing right away, although three of the team's top receivers were coming back.

"If you're afraid of competition, you might want to go to UOP," Beam told Will.

Brown scoffed at the notion. "Oh, this guy—I don't think so. He ain't afraid of nuthin'."

"If I'm like a backup—which I won't be for long—I won't redshirt then?" Will asked.

"No, no," Brown said. "Backup is two-deep. If you're traveling, you're playing."

Brown turned to Stella. A cozy smile crossed his face.

"This kid ain't afraid of nuthin', is he mom? That's what Mac told me, too. Mac sat there and said, 'You know, I looked in his eyes and he ain't afraid.' "

"No, uh-uh," Stella said.

"No way. He's gonna do just fine."

The Buffaloes were less than a month removed from an appearance in the Fiesta Bowl. They lost to Syracuse, but there was a story behind that, too. McCartney had left his first-string kicker at home because of academic difficulties. And wouldn't you know it, the backup kicker cost them the game.

"So that just goes to show you something about Coach McCartney, what he's all about," Brown said.

Brown waited until his stay was nearly over to pass his Fiesta Bowl ring around the room. This was the Shakespearean third act, Brown's moment.

"Here, mom, I want to show you this here—" he said, slipping the ring off his finger and handing it gently to Stella. "That way you know what you can confiscate from him. Our guys are always in the habit of winning a lot of those things."

Stella looked it over, a ring double the size of the average class ring.

"Wow," she said. "Isn't this beautiful? That *is* lovely."

She turned to Will.

"That's mine, Sonny. The first one you get is mine."

Brown sat there, smiling. He wasn't with the Buffaloes during the 1990 season, the national championship season, or else he would have been passing that ring around the room. It didn't matter, though—this one was doing just fine.

During the two hours that Brown spoke to the Blackwells, Will received eight telephone calls. Four were from Payton, the San Diego State recruiter. Three were from Denver-area newspapers and one was from UCLA.

"They all gettin' on my nerves," Will said. "It's time to make a decision."

CHAPTER ELEVEN

ON THE AFTERNOON OF FEBRUARY 3, WILL BLACKWELL AND TWO OTHER Skyline football players sat at one end of a long table in the administrative conference room on the Skyline campus. They were flanked by family members, and each player held a pen that hovered over a national letter of intent to a Division I university. Ayyub Abdul-Rahmann, Skyline's quarterback, wore a Colorado baseball cap. Khalid Shabazz, a running back, wore a University of California hat and sweatshirt. A photographer from a weekly newspaper in the hills was there, ready to capture the traditional posed shot for letter of intent day: Smiling players poised to sign a piece of paper.

Will Blackwell didn't wear a baseball cap. He sat with Stella and Roshanda and looked down at a series of legal documents. He didn't say much, just stared down at the paper and occasionally looked up to share a laugh with his friends. Stella had a frozen smile on her face, the pride no longer capable of staying inside. Some Skyline teachers would walk into the room to extend their congratulations to the students and their parents, and Stella's smile would grow.

"No turning back now, fellas," Beam said, laughing.

After living the typical temporal existence of a seventeen-year-old—the future is dinner, the past is breakfast—Will had made the biggest decision of his life. After nine months of wavering and deciding, of having his mind completely, unalterably settled and then changed time and again, Will's decision was made on simple grounds. After Brown left, Will began thinking about the cold and the wind and the probability of sitting there in Boulder watching somebody else play for at least a year. He remembered Beam's words: *It's always colder when you're not playing.* And Will thought the cold would be downright paralyzing if he was stuck as a practice player that much farther from home. The thoughts ran through his mind, juxtaposed with his trip to San Diego, where it was sunny and warm and within a day's drive of Oakland.

Most everyone, including Beam and the San Diego State recruiters, thought Will was headed to Colorado. He was impressed by the way they handled themselves, and he even talked about some phone numbers he got from some girls there. "That's for later, when I get there," he said. Then, on the Monday before the signing date, he called Sean Payton at San Diego State and told him to clear a space atop the depth chart, because Will Blackwell was on his way.

"When I thought about it, it really wasn't that hard," Will said. "I called Colorado, and they were cool about it. I thanked them, because I did almost go there. I didn't just waste their time."

Stella was pleased with the decision, although Brown's sales pitch had her wavering. "Yeah, she liked those graduation rates," Will said. "That had her going."

Beam said another factor played a part, a factor that Will would never admit. "I'm not sure he's ready for the ocean," Beam said. "I think he'll do just fine in a pond or a lake. The ocean might have to wait."

Signing day is a big event at Skyline. Beam invites officials and administrators from the Oakland Unified School District, although most do not attend. One year the conference table was filled with five Skyline players and their families. That was the year Beam's wife told her husband that she was getting close to the breaking point. He was helping each of the five players through the recruiting process, and he was hardly ever home. He would go from school to one player's house, then rush to another, then another. Some nights he would hit each of the houses, sometimes seeing the same set of coaches three times. The recruiters were forced to stagger their home visits and operate under a tight schedule because Beam was fighting an age-old human failing: he could only be in one place at a time.

"I see everyone's here except for someone from the superintendent's office," Beam said as he passed out overnight-mail envelopes to Blackwell and Abdul-Rahmann. "That's OK, though, we know where they are. They're off making the big money, so they don't have time to be here with the kids. This is where they should be, though—with the kids. But they make the big money and here I am, wearing used sweats."

OAL Commissioner Lou Jones smiled at Beam's remarks. He had heard the same many times before. Some of the Skyline administrators looked a bit uncomfortable, but they managed to chuckle out of courtesy.

"Enough of that, though," Beam said. "We came here for something more important."

Later that afternoon, Will scored 14 points in the second half against Oakland High, in a game Skyline won, 67–60. It was his first game since returning from the foot injury, and he saw to it that everybody in the Skyline gymnasium knew he was back. He danced and gyrated after every basket, making grandiloquent gestures and looking to the stands to see if everyone was as impressed with his performance as he was. Most were.

The game was close throughout, and Donlea lost his cool at the end of the first half when Nick Wimberly tackled an Oakland High player as he attempted a halfcourt shot with one second left. Three free throws later, Skyline went to the locker room ahead by only one point.

Donlea had been riding the officials nonstop, and he stormed into the locker room ready to let loose on new subjects. He spoke calmly about adjustments they would make on defense in the next half, then he stopped and gathered himself. He yanked at his belt, ran his hand through his hair and breathed a big anticipatory sigh.

"Wait a minute, I'm not done. I'm pissed off. You guys can play better basketball than that. I'm not satisfied with a one-fucking point lead. You're not playing very hard. You got to contest every fucking shot. How many times do I have to say that? Contest every fucking shot. If you don't contest the shot, they get hot and it becomes a bitch.

"One of these days we'll get a call. It might not be today, but one of these days. But you've got to forget about that; you've got to play through the officials and through Oakland High."

Donlea felt every game was filled with importance that extended beyond the time it took to play it. This was no different; a win against Oakland High would make Skyline 3–1 in the OAL, and it would make Friday's game at undefeated McClymonds a fight for first place.

With Skyline leading by three in the fourth quarter, Donlea pulled Darren Albert out of the game moments after he ruined a sure breakaway by flinging the ball out of bounds. Albert, normally mild-mannered and contrite after a mistake, stomped to the bench and barked at Donlea.

"I just got in the game, and I'm out already. I been practicing hard all year, and now I don't get to play the games."

"Shut up, Darren," Donlea said. "We want to win the game here. There are twelve guys who want to play every minute."

Albert's playing time plunged when Blackwell returned, and Donlea liked to have Bryant Johnson handle the ball when the game was tight. Albert was a senior, this was supposed to be his year. He accepted sitting on the bench as a junior, but not now. Donlea thought Albert overestimated his abilities, and he had mentioned that his personal feelings for Darren probably earned him more playing time than he deserved.

Blackwell, in his first OAL game, was the difference. He didn't start, but his athleticism and rebounding ability offset Oakland High's height advantage. Skyline beat Oakland High 67–60, and the stage was set for Skyline—3–1 in the OAL—to play undefeated McClymonds. In three days, the Skyline Titans would be playing for first place in the OAL. Despite that, an uneasiness permeated the whole team. The scene after the game made it apparent that expectations had been raised; winning was no longer enough. The locker room was somber. Nobody looked up and nobody spoke. The players sat in the middle of the room, flanked by two rows of five-foot lockers. They seemed to sense what was coming.

Donlea walked in last, his hair disheveled and the gray rings under his eyes accentuated by the room's yellowed lighting. The situation with Albert had an unnerving effect on him. He felt pressured, as if he was being backed into a corner and challenged for no good reason. He was disappointed that the players didn't see what he was doing for them, that they didn't recognize that the team was beating teams with far more talent simply because he had imposed some structure into their games. He knew this job would be hard, but he never imagined winning would be so trying.

"Here it comes," one player said quietly as Donlea placed his clipboard on a locker and stood before them. Albert, already dressed with a baseball cap pulled down low over his eyes, looked off into the distance, more than ready to leave and forget the whole thing. He was sorry for what he had done, but he was not prepared to apologize.

"I want to see your eyes," Donlea said. "I want to communicate to you here. We waste a lot of time in practice—me getting upset, you talking, you shooting around on the side. I told you, the key to winning is to eliminate all those things that inhibit success. All those things, all that little shit—you're out in the parking lot when you're supposed to be dressed, whatever it is. I'm not pointing fingers. That's another thing: I rarely point fingers and I'm rarely negative. Rarely. So if I take you out of the game, I'm not separating you and saying, 'You're shit; you can't play.' Goddamit, this is a team. We win as a team. Everybody wants to play the whole fuckin' game. If you don't, I wouldn't have picked you to play for Skyline. I know it hurts to sit on the bench sometimes. You got to understand: I'm the coach, you're the player. I take equal or more than my share of responsibility when we lose, and when we win all the credit goes to you. That's the way it is.

"So if I'm sitting you down, goddamit, cheer for the guys on the floor. Fuckin' we're winning the goddamn game and the bench is sitting there like this: slouched. You can stand up, you can go nuts—it's OK. Christ, we're three and one. Nobody picked us to get off the floor in league, and we're three and one. We're at least the third-best team in the league, but you know better than that. You know we got a chance to do whatever we want.

"You got to understand something, guys. I'm here for you, as a team, as a group. I want to perform like a group, and you're all part of the group—"

His voice trailed off and he turned toward the wall, slamming his fists into the lockers. The players watched in bemused silence.

"I'm here for you, goddamit! I'm not working against you. Quit fighting me, please. Talk to me. Listen to me. Communicate. Run. Hustle.

"I'm trying to work with you. I need you to work with me."

After Donlea left, Nelson Burns said, "He don't understand. Fools ain't fightin' him. Fools just want to play. It's real simple."

Donlea listened to a tape of his outburst later. He cringed in embarrassment, asking himself why he didn't deal with it the next day, after some sleep and on a clear head. An entire lifetime of sports psychology classes couldn't tell him what he just learned, that it's often best to walk away.

"Sometimes I think I'm talking way over their heads. I mean, what am I doing here? Why did I do that? That was a good win for us, and here I am going nuts? It doesn't make sense."

Listening to the tape, Donlea laughed at himself. He shook his head, then looked up into the night sky. The tape rolled on.

"Don't shoot when I blow the whistle. Be disciplined once in a while. We're getting there. I understand the situation. I know you've had three coaches in three years. But why can't you be disciplined?"

"Shut up, Shawn," he told himself. "Just shut up. Why can't I just shut up?"

This was supposed to be fun. Donlea prided himself on living for basketball, of diving into practice and games and losing himself, forgetting everything—his money problems, his commute, his lack of a social life, his struggle to coach both teams. But this was the fun part. This was basketball. This was devising a game plan and watching it unfold. This was molding a group of kids into players, far better players than he ever could have hoped to be. He could never get enough of it, but now it was pulling him in all different directions. He knew he overreacted. He would go home and watch the game tape three or four times, then plan a team meeting for the next day. Sleep was out of the question; Mack was next, and he knew there were fences to mend before his team would have any chance. He would apologize, clear up the confusion. The players were confused, and he didn't blame them. Christ, he was even more confused.

Donlea didn't call many team meetings. This was the third of the season, and it seemed like a good idea. They had two practices to prepare for Mack, and any divisiveness would have to be purged if Skyline had any chance, any chance at all, of walking into West Oakland and doing something nobody else could do. Donlea brought the team into the coaches' office. The players sat on desks, a table, a cabinet and the few plastic chairs that were strewn about the room. Donlea sat on his desk—small, wooden, unfinished.

"You know, it's too bad that we get a nice win like last night and the coach comes in pissed off, upset, and chews your ass for fifteen minutes."

"Who did that?" Bryant Johnson asked, then laughed.

"That's my perception of what I did. I want your perception of what I did, and then I'll respond."

"I didn't have no problem with it," Will Blackwell said. "I understood where it was coming from when you talk about shooting after the whistle, not making eye contact. And the bench—that damned bench—I looked over there myself. I'm out there dancin' and they're over there like this —" Blackwell put his hands on his chin and stared off into nowhere.

"You're playing, though," Donlea said, "so you can't talk for the bench." He looked around the room. "What about playing time?"

Darren Albert had already apologized earlier in the afternoon. He told Donlea he shouldn't have done what he did, and that it wouldn't happen again. There was no reason for him to speak here.

Donlea looked at Nelson Burns, who squirmed and sat up straight in one of the plastic chairs. This was his chance to stand up for himself, to ask the questions he'd been asking himself since his playing time ended with the preseason. Burns wanted Donlea to know that there was more at work here than a kid sitting on the bench. He wanted the coach to know that basketball is not merely a social exercise; it's deeper than that.

The thoughts began to take over during the summer. As he lay flat on his back on his bedroom floor, flipping the basketball in the air, over and over and over, Nelson Burns ran the upcoming senior season through his head. He would start at Skyline, alongside Strom, his best friend. He would look up at the ceiling and see himself drilling a three-pointer at the buzzer to beat Mack, or stealing an inbounds pass and feeding Strom for the game-winner. He would show everyone that laughed at his dreams, everyone who scoffed at the skinny kid with the basketball. He would, in the end, be the Oakland Athletic League's Player of the Year.

"To some people that may seem unrealistic comin' from me, but I was thinking, I know there's no one else in the OAL who practices as much as me. It's funny; it seems like I have all the tools to do it, but . . . I don't know. I don't know what happens."

He thought about crazy things, too, like how he would take over an entire game—completely change every aspect of it—without scoring a point. Gary Payton did that, and so did Nelson's hero, Kenny Anderson. And now Nelson Burns would do it. He would play balls-out defense, get a few steals, sneak in for a few rebounds and, more than anything, rifle perfect pass after perfect pass through the defense. He could get lost in these thoughts and put everything else aside for hours. Nelson's parents began to wonder if they weren't losing their son to the streets. All the warning signs were there: he would leave the house for hours, he was uncommunicative and he spent a lot of time alone in his room. They eventually realized they were losing him to the game. Basketball was stalking him, like some insidious disease.

He got out of summer school at one in the afternoon, then he and Strom would run the tree-studded canyon behind the University of California at Berkeley. The course is a fire trail that zigzags up the steep side of Strawberry Canyon like a long beige scar. They would run it in the heat of the summer, four miles up, then run down and be ready to play.

They would go down to the campus, where they would run full-court with whoever was around, sometimes the players from Cal. And—if they were really lucky—some of the Golden State Warriors would show up. If the gym was closed, they'd play outside until the sun set, then hop in the car and look for an open gym somewhere in Oakland.

Everything Nelson did was a prelude to his senior season, every pickup game a dress rehearsal. The script called for college scouts to be drawn to his precise, selfless game and flood him with offers. Maybe they would be there to see somebody else, maybe Jason Wright or Michael Franklin, but they would be captivated by Nelson

Burns. That's what would happen, because those were always the best stories.

Halfway through the season, faced with the reality of his lack of playing time, he remained defiantly optimistic. He would go to a junior college, then take his game from there to a Division I program.

"I'll play D-one somewhere," he said. "The way I look at it, I have to. I've wasted too much of my life for it not to happen."

He couldn't get basketball out of his head. It was always front and center, ready to take him out of his North Oakland neighborhood and off into some far-off place—Chapel Hill, North Carolina, or Bloomington, Indiana—places that seemed to exist solely in his imagination. He would lay awake at night thinking about a new move or a way to improve his outside shot. Sometimes he wondered if he thought about it too much, wanted it too badly.

"Sometimes I'll be thinkin' while I'm playin', and that's not good. I don't know what it is, I just think more than I play sometimes. I'm always thinkin' about basketball, always."

Burns's neighbors always knew when he was off the bus and on his way home. The rhythmic bounce of the ball against the sidewalk signaled his arrival as clearly as any siren. Even if they didn't know his name, they knew him. He was the kid with the ball.

He brought a basketball to school with him every day, dribbling it the five blocks to the bus stop, then up the hill to Skyline. He started doing that in eighth grade, and the ball had since become an extension of his hand. His sisters stopped trying to describe their brother to friends who hadn't met him; instead, they simply said, "You know, the one with the basketball."

Everything was to lead up to this point.

Nelson Burns knew he had a lot going against him. He was five-seven and 130 pounds, a slight, friendly kid with a quick laugh, gentle eyes and a half-high fade haircut. One of his brothers was 6-foot-4, but he didn't play basketball. Nelson, as long as he lived, would never understand that. The brother was a good football player, and a good baseball player, but with that height? Nelson figured he would have had to play basketball. Nelson told himself that he could grow some more; just three more inches and he wouldn't have to worry about what anybody said. He knew there were a lot of people who didn't take him or his game seriously, but he thought he would make up for it with desire. Nobody wanted to play more than he did. Nobody.

Darrnaryl Stamps wasn't out there as much as he was. Neither was Kareem Davis or Anthony Byrd or Michael Franklin. Nelson Burns was still looking for a game after those guys went to bed. There was nobody who could tell him that he wasn't going to make it. His dreams would come true because . . . well, because they had to. Nelson Burns didn't have a better answer than that, and he didn't think he needed one. Dreams aren't built on logic.

"There are a lot of people who have told me, you know, 'You can't do that,' or 'You wastin' your time.' But I have a way of not listening to that. It's hard to explain. I like to hear everybody's opinion, but if they trying to tell me something I don't want to hear, I kinda just let it go by and forget about it. The way I look at it, you got to believe in yourself."

Besides, his game wasn't completely without merit. He could ball with everybody else on the playground. He had a nice jump shot and he could handle the rock with some flair. He didn't fully respect Donlea, because he didn't think the coach could play. Because of that, he didn't completely believe that Donlea could judge talent in others. But Burns had trouble when he was pressured, and he sometimes stood at the point and dribbled the ball until it threatened to bore a hole through the floor. Donlea couldn't handle the dribbling; it was as if every bounce throbbed at his temples.

They were all gathered in the coaches' office, waiting on Burns. Donlea waited on Burns. Everyone waited on Burns. They all knew he had something to say, and most of them felt he was justified in saying it. Everybody liked Nelson; they were with him.

"I don't have a problem with not starting or nothing like that," said Burns, his large eyes rising to meet Donlea's. "But if I be coming to every practice for the whole season, and I know I'm not crap, I should be playing. I don't feel there's no reason why I should not have been in any OAL games this year, not only because I feel I can play. I've earned my respect enough to be able to play on this team. There's not no excuse as far as I'm concerned. I should be playing. I heard you saying a lot of players are starting to use the word 'I'.

The only way a person can be selfish is if they already have something and they try to get more. If you don't have nothing, that's not being selfish—that's just trying to gain a little something. I can't speak for other people who sit on the bench, but I know what I do and what I should be doing."

"You don't think you have anything right now?" Donlea asked.

"He said he didn't," Govan broke in.

"You're telling me as far as Nelson Burns is concerned, you don't have anything."

"I ain't played *one* second in the OAL; we've played four games."

"You haven't played an integral part on this team all year long?"

"That's what you're saying, but that's not what I feel."

"He said he wants to play," Govan said.

"If you're not contributing to the team, it's kind of hard to be a part of it," Burns said.

"You guys have to see my position, my job with this school and this team. My role is to put the best possible basketball team on the floor at all times to make us as competitive as possible. Or else I wouldn't have picked the best players in the school. If I wanted to go out and have fun, I would have picked the twelve nicest guys, or the twelve with the best grades. In any group you're involved in, you're not always the star. That's where I differ with you, Nelson. That's where I differ a great deal: that you have nothing. You made this team, for one; that's a lot. That is a lot."

"Like you said, I made the team," Burns said, his voice quavering. "I don't want to be no fill-in, I don't want to be no practice dummy. I want to be me. I don't want to be somebody else's replacement. If I'm gonna play, I'm gonna play. If I'm not, I'm not."

"So you don't find that selfish?"

"No. I don't have no problem with not starting. But after the Sonoma game—I didn't play in that game, I don't have a problem with that—but you said, 'Don't worry, Nelson Burns, you'll be playing big minutes.' If that's not contradicting yourself, I don't know what is."

"I don't remember saying that. If I did say that, I remember you played a lot after that, like six straight games."

"In those six straight games, who else was not playing? Dave Strom. What does that tell you?"

"What does that tell *you*, Nelson?"

"It ain't nothin' against Dave. I'm just sayin, throw me in there when Dave hurt. 'Nelson, go in there and ball.' Next thing I know, OAL comes and I ain't seen a second. Not even a second. That's like an insult for a coach to come up with fourteen seconds to go in the game and say, 'Get in, get in.' It's not like this is Duke and I'm on scholarship or something. This is high school; I'm supposed to be having fun. I ain't even getting the chance to have fun."

"I'm not looking at it like, 'I'm freezing Nelson Burns out.' I don't give a shit who plays. I really don't. I don't care who scores the baskets, who makes the passes, who gets the rebounds."

"You say you're not doing it on purpose; you doing it on accident or something?"

"I'm putting the best team on the floor. Nelson, if you think you should play over David Strom —"

"You never heard that," Burns interrupted. "You never heard the words, 'I should start over David Strom,' come out of my mouth. Never."

"David Strom plays thirty minutes a game—thirty. There's only thirty-two in the game. If I could be frank with you, you've got two people ahead of you. I think if you were in my position, you would think the same way. I don't think you would say, 'Hey, we've got to play everybody, and everything's nice.' You put yourself in my shoes, what would you be doing?"

"I'd be playin'," Burns said.

"I'd play everybody," Govan said.

"I'll say something," Blackwell said. "If I was the coach, I ain't gonna lie, I ain't gonna play everybody. Beam don't play everybody. When I go to college, I got to beat the person out in front of me. I ain't gonna get a chance to do that in a game; I got to do that shit in practice. They're gonna go by how many balls I catch and how many he catches. If I catch more, they're gonna be forced to put me on the field. So what I suggest to you is to do it in practice."

"When you go to college, they'll be paying for your education, you'll have a scholarship," Burns said. "Here, I'm going to school; I'm playing ball to be having fun."

"So what I'm hearing is that it doesn't really matter if we win or lose," Donlea said.

"You never heard me say that," Burns said.

"So I should make exceptions and play everybody regardless of the game?"

"Fuck that," Blackwell said.

"No matter who plays, everybody is important on this team. We don't get better in practice without people like Nelson Burns. We are not the team we are now without the guys who don't play. You do have something. You're part of a team right now that plays Friday night for first place in our league, that has a chance to beat the number-one team in the Bay Area. To me, that's something. Granted, everybody would like to play, but you have to be realistic. Would you want me to put you in for thirty seconds?"

"No," Burns said. "I want to play."

"And why aren't you playing?"

"'Cause you're not putting me in the game."

"No, that's not the reason."

"That's exactly why."

"There's two people ahead of you right now."

"I still don't think that's the reason."

"Well, I do, and I'm the coach."

"Then why you asking me? If you already know, why you asking me? That's what I want to know."

"Are you unhappy with that role?"

"If I wasn't unhappy, would I be saying anything?"

"I'm telling you, things probably aren't gonna change."

"So you're telling me about my part, what is my part?"

"Your part is to be supportive, be emotional, be excited about us winning, that we're a team, that we're a group, that we're a family, that we are Skyline and we're competing and winning in a tough league. Believe me, I think about this. I know there are guys on the bench."

"If I wanted to be a cheerleader, I would have tried out for that last year. I don't want to be a cheerleader. I am supportive, but non-stop, continuously sit there and say, 'Good shot, good shot, good shot'? I don't even get a chance for me to get in and somebody to say, 'Good shot' to me, or 'Good defense' to me. If you say my part is to sit down and cheer for somebody else—I'm not a cheerleader. I'm me, that's who I am. I've been like accepting this, so now you're like comin' down on me. I've been sitting here accepting this, but now that I'm talking to you, you make me feel like I'm wrong."

"I'm sorry if I make you feel like that."

Donlea stopped, and the room fell silent. Burns sat mannequin-still on the plastic chair, his elbows on his thighs, his hands folded between his knees. Tears rushed down his face—big, heavy tears; tears carrying the hopes of a dream that would never come true.

CHAPTER TWELVE

ALL DAY THE SCHOOLROOM CLOCKS SEEMED FROZEN. DARREN ALBERT had a tendency to get nervous before games, but this was breaking new ground. Skyline had prepared all year to play McClymonds, and now it was almost here. Almost.

"We just need to get over there and play," Albert said. "This waiting's no good."

During lunch break, some of the boys behind the 20 building—classrooms at the back of campus—were putting their money on Skyline. The game was big enough to warrant a temporary interruption of the best dice game on campus. Some of the Skyline players jokingly wondered where they stood in the underground point spread, knowing there had to be one somewhere. Nobody in the OAL had come within twenty points of Mack all season.

After school, David Strom stood outside the gym, staring impassively at the pickup games on the schoolyard. He wasn't nervous; at least he wouldn't admit to it. Never change expression, never show fear.

"Have fun and play hard," he said. "There's no reason to be nervous."

Strom knew what awaited him at McClymonds. Everywhere he went, it was the same. *White boy. White shit.* "It's always white something," Strom said. He had learned to blot it out, to ignore it, but he always knew, when he took the court and walked into the crossfire of eyes, that he was different.

"If I forget, somebody's sure to remind me," he said.

Strom's philosophy differed dramatically from the team's strategy. Strom felt the only chance Skyline had was to push the ball, press full-court for 32 minutes and try to beat McClymonds at its own hyper-paced game. When he wasn't playing, Strom spent a lot of his time watching tapes of old basketball games. His favorites involved the Loyola Marymount teams with Bo Kimble and the late Hank Gathers. He thought that was the only way to play. Donlea, of course, thought that was ludicrous. Every team in the OAL had tried to run with Mack, and each had failed. The only way the coach thought they had a chance was to play at a measured pace, run the halfcourt offense and keep from falling into the yawning maw of the blowout.

"We run, we win," Strom said.

None of this was new to Will Blackwell. Skyline had beaten Mack the year before, and Will was more than willing to recount the details. Anthony Byrd had scored some ungodly amount of points in the first half, Blackwell thinks it was 27, before the coach made a defensive switch. Blackwell took Byrd in the second half. Byrd finished with 29. Blackwell scored 18 and Skyline won.

"I think we can win this game, too, I really do," Blackwell said. "If I shut down Byrd? Who knows? Stamps is good, but he don't like to come inside. He don't worry me that much. If we can rebound, we'll be all right."

For Jason Wright, it was another gym full of people to impress and annoy, another place to show his game. If, by the end of the game, they were screaming at him and cursing him and threatening him? Hey, that's what it was all about. He wasn't out to make friends; he was out to make enemies. If everyone in West Oakland hated him by sundown, he'd done his job. At least they'd remember him.

Nelson Burns knew the only way he would play in this game was at the ugly end of a blowout. He resigned himself to that as he got dressed for the game. He thought about Donlea's reaction at the team meeting, and he concluded that he might not play again. He started thinking more about altering his after-school schedule; he might start hitting the playground early and forgetting about practice.

Donlea hadn't slept, of course. The rings surrounding his eyes were beginning to look permanent, the gray becoming more prominent around his chalk-white skin. He planned to start his biggest lineup against Mack. He would put Govan in the backcourt and go with

Wimberly, Blackwell and Calvin Wilson up front. Two days before the game, that plan was lost when Wimberly dislocated his left pinky going up for a rebound in practice.

Without Wimberly, a daunting task grew tougher. Donlea would have to play Mack without a player taller than six-three.

"That really hurts," Donlea said. "Our only chance is to control the boards. If they out-rebound us, we could be dead early."

Donlea felt good about the game, but he had no idea why. The past week had been a tortuous one. He was furious with himself for the blowup after the Oakland High game and disgusted with the way he handled the supposed solution, the team meeting that degenerated into a clash between him and Nelson Burns. But he came away from both episodes with a decision: There would be no more mind games. If he sensed he was losing his temper, he would walk away. Nothing else he had done seemed to make much of an impression on his players, so he decided to try it. The thought occurred to him as he lay awake wondering how to bring everything back together. He had to convince himself that it wasn't an apathetic response; it was simply common sense.

He also felt he was giving the players too much credit, coaching too democratically. He was constantly aware of his newness, of his lack of experience with the inner-city environment. He also felt young. For those reasons he felt compelled to let them have their say, to give them a voice in the process, but that had heaped confusion atop confusion. From now on, he would handle the playing time and the game strategy and the starting lineup. The players would have to deal with it on their own.

"Of course they want to play," he said after the team meeting. "They all want to play. They're in high school, for Christ's sake. Everybody in high school wants to play the whole game. Why don't I just realize that and move on? What would they do if I said, 'OK, we're just going to play everybody and whatever happens happens?' They'd be pissed off. They say, 'We just want to have fun,' but that's bullshit. They want to win as much as I do. It's the American way. That's why you play. Winning is the only thing, and they know that as well as I do. I'm just not going to worry about it anymore. I'm going to do what I know is right."

The day before the game, Donlea was presented with a perfect opportunity to show his new leniency. Jason Wright shot a free throw underhanded during a running drill at the end of practice. Given the team's horrendous foul shooting, it appeared to be the perfect way to ignite Donlea's fuse. As the ball floated aimlessly toward the basket, Donlea's jaw went slack and his eyes rolled back inside his head. He dropped his hands to his knees, looking like a man who had just been given some very bad, and very unexpected, news.

Then, as the players awaited the explosion, he marched from the gym and closed himself in the coaches' office. The players admonished Wright and waited for Donlea to reappear. They expected a tirade, and most of them felt it would be deserving. Donlea was gone for close to five minutes, and when he returned his look was serene, calm. He gave a short, upbeat talk and sent the players home. They looked at each other, amazed, and shrugged their shoulders. They thought they had him figured out.

"It doesn't do me any good to scream and yell," he said. "That's why I went in there. Screaming hasn't worked, so I'm just not going to do it anymore."

Donlea knew what the Mack game meant. Everyone knew Mack's talent was far superior to anyone in the area, maybe even the state. The only way to beat McClymonds was with a plan, and nobody had devised the right one yet. This was his chance to have his team play his game and show everybody that it could work, that structure could win in the OAL. They would run the offense and play what he liked to call "Skyline Defense." They would play hard for 32 minutes; they wouldn't back down. Everyone else had gone with the macho, playground routine: Run with Mack, beat them at their own game. Skyline didn't have the talent for that, despite what the players felt. If Skyline were to win, it would come back to Donlea.

The Skyline players dressed at the school, before boarding the bus.

"What if we win this game?" Darren Albert asked. "Those people ain't gonna like that. If we win, we gonna have to get out of there in a big hurry."

There were six Oakland Police squad cars in the McClymonds parking lot when the bus pulled in. The players joked about who would leave the bus first. Damon Gardner walked out holding his hands over his head. They got nothing, not even a dirty look, from the crowd waiting to pass through the security outside the gym.

A lot had changed at McClymonds over the past three years. Some coaches in the OAL now considered it the safest place to play. The school district's crime statistics from July to December of 1992 showed nineteen weapons seizures at the six Oakland public high schools. The only school with less than three was McClymonds, which didn't have any. Skyline, the privileged school on the hill, had three.

The McClymonds principal, Oliver Chambers, did not believe that an inner-city high school had to throw up its hands and surrender to the evil forces swirling around it. He believed in self-reliance, and self-control, and he didn't accept conventional excuses. The students would learn or they would get out. Chambers had devised a pre-collegiate program for the school. Students would choose a major in tenth grade and take as many courses in that field as the school could provide.

"We don't need any more excuses in the inner city," he said. "Students need to work hard, because they will be amazed at what happens when they do."

According to statistics provided by the Oakland Unified School District, 99 percent of the students at McClymonds came from families that receive Aid to Families with Dependent Children. The schoolwide average grade-point average was 1.83. In standardized tests, the senior class at McClymonds in 1991–92 scored in the 14th percentile in reading, the 17th percentile in language and the 31st percentile in mathematics. Just twenty-three McClymonds students bothered to take the Scholastic Aptitude Test in 1992, and their average combined score was 652 out of a possible 1600. The three-year dropout rate at McClymonds has varied from 28 percent to 50 percent.

In his fight to change expectations at McClymonds, Chambers was fighting history, a history that Bill Russell described in his autobiography, *Second Wind*. Russell wrote:

> *None of the kids was expected to go to college, and very few of the faculty expected to go anywhere either. It was not a school that inspired high hopes for anybody, and most of*

the teachers were bitter about it. They ran kids through 'job-training' classes that consisted mainly of personal errands. They prepared kids for the harsh realities of the outside world by deflating their dreams with cynical comments. Once I almost told a teacher I wanted to be an architect, but I stopped myself. I knew what she would say."

West Oakland is the other side of The Grapes of Wrath, the side that didn't get its book or its movie or its Broadway play. It is a place that seems to be forgotten by history, abandoned and left to decay like one of its many ill-conceived housing projects.

During the wartime boom, as more and more blacks migrated to Oakland searching for the industrial motherlode, West Oakland began to overflow. For entertainment, families would congregate at the 16th Street train station and watch as the cars unloaded, carrying prospective workers and their families.

One diary from a McClymonds student in the late 1940s typified the scene:

> *"I can remember we'd go down there . . . after school to watch the people get off the trains, and it was like a parade. You just couldn't believe that that many people would come in, and some didn't even have any luggage; they would come with boxes, with 3 or 4 children with no place to stay, and then there would be people there, and they'd ask everyone if they had any place to stay or could they make some space into rooms."*

The black men who migrated from the South and East to take part in the wartime manufacturing boom in Oakland were given the opportunity to work alongside whites. Russell's family was typical; they moved to West Oakland when he was nine years old, and they chased a dream that was utopian and color-blind.

Russell wrote: "We were pulling up stakes, and maybe we'd become like those families who return every summer to visit from the North, driving long cars, wearing shiny clothes and making people feel uncomfortable."

The need for workers was desperate, but blacks received a hugely disproportionate share of the dangerous tasks. Black faces filled the graveyard shifts. Black workers could become union members, but they were not allowed to vote in union elections. The influx of black workers was blamed for the shortage of housing and consumer goods. The crowded homes and streets of West Oakland also made them easy scapegoats for the housing shortage.

Inevitably, confrontations occurred. There were minor altercations at the shipyards and on the city streets, but in early March of 1944 a riot between black workers and white policemen brought the issues to full boil. An editorial from the weekly *Oakland Observer* of March 11, 1944, outlines the prevalent feeling toward blacks at the time:

> *That riot on Twelfth Street the other day may be the forerunner of more and larger riots because we now have (a) a semi-mining camp civilization and (b) a new race problem, brought about by the influx of what might be called socially-liberated or uninhibited Negroes who are not bound by the old and peaceful understanding between the Negro and the white in Oakland, which has lasted for so many decades, but who insist upon barging into the white man and becoming an integral part of the white man's society.*
>
> *Thus we see, in Oakland, white women taxicab drivers serving Negro passengers, and white women waitresses serving Negroes in white men's restaurants. If that is not a potential source of trouble, we do not know what is.*
>
> *There is no intention here to blame the Negro. That riot may have been entirely the doings of white men. We do not know. We do know, however, that the influx of the exuberant Negro has brought up the problem, and it is certain that the white man is not going to be pushed around in a civilization that is predominantly white.*
>
> *There is no doubt that a Negro can get just as hungry and thirsty as a white man. The Negro's money is as good as a white man's, coined by the same Government. The Negro needs transportation as much as the white man, and he is just as entitled to work as the white man. He is entitled to every right that our forefathers fought for, and which*

many honorable members of his race are also fighting for today.

But the trouble is that the Negro newcomer does not concede that the white man has the right to be alone with his kind. If the white man does not want the Negro sitting alongside him in the white man's restaurants, or does not want the association of the Negro anywhere else, this may be attributable to race prejudice. Yet, in the final analysis, the white man has the right of race prejudice if he so desires. If he does not care to associate with anyone, he is not compelled to do so.

Right there is where the Negro is making his big mistake. He is butting into the white civilization instead of keeping in the perfectly ordered and convenient Negro civilization of Oakland, and he is getting himself thoroughly disliked.

It might be well for the more orderly and respectable Negroes to tell the newcomers about the facts of life. Otherwise we are going to have some more riots.

Race riots never became the problem some anticipated in West Oakland or anywhere in the flatlands. The solution was simple: the white people moved out.

The fans inside the McClymonds gym were awaiting Skyline's arrival. Another game, another victim. Mack's success had brought the community closer together, and each game brought greater anticipation. They regularly had to turn spectators away from games, and some of them responded by standing in the parking lot, listening to the crowd reaction. The week before, when Fremont High came to McClymonds for the showdown of undefeated teams, more than 100 people spent the game in the parking lot.

As soon as the Skyline players walked from the bus to the court, the public-address announcer was ready.

"We'd like to welcome Skyline to the flatlands," he yelled above the thump and thrash of the rap music. Some of the fans, sensing the ironic intent of the message, laughed and waved placards reading, "Dunk 'em, Warriors."

The Skyline Titans huddle before a game. (Dave Nielsen)

ach Shawn Donlea barks instructions from the sidelines. (Dave Nielsen)

A sign of the times. Security guards search all fans for weapons at Skyline home games
(Dave Nielsen)

Ever present, armed police officers keep a careful watch on the crowd.
(Dave Nielsen)

avid Strom and Beverly Palley, a Skyline teacher. (Dave Nielsen)

Will Blackwell (*right*) lends some advice to Eric Govan before the start of a playoff game. Calvin Wilson is at left. (Dave Nielsen)

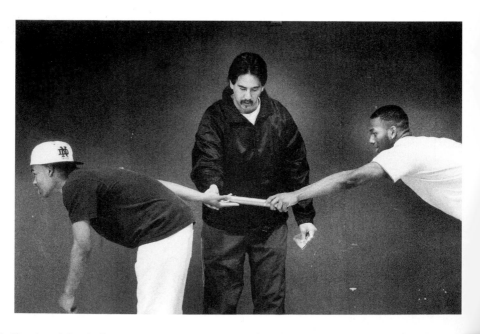

Skyline head football coach John Beam works with two members of the school's track team. (Dave Nielsen)

McClymonds head coach Willie Hearnton. (Dave Nielsen)

High scorer Jason Wright slams home two more points. (Dave Nielsen)

Junior varsity players Mike Scates (*left*) and Montise McKinley. (Dave Nielsen)

Coach Donlea paces the sidelines as players (*from left*) Nelson Burns, Bryant Johnson and Rod Ponder take in the action from the bench. (Dave Nielsen)

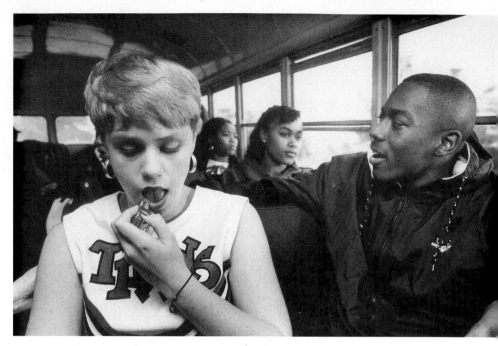

Will Blackwell shares a seat on the team bus with a Skyline cheerleader on their way to a playoff game. (Dave Nielsen)

During a game against Castlemont, Maggie Wimberly encourages her son Nick (#40). (Dave Nielsen)

•••

Donlea paced in front of a blank chalkboard in Mack's wrestling room, just off the court. Not even he could stand still before this one. He wanted to get a few technical points clear, but he realized the futility of the effort. He couldn't bring himself to discuss the 31 defense or the 22 set or the importance of setting a back pick for the cutter in the Brown offense. His mind was racing, the thoughts whipping through and clearing out as fast as he could think them. There would be emotion out there, so there was emotion in here.

"You have nothin' to worry about today—nothin'," he said. "Go out and play your game. You play it smart, you have fun with it, you pass the ball, make sure everybody's involved, take the shot that's there, run the offense when it needs to be run, break the press with the pass, get the ball out of the trap before the trap gets on. Hey, we're ready for this game. We've been preparing all year. I've prepared you all year to play this team. You've prepared all year to play McClymonds. You're ready to play! You go out, you have fun with it. Play it smart and go after it, guys."

The players started moving forward, getting into the rhythm of Donlea's words. The scene took on the appearance of an ad-lib revival meeting.

"Hey, people been tellin' me, 'Yeah, your boys are gonna go down to McClymonds and the fans are gonna scare 'em'—"

"Fuck that!"

"We ain't afraid of their shit."

"They say if we start getting a lead, people are gonna start saying, 'You guys better not score a basket or we're gonna kick your ass after the game.' "

"That's bullshit—bullshit."

"We here to play."

"You guys don't have to worry about that shit. You just go out and play. They're just kids just like you are. They're nothin' else, nothin' different. They're high school students just like you. The score's zero-zero right now. Play, have fun, play hard. There's no substitute for that."

They extended their right hands overhead. They met in the middle, forming a human triangle of stillness. It would be the last moment of calm. Donlea crouched in the middle, the nervousness and anxiety a palpable presence. The adrenalin needed an outlet.

"OK," Donlea said, his voice barely above a whisper. "Let's have a moment of silence for their winning streak."

They dropped their heads briefly, then broke the huddle and lined up, Strom in front. This was the last moment of peace. They opened the doors to the gym, and it was like throwing open the doors of a blast furnace. The music and the heat rushed into the room like a stumbling drunk. The air was hot, heavy-hot, redolent with the sickly sweet smell of marijuana. The music vibrated off the orange walls, its bass pumping through the room like a massive heartbeat.

Donlea walked across the court to the Skyline bench, his mind racing, his stomach tightening. He looked to his left at the Mack players. *Strong. Tough. Big.* He looked at his players as they circled the floor to his right. *Small. Soft. Smart.*

There was a group of McClymonds fans sitting behind the Skyline bench, obviously positioned there for a reason. They wore the looks of tough people who had lived hard lives, their faces fixed in a street-corner stare. Donlea saw them and walked straight for the bench, reminding himself that he knew this was coming. He had actually expected it sooner. He kept walking, stepping through the center circle ringed with the words "Home of Champions," his clipboard in his right hand, his face stern. He hated the analogy, knew it could never be taken the way he honestly meant it, but he talked about the way animals sense fear or weakness in other animals. He thought that could relate to his situation. He tried not to show weakness.

They leaned forward, their bodies forming tight C's as they strained their voices to be heard above the din of the crowd and the music.

"Hey, whitey. Hey, white man coach. Nineteen and oh, whitey. Nineteen and oh and ain't nuthin' you can do about it. You'll see what happens when you come down off that hill."

He looked up into the stands, making brief eye contact before turning away. There was a big difference between bravado and stupidity.

• • •

Mack took the court, each player coming out with a slow, confident walk, the walk of eighteen straight wins. Willie Hearnton followed, his head down and his walk purposeful. Hearnton is the McClymonds coach, a tall, serious man with a body so thin it appears improbable that all the necessary working parts could be contained within it. He had been grooming this team for three years, since he saw an uncommon amount of talent in one particular tenth grade class. Darrnaryl Stamps, Kelton Runnels, Renard Monroe, Anthony Byrd, Kirtus Clanton, Louis Jackson—they all arrived together, a staggering amount of basketball talent made even more staggering by McClymonds's combined boys and girls enrollment of roughly 600 students.

"I saw this two years ago," Hearnton said. "We've been leading up to this."

Stamps got the tip, easing his body into the air and softly directing the ball to Byrd, who took two dribbles before Govan picked him clean. Strom took a pass and drove, right to the hoop, with the full force of his being. He knew from experience that he had to establish himself, every game the same challenge. He drove hard to the hoop, ducked under Runnels and flipped it in off the board. Runnels barked something at Strom as he headed back downcourt.

Byrd committed another turnover and Stamps's first shot was off the glass and nothing else. A hopeless brick. Govan rebounded and tossed the outlet to Blackwell, blazing down the right side. He took it in full stride and headed for the basket. Stamps came from the middle, the only obstacle between Blackwell and the basket. Blackwell saw Stamps and leaped toward the hoop, his 5-foot-11 body stretched to the limit. There was a decision to be made here: he could stop and fake, hoping that Stamps would fly past and leave him with an open basket; he could stop and take a ten-foot jump shot; he could slow it down and back it out.

Or he could dunk. For Blackwell, that was the only legitimate choice, the only true option. Somebody else might have stopped and head-faked, but not him. He had to make his statement, Skyline's statement, and he did it the only way it could be done. He took it to the basket, as if trying to dunk Stamps along with the ball.

Stamps went up, but Blackwell seemed to stay up there as Stamps descended. He ripped it down, but the ball bounded off the back rim. The fans howled. Donlea clapped.

"Thatta baby, Will!" he yelled from the sideline. "Thatta way to take it to 'em." He turned to the players on the bench. "We're here," he said. "Skyline's here."

The next trip down the court, Jason Wright took a pass from Strom and threw down a hard two-handed dunk. He looked to the Mack cheering section and raised his long arms up and down at his sides, exhorting them, asking them to respond. Mack raced the ball downcourt and Blackwell came from nowhere to reject Byrd's driving layup. Wright continued to raise his arms and Blackwell went into his dance routine—"The Shake"—as McClymonds tossed the ball inbounds.

Will Blackwell and Jason Wright loved the theater of the game, especially in the other guy's gym, in front of the other guy's fans. Both seemed to have an inherent desire to be both remembered and disliked, although, underneath, they were vastly different.

Blackwell's cockiness was born of his success, both on the football field and on the basketball court. He was known around Oakland, maybe the city's best high school athlete, and he felt it was incumbent upon him to announce his presence.

Wright was merely pumping himself up, getting involved in the game. Donlea tried to get both of them to subdue their acts, but he was more concerned with Wright. He told Jason that scouts would take his attitude into consideration, and some might forget about him. *Great player, bad character*, they would write in their notebooks, even though it wasn't true. He wasn't a bad character; he was a bright, thoughtful kid who happened to be extremely excitable on the basketball court. Donlea thought Wright needed to purge the playground attitude from his system before thinking about his dreams.

"Sometimes I wonder, what does coach think when Will and me out there doing something stupid?" Wright asked. "I know he don't like it, but I can't help it. That's just me."

Wright had cleared a huge barrier with his teammates during the

OAL season. Before, they questioned his heart. During the preseason, Blackwell described the difference between the two: "See, I talk on the court, and so does Jason. But when I stop talkin' and start playin'? Jason's still talkin'. That's the difference."

Then, two games into the OAL season, as the injured Blackwell watched from the stands and Wright piled up huge statistics, Blackwell said, "Jason Wright might be gettin' a little heart."

Heart. It's a total, all-encompassing description. It cuts to the very core of a basketball player's existence. Without it, talent is meaningless. With it, talent expands.

Skyline had taken the game to McClymonds, leading 13–7 after Strom drilled a three-pointer from the top of the key. Willie Hearnton called time out. He was glaring now, standing near the free-throw line with one knee bent and his arms at his side. There was a low rumble of noise from the stands; they had expected to be chanting "Nineteen and oh" by now. Hearnton pulled his players onto the court to make his message more pointed and private. He didn't like what he was seeing, but he didn't say much. His eyes, piercing and unblinking, said all that needed to be said.

His players got the message. They immediately went on an 11–4 run, with Stamps hitting a baseline jumper to give McClymonds an 18–17 lead. Five minutes later, McClymonds went to the locker room with a fifteen-point lead at 37–22. It was Stamps one time down the court, Byrd the next. Point guard Renard Monroe tossed in a three-pointer and the place was mad with noise. Donlea tried to slow down the game and deflate the run, but it was no use. He sat down on the bench and wished the remainder of the half away.

As he walked to the team room at halftime, somebody yelled down from the stands, "Whitey, we told you not to come down off that hill."

Back in the wrestling room, back in the quiet, the Skyline players sat on the floor or stood in the corner or lay sprawled on the rubber mat. Donlea had fought to keep his game plan intact, but Mack's late run had frazzled his team; they responded as Donlea knew they would—they tried to run with Mack.

"It's only fifteen," he told them, his hands out to his side, his palms pointed heavenward, as if pleading. "Fifteen points. With the number of turnovers we had, that's not bad. That's not bad at all. This game is not out of reach, by any stretch of the imagination. It's not out of reach. We've got to be together, stay together. We've got to change defenses more frequently this half. You gotta be listening, gotta pay attention."

Donlea rattled off some technical points. As he turned to the blackboard, the players instinctively turned away, their attention gone. Donlea turned back and met their eyes.

"I'm a little disappointed in our man-to-man," he said. "Once they catch the ball, we're going, 'Oh, Shit.' Hey, go out and play. Get in their shit. If you foul 'em, foul 'em. *Get. In. Their. Shit.* Stay close to them. Strip the ball. We got to come out tougher. Come out tougher. Remember: Nobody thinks we have a chance but us. Let's put it all out there. Put your balls on the line."

Stamps scored inside to start the second half. Jason Wright hit a 15-footer and Blackwell stole the ball in the open court and ripped it through with a tomahawk slam at the other end. Fifty-three seconds into the second half, with Skyline just two points closer than they were at the half, Hearnton called another timeout and met his team at center court.

He put his hands on his hips, flaring his brown sports coat at the sides, and glared. The players looked at him, then looked down. He yelled a few instructions in his throaty rasp and sent them back to work.

The timeout showed Donlea that his team worried Hearnton. The McClymonds coach didn't know what to make of Skyline, because Donlea continued to change defenses and the players continued to play hard. Mack was accustomed to running up a score and then having a good time. Donlea decided to use a halfcourt trap and see if the Warriors could handle it.

The game changed. Four minutes later, after three straight baskets by Wright and two three-point plays by Govan, Skyline cut the lead to seven at 48–41. Blackwell was turned toward the Mack fans, gyrating and gesturing, doing a slower and longer version of The Shake. Hearnton called another timeout.

OAL Commissioner Lou Jones was standing under the Skyline basket. He called one of the referees over and told him to speak with Donlea about Blackwell's antics. The referee was one of the few white referees who work OAL games, and Donlea had been berating him the entire game.

"He's intimidated here," Donlea said at halftime. "He's not gonna call anything on them, because he's afraid."

The referee stood in Donlea's face and tried to be heard above the noise.

"Coach, Mr. Jones said you better keep number 13 under control or he's going to ask him to leave. He can't do those things here."

Donlea called Will over.

"Tell him that," Donlea said to the referee.

The referee repeated Jones' words. Will laughed and motioned across the court, toward Jones.

"I'll be cool," Blackwell said.

The referee spoke with Blackwell while holding the basketball with in his right hand, with his palm up, like a waiter holding a tray. After Blackwell walked away, the referee turned back to Donlea.

"I think he's seen too much Big East basketball," the referee confided with a laugh.

"I don't think you've seen *any* Big East basketball," Donlea said as the referee jogged away, out of earshot.

During the timeout, a Skyline cheerleader turned to Skyline teacher Heather McCracken and said, "We might win this game. What do we do if we win?"

McCracken, the school's cheerleading coordinator, said, "I don't know about you, but I'm running out of this place as fast as I can."

After the timeout, an orange aimed at the white referee came out of the bleachers. The referee stopped the game in the middle of a Skyline possession, as Strom was penetrating to the basket.

"What's going on?" Donlea screamed. "We've got the ball! We've got the goddamn ball!"

Donlea ran up and down the sideline, waving his arms frantically. Hearnton stood near the scorer's table, his arms crossed, watching Donlea.

On the bench, Nelson Burns said, "Coach be having a heart attack here. He better calm down. He's way too excited."

In the fourth quarter, McClymonds showed how it had built an undefeated record. The full-court press came alive, and Skyline looked to be playing against six or seven defenders. A steal led to a dunk, which led to another steal and dunk. The game never looked so easy. Skyline's chances evaporated as quickly as they had appeared. Blackwell picked up his fourth foul less than a minute into the quarter. Stamps scored inside, Byrd hit two three-pointers and Runnels slammed one hard. Mack led by seventeen, and Skyline was finished. The rest of the game was exactly what Donlea hated the most: a rag-tag waste of time, with everybody trying to dunk. McClymonds won, 74–50.

With two minutes left, the Mack fans began the chant.

Nineteen and oh
Nineteen and oh

After the game, the fans were on Donlea again.

"White man, we told you not to come off that hill. Why don't you listen?"

Donlea walked over to shake Hearnton's hand, then looked up in the stands, in the general direction of the comments.

As he walked off the court, Donlea said, "I expected more of that this year, but it still bothers me. I mean, look where I am. I'm really a racist, aren't I?"

Donlea told his players that they would get another chance at Mack—and maybe two.

"We can beat them," he said. "There are things we have to work on, but we can do it."

After the players had left, Donlea said, "That's a great high school basketball team we just played. If we play them ten times, they'd beat us ten times."

Hearnton stood outside the gym, leaning against a graffiti-filled beige stucco wall and smoking a cigarette. Dusk was beginning to settle on the city, and the movement on the streets surrounding McClymonds had begun to pick up in intensity. Cars passed slowly, the bass pouring from the open windows like musical exhaust. Hearnton talked about what his basketball team had done for the community of West Oakland, and his words were constantly interrupted by spectators extending their hands in congratulation.

He tried to explain how important basketball can be when played against this backdrop. Darrnaryl Stamps lives in a home for boys in East Oakland. Backup point guard Richard Hardman had perhaps the hardest life: his mother was beaten to death by a boyfriend, and his father took his own life.

"This team's done very well for the community," Hearnton said. "We have a nice crowd every game. Now we have to more or less restrict parking. I've even got friends who take off work to come watch us play. It's been uplifting, and we appreciate it. We just want to try to keep everything up, keep everything positive, keep everything going in a positive vein. This is a maligned community—many times erroneously so—it's just not that way."

Hearnton stood outside the gym where Bill Russell found his athletic ability, where Paul Silas learned to rebound. A short walk away, on the baseball field, Frank Robinson learned his competitiveness and Vada Pinson ran down fly balls across a clod-covered outfield. It was near dinner time. Darrnaryl Stamps would head back to the boys home. Richard Hardman would go home with teammate Renard Monroe. They were 19–0, intent on making history repeat itself.

"I don't have to tell them about the history here," Hearnton said. "People in the community take care of that. We're about making our own history, making our own niche. That's what I tell them."

The Skyline players boarded the bus that would take them back up the hill. From there, they would descend it again and head home.

CHAPTER THIRTEEN

CALVIN WILSON WONDERED HOW MUCH ONE PERSON COULD TAKE BEFORE everything inside snapped. He had seen so much and lived through so much that it was hard even for him to realize he was just seventeen years old. He looked thirty and felt even older.

He wanted one thing: out. He wanted out of the formless, nomadic life he was leading, out of the stink and rot of the city. He wanted to get away from a two-hour commute to high school, *high school*, and into a place where he could walk to class and talk to people and play football. More than anything, Calvin Wilson wanted a new life, because the one he had wasn't worth a damn.

He was a tough-looking kid, with a furrowed brow beaten down under the hardships of his life. He wore a Fu Manchu that accentuated his glare, his *attitude*, and his long sideburns floated free under a shaved strip above his ears. But that face could break into a wide smile with little provocation, his eyes narrowing and nearly getting lost as the smile broadened. He was confused and wary, because he knew of no other way to be, and the exterior was simply a safeguard, a facade for the turmoil that lay underneath.

Calvin's senior year in high school had been one trial after another. He often thought there was some force out there in the world conspiring against him. He laughed at the litany of misfortune that had plagued him throughout the year; the sheer absurdity left him no other choice.

He started the year normally enough, living in Oakland with his mother and stepfather in a house just down the street from Jason Wright, on the flatlands side of the MacArthur Freeway. In January, his stepfather left and his mother couldn't pay the bills, so she was forced to move to San Francisco to stay with her sister. Calvin went along.

Shortly after the move, they went back to Oakland to get their belongings. They found that somebody had broken in and stolen whatever they could handle, including a sofa bed and the family's refrigerator.

"They must have taken 'em right out the front door," Calvin said, cocking his head to the side in disbelief. "I don't understand it; they took our refrigerator. Our *refrigerator*. And it wasn't even new. Oh, they were nice enough to leave us the food. They took all that out and put it on the counters before they walked out."

Living in San Francisco and going to school in the hills of Oakland became a public-transportation nightmare. It would have frayed the nerve endings of the most seasoned commuter. Calvin left his house at 5:30 in the morning and walked to the nearest San Francisco bus station, about four blocks away. The bus weaved its way through the southern edges of the city, stopping every few blocks to pick up the area's blue-collar workers who relied on the early bus to get to work. Calvin got off the bus at the Bay Area Rapid Transit's Balboa station and took the high-speed rail train underneath San Francisco, through the tube under San Francisco Bay and onto the Oakland side. He got off at the Fruitvale stop in Oakland. He walked from there to the bus stop and waited to be taken to 35th and MacArthur, roughly three miles from Skyline. He would wait there anywhere from ten to thirty minutes before the bus arrived to take him up the hill to Skyline.

Calvin Wilson's commute to high school dropped him off at school at approximately 7:45 every morning, barring any delays. The one-way trip lasted just over two hours. His cost for getting back and forth to high school each week was thirty dollars.

His year got worse when his mother became ill the night before the Fremont game. Calvin was at her bedside until the small hours of the morning before going home to seek out a few hours of sleep. He went to school that day in order to play in the game that afternoon, but when he forgot his uniform, that didn't even happen.

"You start to wonder just what else could go wrong," he said.

His mother recovered, but Calvin decided to move to his father's house, near the southern edge of San Francisco, even farther from Oakland. One of eleven children, Calvin felt it would be best if he lessened his mother's burden by one. While living with his father,

Calvin got the use of an older van with curtains that covered the side and back windows. He could be found dressing for practice in it nearly every day, and some of his teammates referred to it as his "mobile home." He didn't care what it looked like; the van allowed him to sleep past six in the morning, and he didn't have to worry about buses or trains or anything but the gas gauge.

After the loss at Mack, Wilson went to a friend's house in Oakland to relax after the game. It was about eleven o'clock and he was tired when he left the house. He nodded off briefly on the Bay Bridge. As he took a right turn onto the Cow Palace/Third Street exit from Highway 101, less than two miles from his house, he fell asleep at the wheel and drove the van into a clump of trees that serve as a median strip separating the offramp from the freeway. He wasn't injured, but the van was out of commission and he was back on public transportation.

He laughed when he talked about the accident, saying he didn't think he was that tired. He shrugged his shoulders ("The van's no longer," he said) and chalked it up to fate.

"After all he's been through and he's laughing about that?" Donlea said. "I'd be crying, really crying. And he laughs. I guess it's perspective."

It would have been the easiest thing in the world for Calvin to quit the basketball team, or not to have gone out to begin with. But he lived for the feeling of being on a team, of belonging to something that presented him with a tangible goal. He had to have that bond, that link to normalcy.

He loved working hard, and working up a sweat. He would sweat so much that he would stop to wring out his T-shirt two or three times during practice. Nobody wanted to guard him. He practiced in the same shoes he wore to school, a hybrid hiking boot-sport shoe. He borrowed an old pair of Blackwell's basketball shoes for the games.

He didn't care about any of that, though. He didn't care that he got home at nine o'clock every night, often too tired to do anything but go to sleep and get ready to do the routine all over again. That wasn't the point; the point was he was part of a team, someone to be counted on, a part of the whole.

He missed practice on occasion. Donlea would look at the circumstances and let it ride, stretch the rules a few inches. Some of the players believed Calvin got away with too much, that he abused the rules and let the team down. Donlea, who had learned to adapt from his staunch stance as the season progressed, looked at Calvin's situation in broader terms. Donlea didn't know everything about Calvin's life, but he learned more after the two met early in the OAL season.

Calvin had missed three practices and a game, and Donlea called him into the office. Coach Beam, intimately familiar with Wilson's situation because of football, sat at his desk and listened.

"I'd love to have you, Cal, but you've got to make a choice," Donlea said. "You've got to ask yourself what your priorities are right now. Are they going to school and playing basketball, or are they somewhere else?"

Calvin looked down at the table, occasionally shaking his head slowly. He didn't know Donlea that well, and the look on his face said he wasn't sure his coach would understand.

"I want to play," Calvin said. "But there's just some *things* . . . I don't know."

"You've got to get those things straightened out, Cal, because I can't put up with it anymore. I have to be a little selfish. I have to look at what's best for this team, and I can't always be wondering whether you're part of it or not. I've let things slide a little bit, but I can't anymore. We need to figure this out, to decide what it is you want to do."

Wilson nodded slowly and got up to leave. He looked at Beam, who shrugged his shoulders and pointed to Donlea. This was out of his jurisdiction.

Donlea later talked with Beam and learned a little more about what Calvin meant by *"things."* Much as he wanted to, Donlea hadn't had the time to delve into each player's background. He was busy enough coaching two teams and trying to scare up a few substitute-teaching assignments. He desperately wanted to be on campus more often—to be on staff, as a matter of fact—but it just wasn't possible under these circumstances. What Donlea heard about Calvin from Beam told him enough. Donlea realized that the alternative was worse than a gradual loosening of the team's rules. If Calvin didn't have basketball, he wouldn't have much of anything.

There would be no incentive to respond to the alarm every morning. The bus ride would be longer and even more inconvenient. He would find another way to spend the thirty dollars a week. Without basketball, there would be no carrot at the end of a long and jagged stick.

Basketball wasn't going to take Calvin anywhere, and he knew that. He played center even though he was a shade under six feet tall, but he was surprisingly quick and had good lateral speed for a 235-pounder. He also had a deft shooting touch and a high release that allowed him to get shots off against much taller players. Still, there was no mistaking what he was, a football player playing basketball. His teammates sometimes called him "Mini-Barkley."

"When I'm playin', I can forget everything, all the problems. Be around spirited people, fun people. I ain't gonna do nothin' at home, just sit around. I like playing basketball. Besides, it's my senior year and I ain't gonna be able to do this again."

Donlea loved Wilson as a player, mainly because he was quick to pick up on conceptual matters. Despite missing the first two months of basketball because of football, Calvin picked up the nuances of the offense almost immediately. He was also a strong rebounder who used the width of his body to its biggest advantage.

Calvin kept to himself for the most part, silently walking through life with little in the way of true friends. His toughness had earned him respect, the kind of respect that kept some people at a distance. He had learned not to rely on anybody. He was self-reliant, and that's the way he wanted it to be.

"I can only trust a few people. I don't know what it is, but it's real *hard* for me to trust someone. That's just because I seen so much. My body just don't let me. I'm always on guard, automatically. I don't even got to think about it."

Football was an outlet for everything—anger, fear, confusion. It was as simple and clear-cut as anything in his life: you hit, they fall down. College scouts liked what they saw from him, both as a fullback and a linebacker. He didn't command immediate attention, like Blackwell, but he was the type of player who gradually but repeatedly sent the recruiters back to their notebooks. He could block, he could plug a gap on defense and he was strong in a way that few high school students are.

"You ask any running back about Calvin," said senior Damon Gardner, who gained more than 1,000 yards as a tailback during his senior season. "Calvin opens holes like you wouldn't believe. And he fast for a big man, so he don't clog up the holes. I never ran up Calvin's back, 'cause he was already through the hole and his man was on the *ground*."

Wilson didn't want to think about what his life would be like without football. When asked, Beam let out a slow sigh and said, "He wouldn't be in school, I know that much."

Calvin took recruiting trips to several Division I universities, but he was captivated by New Mexico. He liked the atmosphere, the openness. He thought it would be the perfect place to start over, the perfect place to play football and work his way toward a degree in civil engineering. New Mexico was unlike anywhere he'd ever been. He didn't find the distractions or the temptations of his life there, and although it may have been fantasy, he felt a drastic change in environment would make the difference. He wanted to be alone, known by nobody. He wanted to sever the link to anything that happened before and let people judge him without preconceived notions. He thought it could work, too, if he only got a chance.

The coaches at New Mexico were interested, too, but Calvin wasn't at the top of their list. His trip to Albuquerque had been a safeguard: if somebody else didn't work out, Calvin Wilson would be a serviceable alternative. The Lobos filled their freshman class before that happened, so Calvin had to look elsewhere.

"That hurt," he said. "If I went to New Mexico, I don't know if I woulda came back. You know how people come back for the summer? I don't think I woulda came back. I woulda just stayed out there and done my thing. Go to school and work hard."

He had always struggled for his grades, and now it was becoming even harder to concentrate. By the time he got home, forget it. The thought of waking up in the morning and walking to class, then to the library, seemed like some impossibly wonderful idea. So wonderful, in fact, that he couldn't believe it wasn't going to happen.

"I just liked that environment at New Mexico. I could just go and take care of my business and not have no distractions. Go to the library; I can type a little bit so I could use the computers. They were showing us around a little bit. They've got mentor and tutoring plans. That's what I'm looking for, a school where I could do good academically. I'm not worried about sports; that's not a problem. And I just liked the way it looked down there."

When Wilson was left without a scholarship, Beam went to work, calling college contacts who had expressed interest. He knew the kid could play, but he also knew Calvin's grades didn't help. He had scored the required 700 on the Scholastic Aptitude Test, but his cumulative high school grade-point average was deficient. Beam had to find a school that could look past his transcripts and into that attitude. He found a scholarship for Wilson at the University of Pacific, a university in Stockton, about 75 miles from San Francisco. Pacific, which plays Division I football, would accept Wilson with contingencies; he had to spend one semester at a junior college and pull an A in his senior English class over the final semester.

Wilson expressed his gratitude for what Beam had done, but he found himself feeling empty. He wanted to get away, far away, and this wasn't what he had in mind. He wanted red mountains and dry heat, not more bus rides and more pressure for grades. Even if he made it through that, he didn't like what he saw at the end of the struggle: a chance to play at a school he felt was second-rate. Calvin had been to UOP just once, for a summer passing-league tournament. He didn't even know the name of the coach. And now he was being told to spend a semester in a junior college, pass three classes and be on his way. To Beam, the payoff was worth it. But to Calvin, it meant another full year of the same life. The thought clawed at his insides with the force of a powerful corrosive. He wanted to be out now. He knew he could play—and more than that, he knew how much could happen in a year.

Calvin Wilson could do other things in life besides play football. He could steal a car, any car, in less than a minute. He could pick your pocket or wave a gun in your face or rob you blind or beat you to a bloody pulp. He had done all of those things, and done them well enough to have stayed reasonably clean with the law. He'd been in juvenile hall a couple of times, but his longest stay was a twelve-day sentence he served for car theft.

Calvin Wilson seemed well on his way to becoming a statistic. Young black males are all too often judged by numbers: Murder rate, crime rate, dropout rate. At one point or another, Calvin was near the front of the line for all three.

Stealing cars was so easy. He'd be sitting around with his friends, kickin' it after school, and somebody would get tired of the scene. "Let's go for a ride," one of them would say. So they would.

They would either hotwire a car on the street or flash a gun at somebody sitting at a red light. They'd drive around for a while, then ditch the car and go home.

He went to junior high school in Oakland before attending a San Francisco-area school for tenth grade. In junior high, he carried a nine-millimeter semiautomatic to school with him every day. Went to school *strapped*, in street terms. He was fourteen years old.

"I never had no problems," he said. "I would never say nothin' to nobody. I really didn't want to kill nobody or shoot nobody but I felt I had to defend myself. I felt that I would do whatever it takes to defend myself because I wasn't going to let nobody hurt me. I wasn't lookin' for no trouble, and if somebody was to say something to me, I wasn't going to pay them no mind, because I knowed that I could take their life if I wanted to."

In tenth grade, his life veered farther off course. He continued to go to school strapped, this time with a chrome-plated .45 caliber pistol. He grew his hair long, wearing it in braids or finger waves. School was simply a place to hang in between marinating and fogging his mind. Every day he drank an "eight-ball"—the street name for a forty-ounce bottle of Olde English 800—sometimes before school. He would go to a friend's house during third period and smoke marijuana; his friend sold weed at school and always had a healthy, and free, supply.

"We'd smoke two joints and go right back to school. I had PE third period. And I used to go back to math; that's why I flunked that lady's class. I'd come in there high and couldn't even comprehend. She was a little white lady and she talked kind of fast. She'd be talkin' and doin' the work on the board, be doin' this and subtractin' this, workin' problems. I'm like, *what?* We sat in groups of four, and I'd just sit there and kind of laugh. There was only two black people in that class, and [the other] was this black girl in the same group. She'd just crack up, she'd be laughin' at me, like 'What's wrong?' I'd say, 'This shit is *crazy*.' I couldn't really comprehend in that class. I could have done the work, but when I went I wasn't in the right state of mind."

Calvin says he did "most of the dirt" during an eight-month span of his sophomore year in high school. He was back in San Francisco after going to junior high in Oakland. He hadn't discovered sports. He was aimless. And he always had a gun.

During that time he hung out with members of his family, either cousins or brothers or friends who were considered family. One night four of them, including Calvin, were cruising through San Francisco—out to cause trouble, he says without pretense—and they decided to drive to the East Bay city of Richmond. It was late at night, and they drove to a bank, looking for some easy marks.

"We saw these four white men, late twenties, early thirties," Calvin says, his voice calm and mechanical. "They was sittin' in a car outside the bank at a drive-up cash machine. I was lookin' at 'em and lookin', and then my friend say, 'They don't look like four normal dudes, maybe we shouldn't do this.' My cousin, he crazy, he grabs the gun and says, *'I'll do it.'*

"We get out of the car and he walks up to them with the gun and says, 'All right, don't nobody move.' We got them out of the car and we was pattin' 'em down and everything, and one of 'em had a gun. This one dude had a gun like down his back, behind his belt. I didn't see it, but my friend did. I took his wallet and his watch and stuff, but I didn't see the gun. We left them and the guy started reachin' back there, and my cousin say, 'Get your hands back on that car.'

"He backed up, holding the gun on 'em, and we was just runnin' and runnin' and runnin' down this back street. We was lookin' for my other cousin, who was supposed to be drivin' the car for us. But he wasn't there. We walked down another street, and I was on the left side and they was on the right. This car passed me real slow, and I saw it was those guys. I didn't know what was going on, and I thought maybe they was comin' back for revenge or somethin'.

"They looked right at me and kept on goin'. Then they saw my cousin, and they gunned it up to him and slammed on the brakes. The dude with the gun jumped out and *POP-POP-POP* he shoots my cousin. He got him with one bullet and my cousin, he went down. My cousin had his gun, a chrome .45, against his stomach, but he didn't have the clip in. So he went down like he was real bad, and that's what he wanted them to think. When he's on the ground, he got the clip in and those guys came up. They got there and he shot two of 'em. Then he started comin' toward me, movin' as best he could, and our cousin showed up with the car. He got in and said, 'Get me to a hospital, I'm hit bad.' He got shot in the pelvic area and the bullet came out his butt. Came out his left booty cheek. We never knew what happened to those dudes he shot."

On another occasion, Calvin was the one with the gun. He and some members of his family "got into it" with a carful of men near the San Francisco-Daly City border. Some car windows were broken and threats were made.

"They had broken some windows in my uncle's car, and he knew they was gonna come back," Calvin said. "Sure enough, they came back in two cars. We was making cocktails—we had forty-ounce bottles and we got some gasoline to put in the bottles and put a rag in there. We was ready to blow 'em up. They came down there but I was at the gas station. As we were comin' in, they was tryin' to come out. We blocked 'em, and that was the only way out. They didn't know that, so they turned around and tried to go the other way. The person that was driving their car parked and got a shotgun out of the trunk. Then he got back in the car and started drivin'. They saw there was no way out, and they turned around and came by again. It was *freaky*. I just like took this old shotgun we had—it didn't even have no wooden handle; that was gone—and stepped out into the street. As soon as they got close I just shot and hit the door. They kind of swerved and kept goin'. They ain't never came back after that."

He says he has changed, that what he did was wrong, and that he was lucky he never really had to pay for it. He speaks about the crimes with a detached disbelief, as if somebody had inhabited his body. Despite the problems he's endured, he knows he's lucky—lucky to be alive, lucky to be able to carry on his dreams. And that is why the thoughts of leaving, of getting away and starting over, had invaded every pore of his being. He had learned not to trust anyone—including himself.

"I done some bad things," he said. "Some really bad things."

He lived his life one way: "I didn't think about much back then. I just did it. If I felt like doin' it, I did it. I didn't think about it."

One thing Calvin couldn't do was sell drugs. He tried, but he didn't have the heart or the savvy for it. He went with his brother down to Third Street in San Francisco, behind Candlestick Park in the worst neighborhood the city has to offer, and tried to sell drugs. He stood out there near a bank of pay phones with all the other clockers in their slick jogging suits and high-cost Nikes. His brother could do it. Oh, could he ever. His brother was a pro, a big-timer, but Calvin couldn't get the hang of it. After two or three days, he gave up.

"I see 'em out there every day," he said. "They probably makin' good money, but it's not for me."

His brother's luck eventually caved in under an avalanche of convictions, including several narcotics charges. Calvin says his brother is serving an eighty-seven-year term in prison. Calvin visited him a couple of times, but he was disgusted with the whole prison scene. His brother quickly faded from his life.

As one of eleven children, Calvin says the family ties were strong, like cable. There's a code that goes along with that, a responsibility that doesn't allow for questions or hesitation.

"If I'm out with my family or something and there's a lot of us, you know, something happens and one of them get into it, I have no choice but to defend them, be on they side, watch they back. I got no choice. I feel that's an obligation. I know if I get in trouble, I wouldn't have to say a word and they'd be right there. They ain't gotta say a word; I'll be right there. Sometimes, you know, we might not be lookin' for no trouble, just trying to have fun, and some hardheads who want to act crazy and act ignorant, they want to look at you, what they call 'Mean Mug', and they like to mug you, look at you hella crazy. Like lookin' at you with a frown on they face. And then that's gonna cause you to look back like, 'Why you lookin' at me like that?' And then there's gonna be a word, and somebody's gonna say, 'What you lookin' at?' That's gonna start it off. 'What you lookin' at?' 'I'm lookin' at you, partnah.' 'Let's do this, then.'

"You get a crowd at a party or somethin'—three, four hundred people—you don't know what's goin' through people's minds. You just got to always watch your back. Nowadays they be strapped with guns, automatic machine guns, powerful shotguns."

At some indefinable point, death becomes irrelevant, a passage of life as everyday as sex or hunger or homework. Violence is expected, and everybody who lives the life knows enough not to take it too seriously. Wilson says: "When I go home, when I pass, I think I've done enough good to kind of override the bad."

More than anything, Calvin was tired of watching his back, and even more tired of watching the backs of other people. He would do it if he had to, regardless of his feelings for right and wrong, because, after all, obligations aren't negotiable. Still, for once in his life he was looking for the opportunity to look straight ahead.

Calvin was going to make it in football; he was sure of that, more sure than he was of anything else in life. All he needed was a chance to get out and make his own life, succeed or fail on his own merit, in a situation where everyone started out equal.

"I know I can make it," he said. "I just know. There's no doubt in my mind. I got the heart."

The scholarship papers sat in his room, unsigned. Beam had told the newspapers, and the *Tribune* had added Wilson's name to the list of Skyline players who had signed Division I letters of intent. But two weeks later, Calvin still hadn't signed anything. He didn't want to believe this was all there was. He held out hope that something would change. He didn't care what the newspapers said, he hadn't signed anything. He thought he might forget about the scholarship, go to a junior college and go through the whole recruiting process again during his sophomore year. That meant another year and a half of *this*, but he thought he might take the chance.

He wasn't Will Blackwell. Head coaches and regional recruiting coordinators weren't calling his house or setting up appointments. His business took place at Skyline, where coaches would talk to him and Beam. There was only one exception, and that was a meeting with a University of Oregon coach. It was at a restaurant near San Francisco International Airport, and Calvin went alone.

Studies show that one out of every 800,000 high school athletes goes on to play professionally. Nearly one in a million. Calvin Wilson wanted to hear none of that. The people who take the time to compute those numbers don't know what's inside a man. If it was one in a million, that's OK. He'd be that one.

"From when I was little, I always wanted to live nice, to have a nice house, nice cars—just live nice. Kinda wealthy. I always thought that would be the thing, have a nice house, a nice place for my kids to grow up. I want to have some space, you know? I like living in a city, but not like this. Not where you don't have no room. I want to live kinda near the city, but not in it. I just kinda have to keep thinkin' about those things, because things ain't been goin' too good for me lately. But, you know, I'm livin'. I'm livin' a whole lot better off than a whole lot of other people. That's what I gotta keep tellin' myself: I'm livin'."

CHAPTER FOURTEEN

AS THE GAME CLOCK TICKED DOWN AND THE FANS AT McCLYMONDS began chanting louder and louder, Nelson Burns quietly fumed. Mack's lead grew into the high teens and the clock ground down to below three minutes, and still he sat. His eyes went from the clock to Donlea, back and forth.

Will Blackwell, who had fouled out, sat on the bench and pointed to the scoreboard.

"Hey, these guys should be in there," Blackwell said, his hand pointing back to Burns and Damon Gardner. "There ain't no excuse now. This game's over."

Donlea was defiantly, unrealistically holding out hope. Skyline continued to press and harass McClymonds, even though Hearnton had pulled most of his starters. Then, with less than two minutes remaining, he called on Burns and Gardner.

Burns looked up at the time and reluctantly pulled his warmup top over his head. He thought about turning down the invitation, but he couldn't. He'd give it one more try.

Burns spent that weekend, as usual, thinking about basketball. He thought again about how quickly his hopes for the season had been doused. He and Strom went to Piedmont Park and played a few pickup games, but Nelson's heart wasn't in it. He told Strom he was thinking about quitting. He thought about how much he enjoyed the playground game, and how much easier he fit into the picture there. He could play after school and work on his schoolwork and get in shape for next season, wherever that would take him. Strom said he wouldn't blame him, and that sitting on the bench and going through the motions in practice wasn't doing anything but bringing him down.

"I know I'm gonna play next year; I just don't think I need to stay around here. I just kept lookin' at the clock during the Mack game and I was sayin' to myself, 'I should be in there now. I should be in there now.' I don't know what I'm gonna do, though. I just want to play, and he said things probably wouldn't change."

Burns decided, then and there, that he would quit the Skyline team and spend more time playing on his own.

"It's all I've been thinkin' about," he said. "I can't get it out of my head."

On Monday, Burns wavered. He heard the talk about Friday's game, and thought about how much effort he had put into this season. He decided to give it one more game. He would give Donlea one more chance.

He showed up for practice as he always did, wearing his baggy red shorts and his jacket. Strom had been off campus applying for a scholarship. He walked into the gym and saw Burns. He began laughing.

"What're you doing here?" Strom asked Burns. "You stickin' around?"

Nelson repeated his plan: One more game.

"Man, this ain't doin' you no good," Strom said. "What is this doin' for you?"

Burns shrugged his shoulders and grabbed a ball. He couldn't quit now, because that's what he thought Donlea wanted. To quit would be an admittance, a surrender. That wasn't what Nelson Burns was all about.

"Somebody tells me I can't do something, I'm gonna do it," he said.

That day at practice, Nelson Burns played as if his life depended on his performance. He held his own against Strom defensively and made crisp, authoritative passes. He hit most of his open shots and didn't take any bad ones. He ran the floor harder than anybody, at times making his teammates look bad with his hustle. And, above all, he didn't dribble too much.

Donlea noticed the difference right away. He kept quiet for the first half of that day's scrimmage, but after one particular sequence, when Burns stole a pass, dribbled to the foul line and bounced a perfect pass to Blackwell, Donlea couldn't hold back.

"Nelson Burns! Nelson Burns!" Donlea shouted at him. "You're showing me something."

Nelson heard Donlea, but he didn't react. He wouldn't give his coach the satisfaction. In his mind, he wasn't showing Donlea anything he shouldn't already have seen.

"I'm doing this for me," Nelson said after practice. "Nobody else."

The next day, before the team left campus to play at Oakland Tech, Donlea said, "Nelson's going to play today. He's going to play a lot. You know, I've got a different take on that kid now. He's still not going to play much against Fremont or McClymonds, but he's really come around. Part of the reason he wasn't playing before is because he was pouting and sitting around during practice. Now he's trying to prove me wrong, and I like that. Yeah, he'll play."

It was Skyline's first game since the fevered loss at McClymonds, and Donlea was worried about motivation. The Oakland Tech gymnasium is the nicest and cleanest in the Oakland Athletic League, but Donlea didn't like the color scheme. Oakland Tech's school colors are yellow and purple, and a bright lemon-yellow stripe about eight feet wide rims the walls inside the gym.

"I see all this yellow, and I don't know," Donlea told his team. "I don't want you guys being all mellow because this place is so sterile."

Moments before the game, Donlea pointed to a far corner of the gym, where several Oakland Tech students sat slouched against the wooden bleachers, ready to watch the game. The season's second grade check was the day before, and Toby Harris was one of the spectators. He had left Skyline because he was ineligible, and because the academics were too strenuous. Now he was an academic casualty at Oakland Tech as well.

"That's what happens," Donlea said. "There's my whole philosophy right there. That kid would have been better off staying where he was."

Skyline made it through the grade check with only minor difficulties. Two players had to get grades changed to remain eligible, and they went about the task as if performing intricate covert operations. By the next day, the grades had been changed and they were in uniform.

Donlea kept his word: Nelson Burns was one of the first players off the bench against Oakland Tech. He came in midway through the first quarter and played some tough defense. As was the case the first time the teams met, Skyline had some trouble shaking Oakland Tech, an undertalented team that played hard and with some discipline.

Burns also had two steals and two assists during a third-quarter run that gave Skyline the game. Then, at the start of the fourth quarter, Burns took a pass from Strom on the right baseline and drilled a 17-foot jump shot that gave Skyline an eight-point lead. After the shot fell, Burns stood and watched for a split-second, his right hand extended in the follow-through position as he savored the moment. The Skyline players on the bench rose as one, pumping their fists and turning to high-five each other.

It was Burns' first big moment since the preseason game against Riordan, when he hit a three-pointer that gave Skyline an early lead. This meant more, because this came in an OAL game, and it came because he had earned his way onto the court.

This wasn't what Nelson Burns had in mind when he was flat on his back on his bedroom floor, flicking a basketball into the air and watching the backspin. He had loftier goals, visions of his name appearing in headlines and being spoken around Oakland playgrounds. But he would enjoy this sliver of success, this feeling of helping his team when it needed him. Nelson Burns would end his senior season with only two points in the Oakland Athletic League, but he would walk away knowing they were big points.

Michael Donlea and his wife drove to Oakland from Lompoc—about a five-hour drive—to watch Skyline play Castlemont on February 12, a Friday. It was the first time he had seen his son coach the game they both loved.

This was, in a way, a family rite of passage. Michael and Shawn Donlea had their differences and had endured hard times, but this game provided a bond. Basketball was always there to cut a swath through the differences and unite father and son.

Shawn wanted his father to see what he had accomplished, and this game would be his testimony. The Skyline players would take his concepts and his philosophy and incorporate it on the court. How they did would tell his father everything he needed to know about his son. They would be playing through Shawn to Michael.

A win would clinch third place in the OAL and ensure Skyline a spot in the playoffs. That was Donlea's goal from the beginning of the season, but he didn't want to tell his players about the ramifications. Everything in his psychology experience dictated against it. He would wait until after they won, then inform them.

"From all I've read, it's not a good idea to bring something like that up," he said. "It doesn't aid performance. Instead of thinking about what they have to do to win the game, they start thinking about the playoffs. It can become a distraction."

The Castlemont fans filed into the Skyline gym about fifteen minutes before the start of the game. The security was heightened; something was expected to come down during or after the game. The anxiety was fueled by the restless energy of the impending weekend.

"Word is they know they can't take us on the court, so they's gonna fight it out," a Skyline student reported to some of the players.

"That's bullshit," Will Blackwell said. "That's what they always say when we play Castlemont."

The campus security officers and the uniformed police searched with more diligence than usual as students and spectators entered the gym. Donlea was unable to get into the gym at first. Apparently, the officers weren't convinced he was telling the truth when he told them he was Skyline's coach.

"The gym's not open yet," one of the officers told him. "We're not letting fans in for a few minutes."

"I'm the coach," Donlea said.

Another Skyline teacher walked past and vouched for Donlea, and he was allowed in to coach his own team, in its own gym.

"They're talking about a fight, with knives and stuff," Donlea said nonchalantly. "I don't worry about that stuff anymore. It seems like we go through this every game, and nothing happens."

Michael Donlea and his wife passed through the metal detectors and filed past the security guards and the uniformed officers. They walked into the gym and sat on the Skyline side.

"To walk into that situation, that was a little bit scary for us," Michael said. "We're from Lompoc, you know. There were five cops standing around ... yeah, that's a little bit scary for us. We sat down and looked around. There were about 400 people there, and we're just about the only white ones. But once the game started, it was fine. Everybody had a good time. Nothing happened."

In the second half of the OAL schedule, David Strom took the ball to the basket with an intensity and purpose that had been missing in the first half. The game started, and Strom was the focal point, shifting through the traffic, dribbling behind his back and between his legs. The fans howled and hooted and looked at each other in disbelief. The white kid was all right.

He shredded Castlemont's defense and continually found a team-mate, usually Blackwell, open for a layup or short jump shot. Strom's performance wasn't accidental: he had decided to play the game his way, on his terms. He was directing the offense when the situation arose, but he was making chances for himself and his teammates by taking the initiative. He felt it was the only way Skyline would improve.

"I knew coach didn't want me taking it to the hole," Strom said. "I really didn't care what he had to say. I'm a senior and this is my last year. I sold out last year. I was the pass-boy last year. I'm tired of being the good guy."

Besides, Donlea's instructions before the game gave Strom the opening he needed. Donlea had said, "It's gonna be a fun game tonight. Very up tempo, just like you guys like to play. But I don't want to get into a run-and-dunk drill. Play Skyline defense and run, run, run."

Skyline ran, and at the end of the first quarter it was 35–14. Blackwell was scoring inside with the ease of a player all alone on a playground.

This was Jason Wright's return match with Michael Franklin, and it wasn't going Jason's way. Along with Govan, Wimberly and Calvin Wilson, Wright picked up two quick fouls and found himself in an unusual position: on the bench. He sat and sulked, waiting to return to the game. Both teams were flying up and down the court, playing *his* game, the Allendale, Mosswood, Brookdale game, and he was being sacrificed for the good of the team. Because of the wide-spread foul trouble, Donlea felt he had to save someone for the second half, and he chose Jason. Jason didn't like it because Jason wasn't used to it.

It was plainly evident by the way Wright sat on the bench—slouched, impatient, unobservant—that he was unhappy with Donlea. After a second-quarter timeout, when Donlea again left him on the bench, Wright walked away from the bench with an irritated look on his face.

"You're not special, Jason Wright," Donlea told him in front of the rest of the team. "You're a member of this team just like everybody else. You don't get any special treatment."

Donlea continued his tempestuous relationship with the referees in the OAL. He had refereed more than 1,000 games over the past five years, and the inconsistencies were driving him to the brink.

It was as hard to find officials who were willing to referee in the OAL as it was to find qualified coaches.

After Govan was called for a reaching foul—his third—in the second quarter, Donlea stomped down the sideline and said, "I'm tired of getting screwed in this league."

Skyline led by 16 at halftime, but Wilson, Govan and Wimberly each had three fouls. Castlemont finished the half on a minor jag, scoring six of the final eight points. Donlea could see Michael Franklin taking the game into his own talented hands, and there was a sense of uneasiness in the Skyline locker room, an uneasiness not normally associated with a 16-point lead.

"They're feeling good right now," Donlea said. "They're only down 16 and we're in foul trouble. They're gonna come right back out and take it to Skyline. They've got nothing to lose. They're gonna slap and hack and probably get away with it. We get every call against us. But forget the foul trouble. Forget it."

Donlea's senses proved correct. Castlemont made a tremendous comeback in the third quarter, with Franklin scoring at will. They came on like a full-force gale, pulling to within three points late in the third quarter.

Franklin has a strong, brooding face and a lean, powerful body. He scored from outside and inside. He scored on incredible leaning, one-handed jump shots from deep on the baseline, and he scored on twisting, spinning layups in traffic. He did everything smoothly. He scored 27 points, and he never seemed to exert himself.

Jason Wright returned in the third quarter, but he never got it going. Later in the third, he picked up a technical foul when he spiked the ball at one of the referees. He felt he was hit on the arm while driving for a layup, but no foul was called. He was at the free-throw line in the fourth quarter, being jeered mercilessly from the Castlemont fans. He hit the first free throw, then flipped off the jeering fans with a drumroll beat of his middle fingers. Anyone who knew Jason Wright off the basketball court would have found it impossible to believe this was the same person.

Donlea yanked Wright out of the game immediately.

"J Wright, you play basketball or they'll throw you out of here," Donlea said. "That's no class. You're taking a chance on getting your ass jumped after the game."

Michael Donlea and his wife sat placidly across the floor from Shawn, about six rows up the wooden bleachers. Michael watched Jason Wright and remembered why he left coaching.

"I watched that and I knew I couldn't have handled it," Michael said. "Shawn does a good job with that; he understands those kids. I don't. I don't have the patience."

Wright's actions occurred as Skyline was beginning to pull away from Castlemont. Strom led the comeback with a quick burst early in the fourth quarter. He hit two free throws and a pull-up 15-foot jump shot to turn a four-point game into an eight-point game. Jason followed with a breakaway slam and Skyline led 78–68.

Still, this was Blackwell's game; he had 28 points and 16 rebounds and several spurts of unparalleled athleticism. Donlea was reminded of the conversation he and Blackwell had early in the season, before Blackwell had practiced.

"I guess he is the best basketball player in the school," Donlea said.

They had met Donlea's primary goal; they had made the OAL play-offs. He wanted to tell them they had made the playoffs. He wanted to congratulate them and tell them he was proud. More than anything, he wanted to tell them to be proud of themselves, for all they had overcome to reach this moment.

"Hey, quiet," he said when they gathered in the locker room afterward. "You guys took it to another level tonight; you took Skyline to another level tonight. First ten minutes of the game you took it up, put it together. You played basketball the way basketball is supposed to be played. You took it up there, and then you know what? Gut check. They came at us, we got in foul trouble. Did you have the character? The desire?—"

"Hell, yes."

"—People wonder: What kind of kids do they have? Do they have the character to win games like that?—"

"Hell, yes."

"—We could have folded up the tent and walked off a loser tonight—"

"Nah, coach. Nah."

"—We could have. It's been done. Everything we've done, all the work, has paid off. It was everybody tonight. Everybody. Now you know what's next—Wednesday night, Fremont. Start thinking about it.

"One more thing: You know what? We beat McClymonds tonight. We beat McClymonds playing like we did tonight. Think about it."

He had forgotten about the playoffs. He had the entire scenario scripted in advance, but he also had a junior varsity game to coach. He forgot about the playoffs and went back onto the floor. He spoke to his father briefly and sat on the bench. Halfway through the first quarter he remembered: They had made the playoffs. By then, the varsity players were gone.

About three months later, on his twenty-ninth birthday, Shawn received a letter from his father. It carried a tone of emotion that was rare for Michael Donlea, a man raised in a time and place that dictated that men keep their emotions to themselves. In the letter, Michael told his son how proud he was of him, and how much he enjoyed watching him coach that game against Castlemont. He wrote that he had never seen his son happier. That, in turn, made the father happy.

"I think he's real proud of me, proud of the way I turned out," Shawn said. "That made me feel good. He was right, too. I don't know if I've ever been happier than after that game, because he was there."

CHAPTER FIFTEEN

IT WAS A WARM SPRING SATURDAY IN OAKLAND, AND ERIC ALBERT wasn't about to stay home. His academic problems apparently worked out, Eric was riding a hot streak. He had always been surrounded by an indescribable aura of invincibility, but the previous week intensified the feeling. He had received a letter in the mail on Friday, informing him that he was selected to a preseason Junior College All-America football team. Earlier in the week, he had decided to accept a football scholarship from UCLA.

Darren Albert remembers seeing his brother in front of the house that Saturday morning, the morning of May 9, 1992. Eric was telling the next-door neighbor about the letter.

"I'm about to go to UCLA for football," he told the neighbor. "I'm about to go to UCLA."

Darren and Eric are unmistakably brothers. They both have wide, open smiles and eyes that smile right along. They are both well-built and just about 5-foot-10. Neither could imagine having any trouble finding a date. Eric's skin is considerably lighter, but in black-and-white photographs they could pass for twins.

Eric Albert was feeling awfully good about life on May 9, 1992. It had taken him some time—he was twenty-one—but he had finally realized that football without the grades was as good as no football at all. He had worked at his studies for the first time while he was at Chabot Junior College in nearby Hayward, and now it was finally going to pay off. He was under some pressure, because his father had told him to improve his grades or move out of the house. Eric knew he couldn't play football and support himself at the same time, so the grades improved. There was never any doubt about the football; that was always there.

Eric planned to go out with two friends—Omar Alidaggao and Aaron Pedroni—that May afternoon. Eugene Albert told his son to stay home, maybe work on his car. He was worried about Eric, and the company he kept, but Eric didn't want to stay home. He never did. Every chance he got, Eric was out, kickin' it with his friends.

Omar and Aaron picked Eric up, in Aaron's car. They bought some beer, drank it, then met some people who told them about a pool party at an apartment complex in Dublin, located over the Oakland hills in Contra Costa County. They got into two cars and headed east on Interstate 580, through San Leandro and Hayward. They turned onto I-680 and drove to Dublin. Along the way, they drank some more beer and smoked some marijuana.

Eric and his friends were not welcome at the party. They estimated they were there for less than ten minutes, but they never got beyond the front gate. The manager of the complex asked them to leave, and a police officer was on the way. As they stood outside the gate, Eric and his friends began arguing with the young men who told them to leave. One of them was a 22-year-old black man named Cecil Jason Bell, known as Jason.

The argument was the usual macho talk, fueled by alcohol and wounded pride. As he was leaving, Alidaggao told Bell and the others: "You Dublin niggers ain't shit."

To them, it was all about Oakland. To be tough, truly tough, you had to be from Oakland. Suburban guys couldn't hang with the real thing.

A police officer arrived at the complex. Eric and his friends left the party, but not before they told Bell and his friends where they would be: At another party, on Foxboro Circle in nearby San Ramon.

Skyline football coach John Beam says Eric Albert may have been the best player he ever coached. For pure toughness, there was no doubt. Eric weighed 172 pounds ("Never below 170, never above 174," Beam says) and was uncommonly strong. He could bench press 275 and squat 400. He played defensive back and running back, and he carried a great high school team with his attitude. Skyline went 10–0 in Eric's junior year and made its way into the national rankings.

In the Skyline football program, even the stars have to wait their turn. There is talent upon talent, and being The Man is a result of patience as much as ability. As a senior, Eric Albert was The Man. He had 2,800 all-purpose yards and was the main back in an offense that included Deon Strother, who went on to play tailback at USC.

"Man, was Eric tough," says Beam. "Tough, with attitude. And he ran a ten-five hundred meters in boots. He was our man. Whenever a fight broke out, Eric cleared 'em. He could throw them dogs. Oh, could he throw them dogs. He was something else. Eric could be locked in a room by himself and it would sound like there was a party going on. He could make a blackboard talk to him. He was such a physical guy, everything about him was physical. He wouldn't greet you by saying hello. He'd greet you by giving you a hug. That's just the way he is."

Beam took a special liking to Eric. He worked with him and rode him hard, because he saw the talent. He also saw the attitude, and he worked to harness it and direct it. If Eric didn't have three unsportsmanlike-conduct penalties in a game, he didn't feel like he played.

"It was like, we would score and I would be in somebody's face, talkin' shit," Eric said. "Beam would say, 'You gotta do that every game?' "

Darren was a good football player, too. It just seems he peaked too soon. In junior high he was well ahead of his classmates. He was always the star at Frick Junior High, even with Will Blackwell on the team. He played football for part of his junior season, but he was upset about playing time and eventually quit.

Darren didn't have Eric's temperament. Darren could—to use the street expression—get amped, and he didn't back away from a fight, but he couldn't sustain that controlled rage that seemed to course through his brother's veins whenever he got on the field.

San Ramon is a wealthy Contra Costa County suburb with housing developments named Fleur Du Mont and Vista Pointe. The neighborhood around Foxboro Circle is modest by comparison, a typical California scene. The homes are mostly single-story, stucco with wood trim, and each home has one magnolia tree in the center of the front lawn, like a mast. Like so much of California, the homes are built close together to maximize property value.

Eric Albert and his friends arrived at 10106 Foxboro Circle at approximately 6:30 P.M. on May 9. Eric says he was ready to leave after five minutes, but his friends met some girls and decided they liked their chances. Omar and Aaron wanted to stay. When the topic was girls, Eric never put up much of a fight.

"Even I thought we had a fair shot of getting with the girls," Eric said, "but it was just like, 'It's time to go home.' I was telling them, 'Exchange numbers and call 'em another day.'" They thought they would be safe out here, just three guys from Oakland looking for a good time. They could have stayed in Oakland, hit a few parties there, but San Ramon seemed like the right idea at the time. There was something wrong, though. From the time they left the apartment in Dublin, Eric had the uneasy feeling that everything about this trip was wrong. His feeling of personal immunity was fading.

Eric said, "It was just to get away from Oakland to a place where you would really feel like you were safe going to a party. But out there, everything was all wrong."

About five minutes after Eric voiced his desire to leave, three vehicles pulled up on Broadmoor Drive, the street facing the front of the house. Eric was standing on the lawn when they arrived. One of the vehicles was a small red pickup with a license plate reading "FULLARD." Jason Bell got out of the truck, along with Andre Fullard and Terry Rogers. Right away, everyone knew there would be trouble.

"Before the fight even started, me and Aaron are trying to make peace," Eric said. "Even I know when I'm outnumbered, and I feel like I can handle myself pretty fair. But it's like nine or ten guys against the three of us, and I know Aaron's not a big guy—I'm the biggest one out of the three of us. I'm not all that tall, and I'm like, 'Hey, hold up.' Me and Aaron are trying to make peace and Omar's over on the end, running his mouth off and whatnot. I looked at him and said, 'Be cool; be quiet.' When I turned back around, four guys was rushing me and it was on."

Eric isn't entirely sure what happened after that. Witnesses later testified that Eric was on the ground with Jason Bell, and that Bell was getting the worst of it. Eric remembers parts of the fight, but the girls were screaming and it was loud and hectic. People were coming at him from every angle and he was doing what he had to do to protect himself. He says he hit a lot of people. He didn't think Bell was one of them.

William Finnegan, who lived two doors down on Foxboro Circle, heard the commotion and walked out to investigate. He saw Jason Bell crossing Broadmoor Drive with a gun in his hands. His mouth was bleeding. The gun was a sawed-off .22-caliber pump rifle. It was inaccurate and clumsy, but aimed at a human being, at close range, it could serve a purpose.

The crowd on the lawn had spread out now, as it became known that Bell was crossing the street with his wounded pride and his gun. Eric saw the gun being pointed at him from across the lawn. He stared at Bell, disbelieving. Alidaggao testified that he initially thought it was a toy gun. Eric put his right hand up to his face and felt a bullet tear through his right pinky and hit his right cheek.

There were an infinite number of sociological factors at work following that first shot. Eric stared at Bell, thinking to himself, "Just 'cause you got a gun don't make you a man." Bell had taken the first step; he had fired the gun. Now his friends were pushing him to finish it off. Andre McAlister, one of Eric's new friends, said he was held in a bear hug by one of Bell's friends, who yelled, "Yo, Jay, shoot this motherfucker." Bell pointed the gun at McAlister but didn't fire. McAlister broke free and ran into the house. Eric stayed on the lawn, staring at Bell.

"You know, his aim was real bad, that's what everybody said," Eric said. "So I was thinking, Maybe he didn't really mean to shoot me. Maybe if I would have turned and run into the house, he wouldn't have shot again. I don't know—all I know is, I didn't want to turn and get shot in the back. If a man's gonna shoot me, he's got to look in my eyes."

Bell fired again and Eric was down. He doesn't remember the second shot, but he remembers lying on the lawn, wondering how such a beautiful day could turn out so terribly wrong.

Jason Bell kept coming.

Darren thinks about Eric a lot, Eric lying on the soft lawn of a suburban home with bullet wounds in his hand, face and shoulder, the world spinning chaotically around him as Jason Bell approaches with the sawed-off rifle in his hand and anger in his heart. Darren thinks about Eric at that moment, Eric all alone with his fear and his pain. Eric tried to get up, and couldn't. Jason Bell closed fast, like a middle linebacker with the perfect angle. Eric waited, knowing everything might end—all the cheers and tackles and dreams— on the soft lawn of a suburban home.

Eric knew guys like Jason Bell, guys who held nothing back.

Finnegan, the neighbor, heard the commotion and was out of his house for a second time. He had called 911 and came back to see what would happen now that his peaceful neighborhood had been turned into a battleground. He was about forty or fifty feet away from Jason Bell and Eric Albert, watching in disbelief as Bell walked to within a body's length of Eric, pointed the sawed-off barrel and fired.

Eric was lying on his left side. The bullet entered his body near the back of his right shoulder. It traveled into the base of his thick neck and lodged in his spine. His legs went numb.

"I tried to get up and couldn't. It felt like I was on the football field and I got the shit knocked out of me. I had butterflies in my stomach and everything. I couldn't get up. I thought about what my parents were gonna say, what my girlfriend was gonna think—all kinds of crazy stuff."

There was panic around him and panic within him. He had trouble breathing. The sprinklers next door started with a hiss. He was coughing red. He vaguely remembers the noise and the scattering of bodies. He remembers the sprinklers, the feel of the cool mist on a hot day. He thought about football ("My God, I may never play again") and about his friends and his parents and Darren.

Everyone scattered, leaving Eric on the lawn with the stillness and the blood and the shrieks from the house. An instantaneous and complete calm fell over him. The chaos around him receded, like a pullaway shot at the end of an old Western. He was relaxed and still. The labored breathing stopped. The pain washed away. Eric thought, "I could stay like this; this is cool right here."

This is death, he thought. I'm dying.

"I started thinking, Damn, there's gonna be a funeral and you're not even gonna get to be there. I was just trippin'. There was gonna be all these people there, and you're not even gonna get to say hi or nothing. Then I opened my eyes and I was right back. I was having trouble breathing, I was coughing up blood, I could feel burning sensations in my face, my fingers and my shoulder."

The paramedics were hovering over him, telling him that it would be all right. They began cutting away at his shorts, and he tried to stop them. They were sixty-dollar shorts, and he wasn't even shot down there. He tried to tell them that, but it was like a bad dream; they didn't seem to hear.

A helicopter from the East Bay Regional Parks Police hovered overhead—the rapid *thut-thut-thut* of its blades bringing some sounds of home to the city kids from Oakland. The copter chased Bell as he ran down the side of San Ramon Creek. The police caught him less than a mile from the scene and found the gun in the backyard of a nearby house, 10110 Foxboro. After Bell was arrested, and after Eric was taken away, a blood-stained Nike Air Jordan T-shirt remained on the lawn.

A responding officer heard the call ("Shots fired, people down") but didn't believe it. He thought he had taken a wrong turn and left San Ramon.

Nothing like this ever happens in San Ramon. The police response was immediate and forceful. Before Eric was airlifted to John Muir Medical Center in Walnut Creek, sixteen officers responded to the scene. They weren't used to shootouts here; this was where people moved to insulate themselves from the Jason Bells.

Darren was ready to hit a party that night, too. He was the only one home, and the music was pounding through the house. He heard the phone as he headed for the shower, but it was his parents' phone and not the one he shared with Eric. He ignored it and continued toward the shower. He and Eric operated under a simple system: Anybody who wanted to talk to them knew their number. They used to tell each other that the worst thing that could happen is for a call to their parents' phone to be followed by a call to their phone. That meant somebody *had* to reach them, and that's why the second ring on the night of May 9 pierced the room like a siren call.

An unfamiliar voice asked Darren if he was Eric's brother, and he knew right away that something had gone wrong, horribly wrong. The caller was from a hospital, and she said Eric had been shot.

That's all Darren heard before he felt as if his knees would give out. He explained that his mother was out of town and his father was gone for the evening, and Darren wasn't sure when he would return.

"I'll never forget that night," Darren said. "I was just panickin'. It was like, What do I do now?"

He had to get over there, but how? He didn't have a car, or even a driver's license. He turned the music off and tried to collect himself. He was seventeen years old.

Darren called a friend, his closest friend who owned a car.

When Darren arrived at the hospital, he was told that his brother was paralyzed after being shot numerous times. He thought, "He'll never play football again." That was his first thought.

"I can remember sitting there waiting for the doctor to tell me something, because I was the only one there. They kept saying, 'Are you his brother? Are you his brother?' And I was like, 'Yeah, what's going on?' Then they said, 'He got shot in the spine,' and they used some other word for 'paralyzed.' Everybody looked at him more for his athletic ability than anything else. They were all, 'Dang, he can't play football.' I just remember panickin' so much that I'll never forget that day.

"They wouldn't let me in there for a while, and when they did, they said, 'When you go in there, please don't say anything about it yet, because we want his parents to be here when he finds out.' That was the hardest part."

Their father, Eugene Albert, arrived in the intensive-care ward shortly after Darren. Before he saw Eric, who remained conscious, he was told by a nurse that the shooting occurred after a drug deal went sour.

When he entered the room, Eugene Albert asked his son, "What are you doing dealing drugs?"

"What are you talking about?" Eric replied. "I wasn't dealing drugs. This guy started trippin' and wanted to fight. Then he got a gun."

When Eugene Albert learned the sequence of events, his emotions turned to rage. During Eric's two-month stay in the hospital, Eugene learned all he could about Jason Bell and what happened on the evening of May 9. He was intent upon making Bell pay for his crime.

• • •

The shooting of Eric Albert doesn't fit into a tidy, easily dismissed package. Eric still has a difficult time convincing people that it wasn't gang-related or drug-related. He attended a therapy session in the Bay Area city of Vallejo shortly after he returned home. He wheeled into the room in his electric wheelchair wearing a blue jogging suit. He described the circumstances and mentioned that he was from Oakland. He said everyone had an immediate reaction, a reaction based on commonly held perceptions about young black men and Oakland: gangs and drugs.

"People don't want to believe I'm not a bad person, that I wasn't in a gang, that this wasn't a drug deal or something," Eric said. "They hear about it, and they hear I'm from Oakland, and they automatically think that. I tell them, 'I wasn't even in Oakland, I was in San Ramon.' And on top of that, I lived in Oakland for all my life and nothin' ever happened to me there. I had a choice to go to a party in Oakland or San Ramon. Which one would you choose?"

Eric is sitting in a wheelchair in the living room, talking about football and pain and dreams lost. The Alberts live in a large house on a winding, steep street in a quiet, upper-middle class Oakland neighborhood. Both parents are home and both parents work. They staggered their work schedules to limit the hours Eric would be home by himself.

Although he quit the team during his junior year, Darren would have played football during his senior year. He couldn't because the summer was too hectic and the fall only slightly less so. As the family altered its schedule, Darren had to be free to help out. He was the one constant. He would come home from school in the afternoons and change Eric or help him eat or just sit with him and watch television.

"I wanted to play football, but I saw what my parents had to do," Darren said. "I had to help out, but that was all right. I don't think I'll ever go through as much in my whole life as I did this summer. I always liked basketball better, anyway. As long as I got to play basketball."

After the football season ended, Coach Beam told Darren that Skyline might have gone undefeated with a good strong safety. He told Darren that it would have been him.

"That made me feel good that he said that," Darren said.

Darren wanted to go to the University of Oregon after graduation, but his plans were altered by Eric's needs. Now he was leaning toward a junior college, probably Chabot.

"I would never tell Eric that was the reason I was staying
home," Darren said. "I know how hard my parents work with him,
and I know it would be real hard if I wasn't around. I'll go away
eventually, but now it's probably best if I stay home."

Eric laughs his easy laugh and says, "Yeah, Darren and me are
closer. I'm home all the time now. I didn't ever used to be home."

Eric was close to 190 pounds at the time of the shooting, his
body bulked up through intensive weight training. The muscles
covered his upper body like an exoskeleton. He took great pride in
his appearance and his ability to win over the girls. Now, he says,
he doesn't like to look in the mirror.

"I look at myself and I think, 'Is that really me?'" he said. "Man,
there's no chest there anymore."

Eric can move his arms up and down, but his fingers are stiff
from lack of use. His voice is soft and kind, his eyes clear, his smile
wide. Mostly, he talks about Jason Bell. His arms move as he
speaks, serving to italicize his words.

"If I get better, I might even forgive him," he says. "It was his
fault that he shot, but it was like, I can imagine the peer pressure
he had on him. He's got the dude in his ear yelling, 'Shoot that
motherfucker. Shoot him. Shoot him.' And he's the only one who's
going to jail. I know he's feeling like an ass right now."

On the Monday following the shooting, The Contra Costa Times
published a story that began: "It had the ingredients of the typical
suburban rumble . . . "

"It was so weird how that week went," Eric said. "It was a good
week and a bad week."

The day before the shooting, Eric had a gun pulled on him while
he was walking through a parking lot at Chabot. Two young men
approached Eric with a message for one of Eric's friends; Eric told
them to take it to the source and leave him out of it. They kept
muggin' him and talkin' shit and Eric talked it back. One of them
pointed a gun at Eric. Somehow, Eric talked him into putting the
gun away and settling it with their hands. On those terms, Eric
never lost.

"I whupped him pretty good," he said.

Eric sees now that he didn't always act in his own best interests. He was invincible and untouchable, just like on the football field. He didn't back down. That was for everybody else.

"It would have took a whole lot to slow me down," he says. "My dad, he was always telling me to take it easy, but you know how it goes—nothing could ever happen to me."

Jason Bell was convicted of aggravated mayhem, attempted murder and assault with a deadly weapon. The jury deadlocked 11–1 on the issue of premeditation. In California, aggravated mayhem carries with it a possible life sentence. The prosecution pushed for life. The Alberts pushed for life.

On January 4, the day he was to be sentenced, Jason Bell sat in Walnut Creek/Danville District Court. Eugene Albert was there, too.

Before sending Bell for psychiatric testing, the presiding judge addressed the courtroom: "Well, this is a very difficult case for everybody here. You have two good families here, both suffering terribly as a result of this occurrence here. And both will suffer continuously, I assume, for an indeterminate time in the future."

Jason Bell's attorney asked that his client be allowed to address the court.

THE COURT: Mr. Bell, happy to hear from you.

THE DEFENDANT: I just basically want to let you know that I do feel remorse for the whole situation. And I'm sorry that anybody got hurt on that day. Eric, and even his family. Even though they wish that I would be locked up for a lifetime, I understand, I guess, why. I guess they feel it will make it even. I spend a lifetime.

But, um, I know what with the mayhem charge, very possible that I can spend my lifetime. I just want to let you know that I understand I did wrong. But I want you to understand that's not what I'm all about, you know. I'm definitely not proud of what I did.

That's it.

SPECTATOR: I just want to say—

THE COURT: Come a little closer so we can hear you better.

And just for the record, state your name, please.

SPECTATOR: I'm Nedra Bell, Jason Bell's mother.

THE COURT: Okay.

SPECTATOR: And I want to say on behalf of my son that he's not about violence and, ah, doing bodily harm to other people. We're hardworking people that have raised him, hopefully, to respect others. And we just wanted to say that we're sorry to the Albert family for this.

But I'm also upset that, um, the full blame of this situation has been placed upon my son's shoulders when there were so many other people actively involved in this. And that, um, I know he has to pay, but I hope that you have mercy and that you, um, at least give him a chance to have some life after this.

THE COURT: Thank you very much.

Any other family members on either side want to say anything?

SPECTATOR: I would like to say something.

THE COURT: Go ahead, sir. Come forward.

First of all tell me who you are.

SPECTATOR: Eugene Albert. Eric Albert's father.

THE COURT: You talked to me before.

SPECTATOR: Right.

I would like to repeat the same thing I said so they can understand it, too.

Like I told the Judge before, I never heard of the Bells before. Come to find out that the father works with my wife. And that, ah, I heard all along they were good, hardworking people. But I also heard that Jason had always been an asshole. In high school he didn't get a diploma. They worked out a deal to give it to him.

He had some previous problems. That they used their—this is what I got. That he always been a troublemaker, ever since high school. And I find that, you know, I've grown up in a violent area. I grew up in the ghetto. Seen people like this who have come up from good families who don't act right.

What Jason has done is like walking in to our family and dropping a hand grenade. My son is paralyzed. He will not walk again. The possibility of him living ten years is remote. I think for him to get a life sentence is more than fair.

That's all I have. Thank you.

THE COURT: Could you just tell me—I remember you told me something about this, but just update me a little bit. How does your son get along now? What activities, and how do you take care of him? What has to be done by the family.

SPECTATOR: Okay.

THE COURT: If that's not too traumatic for you.

SPECTATOR: I work for United Airlines. I've been with them for twenty-five years. Now I have to go to swing shift so that I can be with my son in the morning. I change his urine bag. I help get him dressed. I sit him in front of the T.V.

The doctors have told us that he will not walk again. The doctors at Kaiser said that in his condition he can get the flu and die just like that, because with the injury, he does not breathe with his lungs. He breathes with his stomach muscles. Every day is a touch and go situation.

We have a monitor where if I'm in whatever room, I can come in and check on him.

On numerous occasions, I've had to quad-cough him and get his breathing going. And my son, everybody in my family has been affected by this. We are all like paralyzed victims.

So like for me, I can see no problem with him spending the rest of his life in jail, because he did not shoot the person once, but several times. And my son did not touch him. My son did not touch Jason Bell. He—they came to an area where my son was and attacked him, you know. I think that's barbaric. And he should pay, serve time for it.

And to the family, I have no—I feel sorry for ya, I really do, because I know you probably don't want this for your son. You didn't raise him up to be in this position, but there he is.

Thank you.

THE COURT: Thank you Mr. Albert.

On March 3, 1993, Jason Bell was sentenced to seventeen years in California state prison.

CHAPTER SIXTEEN

IT DIDN'T TAKE AS MUCH CONSTERNATION ANYMORE FOR THE VEINS IN
Donlea's forehead to work their way to the surface. They were protruding with more regularity, and with far less provocation, as the
OAL season progressed. By the first week in February, the veins
seemed perpetually present, a bas-relief forehead. He was strug-
gling with his expectations and his desire to turn Skyline into a disciplined, cohesive team. He needed the control he didn't have, and
the battle to acquire it was starting to wear on him.

He knew it was against everything in his constitution, but as the
second game with Fremont approached, he had begun to look forward to the end of the season.

It wasn't just basketball. His financial concerns were becoming
more prominent. The substitute teaching assignments weren't coming with any regularity, and the cost of simply keeping his car running well enough to make the 100-mile round trip every day was
becoming troublesome. He laughed when he received his W-2 earn-
ings statements. After six years of school and an advanced degree,
he made less than $9,000 in 1992.

"That's a guy with a master's degree," he said, laughing. "Boy,
I've really made it big. Of course, my social life sure makes up for it."

Donlea did what came naturally to him: he immersed himself in
basketball. Fremont was ranked third in the greater Bay Area
(Skyline remained unranked), and Donlea thought his team was getting close to a breakthrough game. He knew as well as his players
that they wouldn't be taken seriously until they defeated a team
with a reputation.

He set out to discover a way to make that happen. He looked at
the tape of the first game and saw Fremont make follow shot after

follow shot. Skyline needed to do a better job of blocking out on the defensive boards. Skyline also needed to do a better job of taking care of the basketball. Everything came back to the same philosophy, the one he had been preaching since October, the one he didn't truly believe would ever sink in.

"If we're patient, if we work for good shots and play tough defense, we'll beat them," he said. "I wish these kids would see it the way I see it. We can't match them with athletes, but we can play smarter and better."

He gave that speech the day before the game, and it was met with indifference, just as it had been with every previous delivery. He was going to stick with it, though, because he believed in it with every pore and fiber of his being. He had seen flashes of it against Castlemont, with his father in the stands, and he knew the players had it inside them. He would keep pounding them with it, because Shawn Donlea believed in fundamental basketball just as much as his father did. They believed in it like fundamentalist Christians believe in the Bible.

The Fremont High gymnasium is a monument to funky educational architecture. The basketball floor is on the second floor of the old building, at the end of several wide hallways and a staircase. Inside, it was clean and well-lit, with a smooth and shadowless floor.

An armed security guard ushered the Skyline team into a room off to the side of the gym. Donlea, clearly anxious, started talking as soon as his players had settled in.

"They took the ball away from us inside last time," he said. "They slapped it out of our hands after I don't know how many rebounds. Part of that was lack of strength. You've got to be strong on the boards. Rip the ball down. If they reach in, rip their fuckin' hand off. You got to be a little bit nasty to rebound, and tonight's a good night to be nasty. It's not talking nasty, it's aggressive, strong, rip it down. Rip it down and get it out.

"Don't let your emotions run your game. Above all, stay together. It's going to take all of us to win this game. All of us. Go with your strengths tonight. Do what you do best. Play the whole game with intensity."

Game time was ten minutes away. As the players stood near the door, Donlea walked to the front of the line and said, "You're a good basketball team."

As his team went through its pregame warmup, Donlea cornered the officials and told them to call rebounding fouls on Fremont's inside players. He wanted to see them whistled for climbing on his players' backs and hacking at their arms when they brought down a rebound. The last time the teams played, Donlea felt Fremont got away with numerous fouls inside, and he didn't want to see it happen again.

When Donlea finished his spiel to the officials, one of them looked at him square in the eye and said, "You do your job." They both walked away.

Donlea grimaced, tilted his head and stared up at the rafters. A uniform (number 35) hung unevenly above the center of the court. The inscription read: WESTON HATCH, JR. 1972–1990.

Donlea looked down at his feet. "Great," he said. "I've already pissed the refs off. That was a stupid move on my part. They won't call a thing now."

Of Fremont's first eight baskets, four came on offensive rebounds. Donlea was on his feet constantly, berating the officials and begging for an over-the-back call. Donlea's antics elevated the tension in the game; Govan and Blackwell jawed with several of the Fremont players, and Donlea was too immersed in his own problems to respond. Fremont led by seven at 22–15 when the officials called a timeout and brought the two coaches together near the scorer's table.

"Guess I better calm down," Donlea said sheepishly when he came back to the bench.

Donlea jumped into Jason Wright's face at the end of the first quarter, with Fremont leading, 24–18. Donlea told Wright that he wasn't playing hard, that he was thinking more about the reaction from the stands than the game plan.

"You're better than that, J," Donlea said. "Play the game. Play it right."

Wright clenched his jaw and stayed quiet. He shook his head and adjusted his shorts—downward, of course—as he took the floor. Skyline inbounded the ball and Wright took an entry pass on the right wing. He faked toward the baseline and dribbled toward the free throw line. He avoided Kareem Davis and went straight to the basket. He rose from the floor with the ball curled behind him in his left hand, like a catapult. He propelled the ball through the air and fired it through the basket with force and velocity.

"Takin' it to the cup, J," Darren Albert said on the bench.

Donlea turned away from the game.

"It happens every time," he said. "Every time I try to light him up, he gets pissed and goes off. It's uncanny."

Wright's dunk sent Skyline off, too. Bryant Johnson hit two outside jumpers and sophomore Rod Ponder sliced through the Fremont defense and spun an underhanded flip off the board. Skyline outscored Fremont 22–8 in the second quarter and led by eight at halftime. It was by far the most definitive statement Skyline had made all season.

The makeshift locker room was filled with the pungent smell of sweat, and the air had acquired a thickness that wasn't present before the game. Nobody seemed to notice.

"You see in that first half what it takes," Donlea said at halftime, a newfound confidence in his voice. "It takes this—" Donlea pointed to his head "—and it takes this, too—" he pointed to his feet.

"Hey, we weathered the storm. They came at us and we gave it back. We weathered it. Great job changing defenses. Great job reacting. And we'll do it again this half. They'll try to get easy baskets off the cherry pick, try to make the game easy. You know that. But I'll tell you: You've put in the time, you've put in the work. You're more prepared, you're a better basketball team. You've got 16 minutes to do it. That's only a half, but a damned good one."

"Zero-zero, fellas," Blackwell said.

"That's right," Donlea said. "Let's finish the job off."

Skyline took the eight-point lead and made it 19 within four minutes. Jason Wright scored nine points in those four minutes, and his three-point bomb from the right side made it 55–36. The Fremont players appeared to have lost interest, and coach Clint Williams stood in the coaching box and stared off into nowhere.

Just as Donlea predicted, Fremont's speed and athleticism was lost amid the unexpected precision that his team was showing. They were running the offense and running the fast break; they were making short, crisp passes at exactly the right time.

"They're dying out there," Donlea said of Fremont. "They don't look like they have the heart to make a run."

With four minutes remaining in the third quarter and Skyline leading by 18, Donlea decided to give his starters a break. He took Blackwell and Wright and Strom out, with the intention of putting them back in at the first touch of trouble.

Blackwell was back on the floor within a minute, and Strom followed. Wright sat, seething, fighting with all his might to keep from telling Donlea to get him the hell back in the game. As Wright sat, Fremont awakened. Lamont Brown went to the hoop, was fouled and completed a three-point play. Kareem Davis scored on a break, Frank Knight converted a three-point play and Keith Livers hit two free throws. Skyline's precision was gone, replaced by a harried and frightened style that played directly into Fremont's plans.

The crowd at Fremont was frantic. Skyline ended the third quarter leading by just six at 58–52. Still, Wright sat to start the fourth quarter. Fremont scored the first six points of the fourth quarter to tie the game. Donlea called timeout. Strom walked to the bench and told his teammates, "We're not losing this shit."

With twenty-seven seconds remaining and the score tied at 71, Blackwell committed a reaching foul on Lamont Brown. It was Blackwell's fifth foul. As Blackwell walked toward the bench, Brown got in his face and started talking trash. Blackwell laughed—it took more than words to anger him—and one of the officials whistled Brown for a technical foul for taunting.

Jason Wright had hit six straight free throws, but Donlea pointed at Govan to shoot the two free throws. Wright had been standing near midcourt, pointing at his own chest and pleading with Donlea to let him shoot. When Donlea chose Govan, the team's best free-throw shooter at nearly 75 percent, Wright put his hands on his hips and shook his head.

Govan missed the first shot, causing Wright to walk away and throw his hands to the air. Govan missed the second shot, causing Wright to stand and stare at Donlea.

Skyline got the ball with seven seconds remaining, the game still tied at 71. Donlea called timeout and diagrammed an inbounds play they had run most of the season. It was a simple, screen-and-move play, but—like all Donlea's plays—it depended on total participation. When the players took the court, Donlea tossed his clipboard under the bench and rolled his eyes.

"It comes down to an out-of-bounds play—one of the things I spent the least amount of time on all year," he said.

The play was designed to get Govan open inside or Wright free for an alley-oop dunk. To Wright, this was one big playground, with everybody in the stands waiting for winners. The best way he knew to make sure he kept playing was to do it himself. So, while the other four Skyline players ran the out-of-bounds play, Jason drifted off to the side and tried to get Strom to throw him the ball. Strom looked inside to Govan, who was surrounded. Nobody else was open. Wright had thrown the whole play off, and Strom was unable to get the ball inbounds in five seconds. With seven seconds remaining in a tie game, Skyline had turned it over.

Fremont couldn't score. Overtime. The energy in the building had been rising and falling like the tide throughout the game, and now it was low. Both teams were dragging.

Donlea's voice was hoarse, and it cracked and sputtered like a bad engine when he tried to raise the volume above the crowd noise.

"It's a ball-check right now," he said. "Right now, baby. All balls."

Wright scored four points in the overtime, and Skyline held a two-point lead with twelve seconds left. Fremont's Alvarice Bostick was at the foul line, shooting two shots. The first shot, a hard line drive, fell through cleanly. The second was just as flat, just as hard, but it slammed against the back rim and bounded crazily over Wright's head. Fremont's Lamont Brown grabbed it out of the air and shot it from about fifteen feet away, on the right side. It fell through cleanly. The place erupted in a mad, ferocious cheer. Fremont led, 78–77.

Skyline, with no timeouts remaining, got the ball inbounds while Fremont celebrated. Wright caught a pass near halfcourt. He had a clear path to the basket, but not enough time to get there. He pulled up at the three-point line, straightaway, and let it fly. Wright's shot bounced off the back rim, off the front rim and onto the floor. Wright went down in a crumpled, fetal mass at the free-throw line. The Fremont players and fans jumped and waved their arms and hugged each other reflexively. Donlea sat on the bench, his head down, the coach in still-life. Fremont had won, 78–77, and Skyline would have to wait a while longer to get Oakland's respect.

By the time he reached the dressing room, Jason Wright was furious. He couldn't believe that Donlea left him on the bench during Fremont's comeback. He couldn't believe he wasn't told to shoot the free throws after the technical; he had just made six straight free throws. He scored 21 points in the game, and he felt like he could have had 40. Skyline was now 5–3 in the OAL and 13–8 overall. That might as well have been a losing record.

Jason Wright couldn't understand any of it.

He walked in alone with a trudging, slow gait. He held his warmup jersey loosely in his right hand and trailed it on the floor behind him. He was unable to sit or stand still. He walked around talking under his breath, his head moving from side to side. He didn't make eye contact with anybody in the room.

Donlea stood in front of them, cupping his chin with his right hand, attempting to piece things together in his mind. He knew he had to say something, anything. He pawed at the smooth floor with his right shoe. "Listen now," he said, calmly. He looked down at the floor. "Listen now," he repeated.

"First of all, we will see them again, in ten days. In ten days we will see them again, in a neutral floor, where the referees are more objective, and we will take that game from them. Next game.

"It's not the end of the world. There's nothing to be ashamed of, nothing to be down about. We will see them again, and it will be a different story."

Donlea continued to look down, carefully formulating his words as the thoughts spun through his head. He appeared to be trying to convince himself as well as his players. This was tough, brutally tough, but he couldn't let them know it.

"What cost us the game tonight?" he asked.

Wright, pacing through the room, said under his breath, "You."

"What cost us the game tonight?" Donlea asked again.

"You," Wright said, a little louder.

Donlea didn't hear, or didn't respond if he did. He went on: "We did not execute in the critical times. We did not execute our offensive plan at the critical times. We didn't—"

Wright shook his head and walked to an open window. With his back to Donlea, he watched as the people below filed out of the gym and walked to their cars.

Donlea stopped in midsentence. "Jason Wright, I could rip your ass inside out right now!"

Wright spun around.

"I could rip your ass, too! We lost because of you."

Donlea and Wright stood, about fifteen feet apart, staring into each other's eyes. Nobody moved. Somebody said, "Come on, J. Chill." The air in the room was thick and charged. Neither backed down.

"Jason Wright, you've got to hear me for another year," Donlea said, his voice quivering with emotion. "You know I'm on your side, goddamit! And when I'm talking, I expect to see your eyes and not see you looking out the goddamn window."

"That why we lost? 'Cause I'm lookin' out the window?"

"No, because you didn't execute, OK?"

"Don't worry about it, J," Bryant Johnson said. "Don't worry about it."

"Be cool, bro," Blackwell said.

"You've got to be a member of the team," Donlea said.

"He just mad, coach," Johnson said.

"I know he's mad. Goddamit, you've got to stay within our effort here. One guy or two guys getting out of it, and we're not the team we are—"

He stopped and breathed deeply. The players returned to what they were doing—changing shoes, putting their earrings back in their ears, pulling sweatshirts over their uniforms.

"But you stayed into it most of the game," Donlea went on. "You almost took it away on their floor. You almost took it away. On their floor. And we will see them again. Nothing to be ashamed of. Nothing to be ashamed of, guys."

They couldn't leave individually; they had to leave as a group, with an armed escort. An officer stood inside the room, occasionally sticking his head out the door to see if the whole sequence of events—escorts ready, bus running—was ready to unfold.

Blackwell stood beside him, looking at the gun on the officer's right hip. When the officer had finished another check of the hallway, Blackwell pointed to the gun and asked him, "Hey, is that a nine?"

"No," the officer answered. "It kind of looks like one, but it's not."

"Can I hold it?" Blackwell asked.

The officer laughed. "I don't think so," he said.

"Just thought I'd ask," Blackwell said, laughing. "You know I wouldn't do nothing with it."

Later, Donlea sat in the emptiness of the coaching office at Skyline and made a few notations on a legal pad. His tie was loosened and his face was drained of color. His hair was matted to his forehead by the dried sweat.

"I can't blame myself," he said. "Nothing I can do to change. There's not one thing I would have done right now to change this team, change this program. Maybe if I knew more, there would be more I could have done. If I was older. If I was an older, more experienced coach. I won't sleep tonight. I might as well go down to the ROTC room and watch the film. I won't sleep. It'll bother me all night because we had the game won a couple times. But you know? They started off and almost took the game in their hands. Punch for punch. It's a slugfest, every game in this league. We took every punch; we just didn't get off the mat last. It was close, close . . .

"I knew that was going to happen. I'll think about that all night.

They were just taller. They'll always be taller. There's nothing as a coach you can do to change that."

Darren Albert went home and started his homework. About 10 P.M., there was a knock at the door. It was Lamont Brown, his friend. Brown was still in his yellow and green uniform, still amped from his game-winning shot. He came over to rub it in.

Two days later, Skyline played Oakland High without Govan and Nick Wimberly, both out with ankle injuries. Oakland High had picked up a player in the second half of the OAL season, a 6-foot-5 leaper who was academically ineligible in the first half. In his first game, he had eight dunks and scored 32 points. Along with 6-foot-4 Robert Sasser, the new kid gave Oakland High the second-best frontcourt in the OAL.

"Look at these two teams," Donlea said as they warmed up. "Which team looks like the playoff team? We're a bunch of over-matched kids; they look like men. It's amazing we've come this far."

Donlea feared a major letdown after the Fremont game, and he got it. Oakland High manhandled Skyline inside and led by eight at halftime. Skyline's game plan degenerated into a one-on-one contest.

"The only way they have a chance to beat us is if they play street ball," Donlea said. "We can't go down with them. They've got nothing to lose. I'm sure we'll see some messing around, a little bit of showboat bullshit, some one-on-one crap. But we've got a lot to play for. This game means a lot to us. This means the difference between a .500 season in league and a winning season. We clinch a winning record tonight if we win.

"I've helped you get this far, I've helped you get to the playoffs. Help me a little bit. Be patient. Don't think you can take it to the basket every time."

Oakland's lead reached 13 points in the third quarter. Skyline fought back, calmly and evenly, with Jason Wright and Will Blackwell doing the heavy lifting. With thirty-one seconds remaining in the game and Oakland High leading by four, Wright fought for a rebound underneath his own basket, twisted his angular body through three taller defenders and made a follow shot. Five seconds later, he was fouled underneath and made both free throws to tie the game at 65.

The crowd, which had been quiet and disinterested, got louder and more involved. Members of the Skyline football team jawed with members of the Oakland High football team, and some of them made their way onto the court in the last twenty seconds. What had been a dreary, bored crowd suddenly livened up. Oakland High scored again, to lead by two, setting off a fit of hip-hop dancing on the Oakland High side. By the time Bryant Johnson sank two free throws with no time remaining to send the game to overtime, three police officers were standing in front of the Skyline rooting section, trying to keep a measure of sanity.

Oakland's Robert Sasser scored the first 6 points of the overtime. Skyline appeared to have expended all its energy on the comeback, and now the game was slipping away. But Jason Wright hit two free throws, Blackwell scored inside and Wright hit another tough rebound follow shot and was fouled. With nineteen seconds remaining in the overtime, he stood at the foul line and tied the game.

Oakland High called timeout to set up a play, but Donlea knew it would be no play at all. They would simply give the ball to Sasser and let him try to win the game.

Sasser stood above the free-throw line, dribbling the time away. His teammates posted up or ran the baseline, but it was obvious they would have no part in this. It was Sasser and Jason Wright, two of the best players in town, going at it one-on-one. They had brought the game to this point—Wright with his 29 points, Sasser with his 27—and it seemed perfectly appropriate that they should finish it.

Wright shadowed Sasser as he dribbled to his left, then to his right. With five seconds left, Sasser let fly with a 22-footer from beyond the top of the key. Wright lunged at the ball but couldn't reach high enough. The shot was perfect. Oakland High won, 77–74. Skyline had lost two straight games, and McClymonds was next.

"The knife slices back in a hurry, doesn't it?" Donlea said.

As Donlea spoke to the team after the game, there was a loud and persistent commotion going on outside the gym, on the football field.

Oakland High's football team had upset Skyline in the OAL championship game earlier in the school year, avenging an earlier loss, and most of the football players from both teams attended the basketball game. When the game ended, they got together and challenged each other to a match that presumably would settle the score. There were about thirty of them, and they walked out into the rainy gloom and opened a gate to Jackie Jensen Field, Oakland High's football stadium.

They took off their shirts and stood in the ankle-deep mud, which had been created by a week of solid rain. Their bodies were mere shadows as the rain pelted the ground and dusk brought an enveloping grayness to the city. They squared off one by one—one Skyline athlete against one Oakland High athlete—and wrestled in the mud. It got loud, fiercely loud, with cars passing by on the street above slowing to search for the commotion's source.

Two police officers who had worked the basketball game walked out to check the situation. The rain fell, the football players wrestled and the officers watched. They were tense, no doubt thinking they were watching a situation that could escalate into something dangerous, something they couldn't handle alone.

The crowd grew around the fence, students and teachers and people who happened to pass by. The officers grew edgier, but the sounds of laughter—sheer, unabashed happiness—soon forced them to drop their facade of authority.

"Did you see that?" one of them asked.

"Man, that has to hurt."

They stood and watched through a chain-link fence, along with a sizable crowd, as the shirtless bodies flopped through the air and into the mud. Two would square off, and they would slap their bodies together and wrestle for leverage. One would lose his footing and get slammed to the muddy turf, and the winner would stand over the vanquished with his arms held over his head. The winning side would howl and jump and laugh at the loser, who would get up with a smile that cut through the darkness like the beam of a flashlight.

After about ten minutes, one of the officers turned to the other.

"Let's go, man. Nothing going on here."

They walked away, slowly, occasionally turning back to look and laugh when a loud reaction caught their attention.

•••

School kept bearing down on Calvin Wilson with the force of a wall of water. He had to pull an A in English over the final marking period in order to get a passing grade for the year. If he didn't, he could add summer school into the equation, along with the semester of junior-college work he needed to qualify for his scholarship. He didn't need another obstacle on the road to this new life.

And the scholarship papers remained unsigned, sitting there in his bedroom. He was thinking more and more about forgetting about the University of the Pacific, of moving on and pretending it didn't happen.

"I keep thinking I could go to a junior college and go through the whole recruiting process again," he said. "It might be better that way. Might get me something better, a better ride."

Coach Beam had worked to get Calvin the scholarship. It was as much Beam's word as Calvin's ability that convinced the University of the Pacific to take the chance. Beam wouldn't tell Calvin what to do; he said that wasn't his job. But he fiercely hoped that Calvin would take it and be thankful, that he would see how fortunate he was and use this as the chance to get out of the deep rut that was his life. Beam put his name out there right alongside Calvin's. Whatever Calvin did would reflect on Beam.

"That's the territory," Beam said. "That's how it works. If I go to bat for a kid, he's a good kid. I don't go to bat for a kid if I don't think he's going to make it, or if it's a bad kid. Calvin's a good kid, and he could succeed. It's just so hard for some of these kids to see the things that we might see right away. It's just a different world."

Calvin's English grade—and his immediate future, for that matter—hinged on one project, a ten-minute oral presentation on some aspect of the Renaissance—poetry, art, Shakespeare, something. He liked that period in history, found it interesting how everyone in Europe kind of woke up at the same time. Somewhere deep inside, he felt he could relate. But he had trouble picking a topic. He wanted to focus on the paintings of the period, but he couldn't find a book that would allow him to show the class the paintings while providing a brief synopsis of the work. He decided to do something on the painters themselves, since that seemed to be the focus of the books, but he had problems there, too. He didn't want to do just one painter, and he couldn't locate a book that was general enough to comprehend.

Finally, after he was given a lengthy extension, his teacher explained that it was up to Calvin to interpret the paintings. All along, he had been searching for a book that would do that for him. He had been looking for a way to relay the information to the class. Now he was presented with a more daunting task: he was the one responsible for interpreting the information.

"I didn't know it worked that way," he said. "I was just going to bring in some stuff and talk about it. Now I've got to figure it out on my own."

Donlea spoke to the team before the next practice, a day after the Oakland High game. The players were scattered around one half of the floor, some standing, some sitting, some lying down. Donlea's voice was heartfelt and emotional.

"Sometimes I wonder why I got into this business," he said. "After last week, I really wondered: Why do I put myself through this?"

Jason Wright, lying on his back near the free throw line, looked up and said, "I know why, coach. It's so you can be around the J Wrights of this world."

CHAPTER SEVENTEEN

As the OAL season neared its end, Jason Wright tried to change his ways. He wasn't proud of his actions against Castlemont, and he wanted to pull back from the showboating and outward cockiness. Donlea told him college scouts wouldn't go for that, regardless of the reason. They wouldn't take into account social pressures or the unique circumstances of the Oakland Athletic League. They wanted players, Donlea said, not problems.

"You do some of that stuff," Donlea told him, "and some scouts are going to walk right out of the gym. They're gonna say, 'Questionable character,' and leave."

Donlea didn't expect Wright to listen. He expected to spend the offseason barking in Wright's face, letting him know how good he could be if he listened and learned. Donlea was willing to do this—in fact, he was looking forward to it—because he thought Jason Wright was definitely worth the effort. He also knew that Wright had been caught up in the social pressure to perform as a basketball player and as a *performer*. Wright had tasted crowd adulation, and it would take some work to pull his focus back to the game. The star's chore, after all, is to be as sensational as possible.

Wright got his hair cut after the Castlemont game, got it shaved nearly to the bone. The new cut accentuated the smallness of his ears and gave him an even more streamlined look. He said it was an outward sign of his inner transformation.

"No more foolin' around," he said. "I got to get serious. That's what this means. I want to try to have all perfect games. Like don't fool around and yell and do all of that. Like play good defense and box out and get rebounds with two hands. Maybe somebody will look at me and send me to a camp this summer."

The next game provided perhaps the ultimate test of Jason Wright's commitment. McClymonds was coming to Skyline, which meant many things, among them: A huge crowd, a tense atmosphere, and a chance—once again—to knock off the third-ranked team in the state.

It would be difficult for Jason to keep his emotions hidden in a game like this, but he had been given a good scare after the Castlemont game. He wasn't easily scared; he considered it a sign of respect when he was threatened with bodily harm from the stands. This source was more imposing, however: the dean of students told Jason that he came perilously close to yanking him off the floor against Castlemont and suspending him for the next game. The scare prompted the haircut and the new attitude. Donlea watched this from a cynical distance; he liked to see Jason making the effort, but he also knew Jason didn't leave his unbridled enthusiasm on the barber-shop floor.

Center Nick Wimberly, whose season was rapidly becoming one pain after another, would have to watch from the bench for the second time as his team played McClymonds. This time he was out with a badly sprained ankle, and he was quietly disgusted with the whole thing.

Wimberly was the only Skyline player to gain any preseason publicity. He was mentioned in a few magazines and he had received letters from several Division I colleges. He was invited to play on a California all-star team that would tour Australia in the offseason. He was a shy kid with a kind demeanor and a tattoo over his left nipple—"Nicmeister" it said. As a player, Wimberly was a strong rebounder who played in and out of emotional spurts. Wimberly was something of an enigma to Donlea.

Standing nearly 6-foot-5, Wimberly was Skyline's tallest player, and one of its best shooters. But Wimberly's senior season never lived up to its promise. Donlea's offense didn't feature post play, and Wimberly's teammates didn't go out of their way to get him the ball. But whatever happened, Wimberly never complained, even when he had a legitimate complaint.

Wimberly usually seemed to have something else on his mind.

Several of his teammates found it unbelievable that Wimberly never played on the playgrounds. He enjoyed basketball, but there were other things in life. He worked at a grocery store four nights a week. He worked to help out financially at home and to keep his Audi running.

Nick would sometimes miss practice, especially on Saturdays, because he had to work. Donlea thought he could adjust his work schedule for the greater good of the team, but it never happened. Maggie Wimberly, Nick's mother, explained the situation to Donlea: "I told the coach, 'Nicholas goes to Skyline, but we don't live in the Skyline neighborhood.' He has to work, and if that means he misses a few practices, he just can't help it."

Maggie was Skyline's most loyal fan. A toll-taker on the Golden Gate Bridge, she attended every Skyline game. A friendly, daintily pretty woman with high cheekbones, she took a great interest in her son's athletic achievements. She usually sat close behind the Skyline bench and let her opinion be known. She would plead with Nick to play harder, to rebound, to "go after the ball, Nicholas!" For his part, Nick seemed like he could take or leave basketball.

Before the McClymonds game, after it was clear that Nick's season wouldn't lead directly to a college scholarship, Maggie drew inspiration from an article in the *Tribune*. As part of a series on Black History Month, the story told of Bill Russell's twisting, fable-like ascension from a high school nobody to the greatest basketball player of his era.

Russell failed to make the McClymonds varsity as a junior, then tried out for the cheerleading squad and didn't make that, either. He made the team as a senior, but spent nearly the entire season on the bench. Following his senior year at McClymonds, Russell went on a barnstorming tour with a group of Northern California all-stars. He was invited to play on the tour because he was the only eligible senior on the McClymonds team, and each high school in Oakland had to be represented. It was on that tour that Russell emerged as a player, learning how to block shots and use his gangly body to terrify the opposition.

Accompanying the story was a picture of Russell wearing an Indian headdress in his tryout for the McClymonds cheerleading squad.

"I was reading that article about Bill Russell and I had a vision," Maggie said. "That could be Nicholas."

She said the story made her adamant about getting the money together to send Nick on the all-star tour of Australia.

Skyline had made the playoffs, so the game against McClymonds was essentially meaningless. It was the last game of the OAL season, the last game before the return to the Henry J. for a playoff game against Fremont. Wimberly was out, and so was Eric Govan, who also had a sprained ankle. Govan's rebounding and scoring had been the one constant for the team all season. Govan's efforts sometimes became like background noise amid the clamor of Wright's dunks and Blackwell's athleticism. Govan was as unnoticed as an electrical hum, missed only when it isn't there.

Donlea had reached the goal; he made the playoffs. He thought this game presented a good opportunity for his team to have some fun.

"Everybody's going to play, and it'll be a lot of fun," he told his team the day before. "It'll be a game you guys like: we're going to run, there'll be a lot of dunks. I just want you guys to have a good time."

This was a dramatic, almost unbelievable departure for Donlea, who didn't normally think basketball was a purely social exercise. He wanted to win. He wanted to show everybody that he could take an undertalented team and beat an overtalented team. He had said that McClymonds would beat his team ten out of ten times, but he didn't really believe it. He didn't believe that Willie Hearnton, the McClymonds coach, could beat *him* ten out of ten times. It was nothing personal; he expected Hearnton to think the same way about him.

Then there was the reality of the situation. Skyline couldn't rebound well against McClymonds with its best and biggest team on the floor. With this team, without Wimberly and Govan, Donlea would have to play junior Kenneth Forward, up from the junior varsity team, for some serious minutes. Donlea thought the game would turn into a 32-minute tip drill for McClymonds.

"We can't beat McClymonds with this team," he said. "I'm going to play everybody and let them have a good time. I hate to take that attitude, but we need to get healthy for the playoffs. This game doesn't really mean anything."

But once the game started, the game meant something. Donlea forgot all about his team having fun and enjoying life. The Skyline gym was jam-packed, and the feeling in the air was one of immediate importance. McClymonds had acquired a devoted following that traveled throughout Oakland to watch the Warriors lay waste to their OAL opponents. They walked in with an important swagger, their connection to their team bolstered by twenty-three straight wins. Many were men, either McClymonds graduates or people from the neighborhood. This was not like rooting for the Oakland Athletics or the Golden State Warriors; this was more personal, more gratifying. It gave them something they couldn't get anywhere else.

"See them guys from Mack?" one Skyline player asked. "Man, finger waves and jheri curls must be comin' back in West Oakland."

"That the only place," another player answered.

Nobody had beaten McClymonds, and there was a rumor swirling through the Skyline campus that Mack already had designed and ordered T-shirts proclaiming their OAL title and a 24–0 regular season. On the surface, this was an almost risk-free decision. But to the Skyline players and students, it was a highly presumptive move, a disrespecting of the highest order. True or not, there were neighborhood rules to be followed here.

Willie Hearnton admitted that his team was a little bored with the Oakland Athletic League. He meant no harm to anybody, he just told the truth. The talent on his team was so far superior to everybody else that his players sometimes lost interest. But Hearnton had developed a strong respect for Donlea, and Skyline was the one team in the league that scared him. He saw the way Donlea changed defenses and controlled the flow of the game, and he knew that's where his team was vulnerable.

Donlea didn't expect to slow down this game. He was more than willing to let Skyline push the ball and run the floor; if they slowed it down, they would have to make every shot to have a chance, because they certainly weren't going to get many—or any—offensive rebounds.

Skyline's lack of size was painfully obvious from the start. Darrnaryl Stamps grabbed a missed shot by teammate Anthony Byrd—the first shot of the game—and banged his follow shot too hard off the glass. Blackwell and Calvin Wilson were clawing up at Stamps's 6-foot-8 body as Stamps grabbed his own miss and missed again. On the second follow, Blackwell slapped Stamps's arm and was called for a foul. The game was nine seconds old.

"Is that what we're going to have to look at all game?" Donlea stood up and asked nobody in particular.

McClymonds scored eight straight points to take a 15–7 lead, and Donlea sat back and watched. When they played well, as they were now, the McClymonds Warriors were a lot of fun to watch.

At the end of the first quarter, with the game caught in a seemingly inexorable tide of McClymonds' highlights, David Strom stood with the ball on the right wing and lofted a pass over the basket. Jason Wright appeared from nowhere, leaping from outside the key to catch the pass and dunk in one motion as the buzzer sounded. Donlea jumped reflexively, amazed that the play they had practiced all season had finally worked.

Despite the scare from the dean and the commitment to the revised attitude, Jason couldn't help himself. He was caught in the moment again, swept up in the commotion over his own ability to play basketball. As he ran downcourt after the dunk, he shot a finger—his index this time—at the McClymonds bench.

"That was our offense," Donlea screamed between quarters, a huge smile crossing his tired face. "We're running the offense. That was actually our offense."

Blackwell looked at Wright on the bench.

"Let's do it again, J," he said. "We got the ball, let's show 'em again."

Blackwell stood almost exactly where Strom had stood and flipped the ball up toward the hoop. Wright caught it at the peak of his jump and slammed it down with a scream. He hung long enough to pull his knees even with the rim. The place went nuts.

• • •

Every OAL game is a game of retribution. Stamps saw Wright's two dunks and saw the wild reaction of the crowd. In this setting, with McClymonds' reputation on the line, it was incumbent upon Stamps to give a little back. He found his chance late in the second quarter, when Donlea sent Kenneth Forward into the game to guard Stamps for the final three minutes of the half.

Forward was on the junior varsity team all season. An introspective kid with a muscular body and a long, thin ponytail held together in three places by rubber bands, Forward was a good defensive player. He was also giving up about seven inches to Stamps.

Stamps got the ball on the right baseline, about fifteen feet from the basket. Forward was the only obstacle between Stamps and the basket, but Stamps didn't pay much attention to Forward. He took one dribble and leaped, spinning his body toward the baseline. In defiance of most laws of physics, he hung in the air long enough to throw down a backwards slam. Forward got a good look at Stamps's shoes.

Push it! Push it! *Push it!*," Donlea yelled, his voice growing hoarse as it tried, but failed, to rise over the crowd's response. He turned toward the bench. "Goddamit, they stop when there's a dunk. They just freeze. We should have a transition basket every time they dunk, because they just stop playing to admire it."

Skyline went to the locker room at halftime trailing by eight at 38–30.

"It could be worse," Donlea told his players.

Within minutes, it was.

McClymonds built its lead to 18 before the third quarter was half over. "If they could keep that up for a whole game, nobody could beat them," Donlea said. He had given up on this one.

With less than five minutes remaining in the game, Jason Wright scored inside to pull Skyline to within ten points at 62–52. Stamps followed in a Renard Monroe miss to make it 64–52. The game was over, McClymonds had made its point and seemed content to trade baskets. The fans who hadn't left were losing interest.

Wright squared up on the right wing. He looked inside to Blackwell—nothing open. He looked down at his feet, his toes a hair's-breadth outside the three-point line. He left his feet and let fly, his team's last hopes back-spinning through the air and toward the hoop. The ball went through, all net. Donlea stood up on the bench and yelled, "We're not out of this game. We can get back in it."

Wright's eyes beamed with intensity. Donlea had sat him out early in the fourth quarter, and Wright was trying to make up for lost time. He didn't like to come out of games, because he considered each second on the bench to be a wasted scoring opportunity.

McClymonds threw the ball away. Strom pushed it up the left side and hit Wright as he popped out on the left baseline. No hesitation this time, he dribbled once to gain his balance and lofted another three-point shot. As the ball settled deep in the net, the noise of the crowd swallowed the tiny gym, as if everything that came before was complete silence. Skyline was within six, at 64–58, and Jason Wright wasn't celebrating. He sprinted to his position on the press, as if he was unaware of the fans or the noise or the impact of his play. He wasn't finished.

McClymonds was rattled, for perhaps the first time all season. Renard Monroe tried to force it inside, and Blackwell slapped it to Darren Albert. Byrd found Wright and clung to him, shadowing his every move. Strom dribbled into the forecourt and forced a pass to Wright on the left wing. With Byrd's face practically attached to his chest, Wright turned and shot. The crowd was up by the time he got the ball, and every person in the Skyline cheering section reflexively threw his hands to the sky as Wright released his shot. It went in, Skyline had cut the lead to three with more than four minutes remaining in the game.

Wright had scored 11 points in one minute and twenty-three seconds. McClymonds called a time out. Jason Wright looked only at the scoreboard and raced to the bench, his eyes not wandering into the stands.

Donlea was pumping his fists on the sideline like a man beating a drum. The Skyline bench was laughing and slapping hands. Forget the running and dunking. They were in the game, and *this* was fun. It was 64–61—a game.

Donlea talked about defense. Strom told them to be calm. As the players took the court, Donlea pulled Jason Wright aside.

"Go with it if it's there, J. Don't force it. Take it if it's there."

McClymonds came back and scored to go up by five. Byrd stuck to Wright from the moment the ball went through the basket. The other four McClymonds players set up in a diamond zone. McClymonds coach Willie Hearnton had seen enough of Jason Wright—enough, in fact, to pull his team out of its man-to-man defense for the first time all season.

Wright grabbed an offensive rebound and was fouled by Stamps—his fourth. Wright hit two free throws to make it 66–63. McClymonds brought it downcourt and tossed it inside to 6-foot-5 Kirtus Clanton, who turned on Kenneth Forward and went up for the shot. Forward, still seething from the dunk earlier in the game, anticipated the shot and swatted it out of bounds.

With 2:55 remaining, Anthony Byrd hit one of two free throws to put McClymonds ahead by four points. Skyline needed Jason Wright.

David Strom looked for Wright, but Byrd was playing defense like he meant it. Blackwell was nearly lost inside as he attempted to post Stamps and Clanton. Strom knew he wasn't Donlea's first choice to take a shot in this situation, but he had long since stopped worrying about what the coach wanted. They needed a basket, nobody was open and he had the ball. Renard Monroe slacked off Strom, expecting a pass. Strom came to a jump stop sixteen feet from the basket and lofted it through cleanly. Skyline was within two points. Suddenly, McClymonds looked a bit less invincible.

Willie Hearnton stood up off the Mack bench and stared out onto the floor. It was his trademark look: hands on hips, head tilted slightly to the side. His eyes were like burning embers. One by one, the Mack players looked over toward the bench and understood the message. Stamps got the ball inside and slammed one. The defense picked up and forced a turnover. Renard Monroe hit two free throws and Strom traveled the next time down. There was 1:02 remaining, and McClymonds had built a six-point lead.

With thirty seconds left, the chant began:

Twenty-four and oh
Twenty-four and oh

Willie Hearnton allowed himself the slightest hint of a smile.

McClymonds scored the last eight points of the game and defeated Skyline 77–67. After his gluttonous scoring run, Jason Wright didn't get another shot from the field. He should have been flattered, but instead he was frustrated beyond consolation. Byrd trailed him all over the court, with no regard for anything or anyone else. Jason finished with 31 points, but he played the last three minutes of the game trying in vain to shake Anthony Byrd.

"I didn't want to do anything special defensively, but he deserved a special defense," Hearnton said.

The OAL regular season was over. Skyline won five and lost five.

Jason Wright sat by himself in the dark, cold Skyline locker room. He was still in his uniform, and the game was still inside him. Many of the overhead fluorescent lights remained burned out or broken, and the gray metal lockers and the uneven concrete floor emanated frigidity. Jason sat at the end of one of the thin wooden benches. His head was down and he was staring intently at his shoes. His teammates filed by and congratulated him on the game. Most of them knew Jason placed significant importance on scoring 30 points in a game. He had scored 28 and 29, but never 30. Still, they were struck by how hard he took the loss, and how disillusioned he was by Byrd's ability to take him completely out of the game. He didn't think that was possible.

Will Blackwell put a hand on Wright's left shoulder.

"Hey, J, it's all right," Blackwell said, his voice animated and loud. "He was playing a box-and-one. That's the easiest defense in the world. He ain't gotta worry about anything else but you. He don't worry about the ball, he don't worry about the rest of the team. He just shadows you and gets help when he needs it. I wish I could play that defense every game—ain't nobody *ever* score on me."

Wright eventually got dressed and left the locker room. He shook hands and accepted congratulations from some friends, and he was immediately transformed. He found Donlea rushing out of the coaches' office before the junior-varsity game. Jason asked if he could take the videotape of the game home with him. Donlea laughed and gave it to him, saying, "J Wright, you amaze me."

Jason took the videotape home and watched it over and over on the 52-inch projection television screen that rules the living room. Strom and Burns came by to watch. They left and Jason kept watching. He dissected the two alley-oop dunks, stopping the tape to find the spot where he left the floor. He amazed himself when he saw that he left the floor from outside the key on the first one. He would watch it and rewind, then watch it again and again, mesmerized by his ability to do just about anything he wanted on the floor. He also watched and listened as the fans responded to his dunks, the way the roar rose abruptly, like an explosion, as his hands caught the ball and brought it down hard. He watched how the Skyline students in the stands—and even some adults—put their hands over their heads and *whoosh!* brought them down hard in imitation.

"I watched that first dunk hella times," he said.

Donlea picked up the *Tribune* the next day and shook his head. At the end of the game story, there was a quote from Jason Wright about the upcoming playoff game against Fremont.

"We'll be ready this time," Wright said. "There's no way Fremont is going to beat us three times in a season."

Donlea felt the same way, but he didn't want it publicized.

"Stupid, Jason," he told him. "I'm glad you feel that way, but you've gotta learn what to say and what not to say."

"Coach, what I said's true. Fremont know that. Don't worry about it; I'll take care of it."

In the days following the McClymonds game, Wright began staying after practice. He would jump rope and do some extra running, and he began talking about being anxious to start a weight-training program in the offseason. He had his little name around the OAL, averaging 21 points a game to lead the league, and now he thought that might have been a little near-sighted. The way he'd been playing, the OAL seemed insignificant. Jason Wright caught wind of a feeling: He just might be able to make a bigger name for himself, one that would extend far beyond the neighborhood rivalries of the OAL.

After practice, Donlea usually would keep the gym open for about an hour, allowing players to get some work done on their own. At the beginning of the season, Strom and Burns might be the only two to stay, and even they were more likely to be heading to an open gym in the city for a pickup game. Now Wright was staying behind.

As he watched Wright jump rope the day after the McClymonds

game, Donlea stood in the doorway to the gym and said, "I think he's getting serious about basketball. I think he's seen in the past couple weeks what he's capable of doing." Still, Donlea was worried about Wright's attitude. He thought a little success on the court had traveled a long way in Jason's mind.

Strom and Burns were there, too, working on their games. Donlea's attention was on Wright.

"I'm going to work my butt off with Jason this summer. You know what I was thinking last night? Stanford doesn't have a guard right now who can take somebody off the dribble and slam it down like Jason can. If he can get to a thousand on his SATs, he can go to Stanford. They'll take him. I've decided that's what I want for him."

Wright finished with the rope and walked toward the coaches' office. Donlea stopped him in the corridor.

"You're gonna practically live with me this offseason, Jason," Donlea said. "We're gonna work on all your weaknesses."

"That's gonna be a pretty short workout, then," Wright replied.

"No, it's not. That's what you've got to understand. I'm thinking Division I for you. You have to become a better defender, a better rebounder and you have to be stronger with the basketball. I'll tell you what I'm thinking, Jason. I'm thinking that if you do well in the classroom and get a thousand on your SATs, I'm thinking Stanford. What do you think about that?"

Wright was clearly flattered. He turned his head away and smiled at the wall.

"I know I can do the basketball, but I don't know about Stanford."

Donlea expected that response. He knew the prospect of Stanford's academic reputation struck a chord of abject fear into a lot of inner-city kids.

"That's the best thing in life, Jason, to reach your potential. If you can do it in the classroom, J, they'll take you. But you've got to improve on the court, too . . . That's what I'm thinking."

"The one college I want to play at is UNLV," Wright said.

"I'll tell you right now, you've got to play better defense to play at UNLV. You know what? You guys should love me, because I'm getting you ready for that next step. The other guys around this league? They'll go to a Division I program and the coaches will say, 'This guy's footwork is terrible. They don't know how to help-side defense. They don't run very hard because they think they can get away with shit.' I'm getting you ready for the next level, and those other guys aren't gonna be ready. The guys at McClymonds aren't ready. Stamps is not ready. He's gonna go to San Jose State and think, 'Shit, I got it all. I know how to shoot, I can run, I can defend.' Look, he's weak as a pussycat. He's not tough, he's not good defensively and he doesn't block out. He had Strom on a two-on-one and he jumped up in the air and passed it? Fuck that. You go down there and ram that shit down Strom's throat. David will say that much himself. I'm telling you, Jason, I'm not going to let you slide. I'm going to be all over your ass, because I have high expectations for you."

"I do, too."

"You're gonna have to be a real leader next year."

"I will."

"I mean effort-wise."

"Coach, this ain't my team. This Dave's team and Will's team and Eric's team."

Donlea nodded and leaned back against the wall next to the soda machine. His head came to rest just below a graffiti tag from "Entro" and a large brown saliva stain shaped like a teardrop.

"It goes like this in groups: If the most talented person in the group doesn't have a good ethic, then that shows everybody else that they don't have to. But if he works his ass off? That shows the guys, 'Shit, I better work my ass off. He's got all this talent and he's working his ass off.' Then you got a team. Then you got a chance to win. I'm tellin' you, that's how it works. The truly great players are the ones who work their asses off."

"I work harder in the offseason than I ever do with the team. I don't know why it is, but that's the way it is."

"You know you have to be consistent. You have to show these new guys. If Phil is eligible next year, you're gonna have to show him what it takes on the basketball court."

Jason mentioned the name of one of his friends, another strong player who had grade difficulties and never became eligible.

"Coach, you've got to find a way to get him out here to play. He can play."

"I know. Did I pick him for this team?"

"Yeah."

"Damn right I did. From now on, guys who come in will have to fit into our program."

Donlea was making plans for his summer-league team, and he decided to throw in a novel twist. An idealist to the end, he decided that everybody on the summer league team had to be academically eligible after the final semester of the year.

"Nothing's easy," Donlea said. "That's just the way I think it should be."

Donlea was constantly reminding Jason of that. "There's always somebody better than you are," he told him. Jason's 31-point game against McClymonds had served two purposes, Donlea thought. It had showed him how good he could be, but it had also given him an inflated idea of how good he already was. Donlea's plan for the summer was to build Jason up and, at the same time, tear him down. He was planting a few seeds for that right now, on a cold night in a nearly empty gym.

"I love you guys like sons off the floor, but I'm gonna yell at your ass on the floor, and in practice," Donlea told him. Wright nodded quickly, as if trying to move Donlea off the subject. "You guys— especially you, Jason—have to live with that."

"I think next year you're gonna have to let people know that early," Wright said.

Donlea's eyes shot up to meet Wright's.

"Did I do that this year? Did I throw fits, did I fuckin' chuck balls against baskets—"

"You did, but it was too late in the year, I think."

"Too late?"

"Yeah, I think you should have started at the beginning, that's why I think next year—"

"Did I throw shit? I went ballistic several times. You don't realize how far we've come."

"No. I do. I do. Just be consistent."

"I will. I'll go ballistic again. I'll get in your face. I was consistent this year. More consistent than you think. I really worry about that, because I expect to treat everybody as equal as I can."

"No, you treat everybody equal, but just have stricter policies from the get-go. Like missing practice, sit people down in the pre-season."

"Did I? Who started against Riordan?"

"Nah. I'm talking about before that. I'm talkin' early in the season. You let guys get away with stuff. I know I missed practice, but Bryant—I don't know."

Donlea saw talent in Bryant Johnson that kept him from being as strict as he should have been. He also liked Bryant and thought he was a fun kid to be around. When he was there, he played hard and did as he was told. Donlea saw Bryant's incredible quickness and his open-court inventiveness. So he stretched the rules.

"This year has not been a building year for Bryant, in a large sense," Donlea told Jason. "It's coming around a little bit."

"He be in his own little world out there on the court, coach."

"I know he is. We all tend to go into our own little world, though."

"I don't go into my own little world unless I'm real tired."

"Let the game come to you, J. Don't force the game. Because it always comes to you, J. It always does. You're that good, that's why. Bryant's the same way, if he lets the game come to him and doesn't force it. That's what you have to remember this week. These are the playoffs, J. A lot of people are going to be watching you. This isn't the time to go off on your own. Stay with it. Stay with what we're doing, because if we're a little bit healthy going into these playoffs, I know we can win. Because it's a mental game, it's composure. It's decisions."

"We be gettin' too wrapped up into the, like in the heat of the game? Bryant, Darren—they get too wrapped up in the crowd."

Donlea burst out laughing. Was this the same Jason Wright who carried on a running dialogue with every crowd in the OAL? Jason Wright—the player who left a vapor trail of enemies from gym to gym?

"That's coming from you, Jason Wright?" Donlea asked.

"I mean, showboatin' is showboatin', that ain't what I mean."

"I don't say showboat, but you get into the crowd. I think it turns you on a little bit. I think I turn you on when I piss you off and sit your ass down. Shit, I pulled your ass out last night, you got pissed off and went back out there and lit it up. How often has that happened? That happens a lot when I yank your ass out. You go back in and kick some ass? Don't ya?"

"That's just natural ability, coach. If I sit on the bench, this is what I think of: All that time I sit on the bench, I could be out there going to work. So when I get in there, it's like I'm already behind. I feel I've to get back out there and get right back in the flow of the game. It's like going to the park and playing a full game and then comin' out. I can't handle that. I need to go back in."

In the background, two basketballs continued to beat against the hardwood. On the far court, Strom would start at halfcourt on the right sideline. He would dribble toward the middle, his shoulder down as if breaking a double-team. He would go behind his back to the right, then through his legs back to the middle, where he would take two dribbles and shoot a pull-up jumper from the free-throw line. If he missed, he'd follow it in and dribble back to halfcourt. If he made it, he'd go back and do it again. Burns was on the near court, trying out a new playground move. Starting near the top of the key, he would go behind his back with his left hand, then behind his back with his right hand, then spin with a reverse pivot and lay it off the glass. It was hard to imagine the move working with a defensive player anywhere in the vicinity.

"You think you're gonna grow some more?" Donlea asked Wright.

"I think I can squeeze out about two or three more inches. Go hang in the backyard."

"That'd be nice if you were about 6-5, 6-6."

"I think I can get about 6-5."

"You've got to work on gettin' a jump shot, too. Shooting on the move."

"Right now I just shoot it because it's open. I need to be able to look for my shot."

"We've got a lot of work to do this summer, J. We're going to spend a lot of time together. A lot."

"Yeah," Wright said, pausing. "Yeah, I guess we will. I don't know what it is, but I'm looking forward to the end of the season. I want to play the playoffs, but . . . I don't know. I get some serious work done in the offseason. I'll be kind of glad when it's over."

"So will I, Jason," Donlea said. "So will I."

"I got a lot of things to take care of."

"So do I, J. So do I. For one thing, I've got to get a life."

CHAPTER EIGHTEEN

THE EMOTIONS WERE STRONGER NOW, BURNED INTO HIS PSYCHE BY FIVE months of constant conflict. Shawn Donlea was obsessed with the game, this one game, and he wore the obsession on his face: his eyes were framed by dark circles and his complexion was ashen. The season had taken a lot out of him.

The game against Fremont was just one of hundreds of high school playoff games taking place across the state during the first week of March, but because of Donlea's approach, it was hard to imagine any of them meaning any more to any single person.

He had been, in many ways, a tortured soul. He had abused himself emotionally, taking his mind through trips of trepidation, disgust and helplessness. He was imprisoned by the lofty expectations he held for himself. Now he was just plain angry; it was all he had left. The anger had been roiling inside from the first half of the season, and it had accumulated to the point of distraction. In order to justify himself, in order to feel he belonged, this had to work, this game *had* to be won. If it wasn't, the season would be a failure. If Skyline won, the season would be a success. He had shaved everything down to that simple equation.

"This is it," he said. "The season."

His initial goal was to bring Skyline to the OAL playoffs. At the time, he thought four teams qualified for the postseason. When he found out it was three, Skyline had already clinched a spot.

"That's a good thing, too," he said. "If I knew only three teams made it, I think I might have been overestimating the team to think we would make the playoffs."

Once a goal was met, however, a new one took over. Skyline led Fremont by 18 points in the second half the last time they played, and still they lost. The players blamed Donlea for that loss, and now Donlea had come to agree. At first he said he wouldn't have done anything differently, but that was pure stubbornness. He looked at the tape again and readily admitted that his substitution pattern— especially leaving Jason Wright on the bench for much of the third quarter—had cost Skyline the game. It had also cost him some respect.

"That won't happen again," he said. "There's no way they can beat us if we play our game. No way. They've got great athletes, but they can't handle structure."

Donlea dressed as well as he could. He wore a white shirt, a peach-colored tie, a pair of beige pants and a brown tweed sport- coat. He wore casual, rubber-soled brown leather shoes. They were scuffed and worn, but they were the best he had. Some of his play- ers laughed at the tie, calling it old-fashioned and sadly out of style.

"There's nothing wrong with this tie," he said. "Especially since I only have three."

Donlea joked about his wardrobe, and how bad it looked next to Fremont coach Clinton Williams, the best dresser in the OAL. Williams wore sharp suits and expensive leather shoes. Donlea sometimes wore a pair of gray polyester slacks that he wore part of a uniform for umpiring softball games.

"If I ever get paid for this, maybe I'll buy some clothes," Donlea said. "But I don't think I'll ever look as good as Clint."

The game was a night game, at the Henry J. Kaiser Convention Center. The security would be tight, and the atmosphere would be charged. The team met at the Skyline gym more than two hours before the game; Donlea would hit them with the technical stuff there, before they met the distractions of the crowd at the Henry J.

Donlea began in his professorial tone. He glanced down occa- sionally to consult the sheet of yellow legal paper in his right hand. He had written down several points he wanted to stress, most hav- ing to do with remaining composed regardless of circumstance.

"The foundation of this program is defense—the footwork, the positioning, the help-side, contesting shots and on boxing out," he said. "And eventually, that's what we're going to rely on—how good our defense is in half-court. We'll get turnovers and buckets out of our press and out of transition. We'll come right at them again, right down their throats. *Right* down their throats. A good defensive team like you are, they won't get much on offense. They'll shoot it up. You better make sure you're rebounding. Especially guards. Why is that?"

"Long rebounds," Darren Albert said.

"That's right—long rebounds. Kareem Davis starts going right, it's going up. Fight through the pick. Box somebody out, get the rebound and look to run. We will control the tempo of the game with our defense, and we will win with the smart decision-making. You play a team game and that's why you're in the playoffs. That's why you're successful. You guys have given up a lot for this—a whole lot. It's going to take your heart, your feet and your head. No technical fouls—composure. If we get a dunk down, get it on, get right into what we're doing. Don't lose focus. Every time you lose focus, you can be hurt. The key is consistency and execution."

Donlea finished and let the players go back to their shootaround. He watched as they went about their business with a quiet seriousness. Even Bryant Johnson, the most loquacious of the group, was silent. Jason Wright was off by himself, working on his free throws.

"They're listening to me," Donlea said. "They're attentive. This is the most attentive they've been all year."

Donlea continued watching. Will Blackwell was rebounding underneath and passing the ball out to David Strom, who was shooting three-pointers from the baseline.

"We're going to win this game," Donlea said. "These guys are ready. I've never seen them more ready."

The bus ride was quiet, with the sound of the yellow beast's struggle eliminating everything else.

There are no locker rooms at the Kaiser Convention Center. It is more suited for concerts (Bruce Springsteen has played there) and stage plays than basketball games. Donlea got an OAL official to let Skyline use the center's makeup room. The room was about eight feet wide and thirty feet long, with a mirror running the length of the long wall. About fifty bare and bright makeup lights ran in a line above the mirror.

The Skyline players sat on the counter, with Donlea standing in the middle of the room, directly in front of them. The mirror and the lights gave the scene a surrealistic look, as if the team had just doubled in size. Jason Wright sat at one end of the counter, staring at himself in the brightness of the mirror. David Strom sat beside Wright, his body totally still, his hands holding tightly to his wrist bands. He made eye contact with no one. Bryant Johnson couldn't sit still, his hyperkinetic body twisting and bouncing on the counter, his face contorted and expressive.

"Come on, fellas," he said in a pleading tone. "We got to get *amped*. We can beat these guys. We got to beat these guys."

Nelson Burns knew he probably wouldn't play. That had been established and accepted. The second half of the season had been much more enjoyable for him, and he seemed glad he stuck with it instead of quitting. He was excited about this game, talking as always about the strategy Skyline needed to employ to win the game. He had an active and sharp basketball mind. Now he sat with his teammates, slapping hands with Will Blackwell and Eric Govan, as much a part of the team as anybody in the room.

Donlea scribbled a few notations on his clipboard and looked up. He was worried about the portable baskets, which weren't equipped with the standard hinged breakaway rims. One of them was bent at a near-comic angle. He was also worried about the shooting background. The building was cavernous, with close to 100 feet of nothing behind each basket. After playing in cramped gyms all season, Donlea worried that they would have difficulty adjusting to the altered depth perception. Mostly, he worried because he knew of no other way to prepare for a game.

"All right, fellas," he said. "Time to get it on. Get out there, get a sweat. Get loose."

"Hey, hey," Calvin Wilson yelled. *"Serve it up."*

"Get used to the depth of the rims," Donlea said. "Let's get on it. When they blow the horn at one minute, come back in here and we'll reaffirm what's going on. Hey, *we're* going on tonight. We are *goin' on."*

They left the counter and gathered in the middle of the room.

"Let's go, baby. Let's go."

"Fire it on up."

"Come on, fellas," Donlea said. "Be sharp tonight—sharp mentally, sharp physically, tough in the heart. Do not worry about the score any time in the game. Don't look at it. Don't worry about it. Play your nuts off. Let me worry about the score. Let me worry about changing defenses. Let me do my job. I'll do it better tonight. You do your job, and we'll be happy in the end."

Donlea moved closer to them, circling the knot of bodies to see each of their faces.

"We're all together in this. We're all together, we're all alive. Now it's time that we arrive."

"Ooh, that *rhymes,*" Will Blackwell said.

They remained together, some with their heads on their teammates shoulders, their right hands meeting in the middle. David Strom asked for quiet. This was a first; he always stood stock-still at these times, his hand upraised and his eyes closed. He let everybody else talk; his motivation came from within. The noise continued after Strom asked for quiet, and Blackwell pulled his head back from the crowd and interrupted.

"Shut up," he said. "The man's trying to talk."

The noise stopped. The rap music from the huge speakers outside in the auditorium vibrated the walls. The circle became tighter. Donlea looked on from the outside with his eyebrows raised, nodding. Strom had the floor. They waited.

There was some history at work here. David Strom's worst moment in basketball occurred under similar circumstances. It was worse than being ignored or hassled on the playground, worse than walking into the hostile gyms of the OAL. It was worse because it was about his game, not his color or appearance.

Strom's sophomore season ended against Fremont, in the OAL championship game. The game was at Merritt Community College. The place was packed. The game, like this one, was carried on local cable television.

Skyline's point guard, Charles King, had fouled out in the fourth quarter. The game was tied. Coach Don Lippi replaced King with Strom, who had played on the junior-varsity team much of the season.

The Fremont team, experienced and tough, seized on Strom. They hounded him from baseline to baseline, screaming at him, telling him what he couldn't do and why he couldn't do it. They attacked him physically and mentally. They told him white boys couldn't play in this league.

"They told me stuff, and it turned out they were right," Strom said.

They rattled him, tearing open his curtain of passivity. Each dribble was contested. He was picked clean at least twice, maybe three times. He has tried to forget the details, but he's kept the overall memory fresh. They had invaded his territory, and he had shown weakness. In his mind, he cost Skyline the game.

"I was intimidated," he said. "Yep, I sure was. I told myself that wouldn't happen again."

He brought that memory with him here, to this room.

"You sophomores, y'all might not get here again," Strom said, his voice low, flat and steady. "You can't take anything for granted. We don't know what's going to happen. You can't depend on what's going to happen next year or the year after. I had a bad experience against these guys when I was a sophomore, and I don't want that to happen again. That *won't* happen again."

When Strom had finished, Darren Albert reached across the clump of bodies and rubbed a hand across Strom's spiny hair.

Donlea never expected to have Albert stay in the starting lineup the entire season. He assumed that, as the season progressed, Bryant Johnson's incredible physical ability would overtake Albert's hustle and determination. It never happened, though, partly because Johnson was comfortable coming off the bench and mostly because Albert continued to provide Skyline with an early boost. He was ready to play from the start, always.

"If I can be immodest, I think Darren's one kid I was able to help," Donlea said. "We went through some rough times, but I believed in him. I told him, 'Good things happen to good people,' and it really worked out for him."

This game, and its repercussions, meant a lot to Albert. He harbored no illusions about playing college basketball. He thought he might try out if he went to a junior college (an option that looked more and more probable as the school year passed), but he knew the end of his high school career might be the end of his career, period. Because of that, he couldn't face losing to his friends three times in a season. The last time was bad enough, with Lamont Brown hitting the game-winning shot and then showing up at the Alberts' house afterward.

"It can't happen three times," Darren said, smiling. "I don't know if I could handle that."

Eric had talked about coming to this game, but he was concerned that he wouldn't be allowed on the floor level. In his wheelchair, a trip to the balcony level—where the fans sat—was impossible. He wanted to see his brother play, but he didn't want to deal with the constant questions and the sympathy his presence engendered. If they hadn't shown interest to this point, Eric didn't have any time for them. He didn't want to spend his time dealing with other people's pity or false concern.

Fremont turned the ball over against the Skyline press four times in the first three minutes, and Darren came up with two of the steals. He scored on a fast break and hit a 16-foot jumper from the right side. He had, once again, gotten his team off to a good start. The first few minutes set the tone; everything was working for Skyline.

Strom broke the Fremont press like an expert skier navigating a beginner's slalom course. He would dribble right, then cut to his left and head upcourt, leaving a trail of defenders in his wake. He would stop and pass to a teammate cutting to the basket and Skyline would score. It looked as if Fremont was running in sand.

Nelson Burns, sitting on the bench, looked out at his friend and said, "He's makin' it look too easy. It's not that easy."

Fremont's inside players were leapers, but none of them were taller than 6-4. Against players such as these, Govan was in his element. He had a seemingly endless supply of head fakes and pump fakes, and each one seemed to work against the Fremont players. They were looking for blocked shots, as Govan knew all too well, and they were left to flail at the air when he ducked underneath to score at will.

Govan scored inside and was fouled midway through the second quarter. After he hit the free throw to give Skyline a 10-point lead at 28-18, Donlea took Govan out. As he walked to the bench and slapped the hands of his teammates, Govan said, "Those babies can *NOT* handle me."

As soon as Govan sat down, Blackwell stole a pass in the open court and powered his way to the basket. He finished it with a one-handed windmill slam from the left side. Although a shade under six feet tall, his elbow was even with the rim when he brought the ball down.

"Superman!" Donlea yelled from the bench. "Superman!"

It was 30–18, almost too good to be true.

"Don't worry about the score," Donlea said during a timeout. "Don't even look at it. Keep your composure. Do not—*do not* give them a reason to get back into this game."

Blackwell scored the final four points of the first half, two of them on an indescribable tip-in from about six feet away. Skyline went back to the makeup room leading by 16. Blackwell had 14 points, Govan nine, Jason Wright seven. Strom had five assists. Everything was working so well that Donlea couldn't help but feel uneasy.

"Wow, that was almost too good," he said as the players filed into the room. They laughed and talked and danced to the heavy beat of Ice Cube's "It Was A Good Day."

Donlea looked back out at the crowd.

"You know, I kind of like that song," he said.

He gave his players a few seconds to themselves while he jotted a few reminders on his clipboard. "I really don't have anything to say," he said before walking into the makeup room. He tucked his clipboard under his right arm and began clapping.

"Great job, fellas," he said. "Great job. Great job executing. Don't abandon anything. Play the same game in the second half. Play hard and play smart."

He had detected a way that Skyline could take advantage of Fremont's athletic ability. Fremont's big players were releasing early whenever Skyline shot, and sometimes it led to easy baskets on the other end. Donlea felt the best way to combat this was to have his big players crash the offensive boards hard while the guards dropped back to cut off the fast break.

"It's kind of a paradox," Donlea told them. Then, as if realizing he had just fallen back into his old habits, he caught himself and stopped in midsentence. He dropped his clipboard to his side and returned to the visceral approach.

"Don't think about winning. Just think about playing. Just think about playing, because there's too much time left to think about winning."

"Can't come out flat, fellas," somebody said.

"Hell, no. We ain't coming out flat," Donlea said.

"No, no, NO, man. Flat. Shit."

"Don't be talkin' that. That's fucked up."

"That's out of the question," Donlea said. "We don't touch anything that's flat. I don't want to hear anything about flat."

Donlea put the clipboard on the floor and bent at the waist, like a linebacker coiled to make a hit.

"HEY, YOU KNOW THEY'LL TRY TO MAKE A RUN AT US, BUT WE'RE GONNA PUT 'EM AWAY THIS HALF."

"Hell yes," Blackwell said.

There was only one anxious moment in the second half, and it didn't last long. With 6:19 left in the game, Fremont cut the Skyline lead to eight. Donlea called a timeout. The Fremont cheering section was alive for the first time. The music started and this time it was Fremont, not Skyline, that walked to the bench moving to the beat.

The concern was evident on Donlea's face. This was what happened the last time the two teams played, and he was worried that a certain sense of fatalism had afflicted his team. He had to remind them that they were the better team, that they *deserved* to win this game. After he was finished, Blackwell looked at Donlea and said, "Don't worry, coach. It's under control."

Blackwell scored on a fast break to move the lead back to 10. Fremont's Frank Knight, a freshman with big-time talent, drilled a three-pointer to bring Fremont to within seven.

Almost immediately, Strom hit Bryant Johnson in the open court. The players on the Skyline bench instinctively leaned forward, knowing the possibilities that awaited. Johnson had one defender to beat. To his way of thinking, that was better than an open layup, because he always liked to have an obstacle to overcome. He dribbled in from the right side and swung the ball back behind him, as if to make a behind-the-back pass. The Fremont defender bit, and Johnson went up, hanging in the air and changing hands to avoid another defender who had caught up. Johnson flipped the ball up over his head, off the backboard and into the basket.

The crowd was silent for a split-second, as if taking a moment to replay what it had just witnessed. Even the Skyline players, who had seen Johnson's act all season, were open-mouthed in disbelief.

Donlea walked to the end of the bench, shaking his head.

"Oh, he can *play*," he said. "He can be *un*believable."

After that, it was over. Strom, exorcising the memory of his sophomore year with a strong game, broke into the open court and flipped a behind-the-back pass fifteen feet across the key, where Jason Wright caught it in full stride and glided in for a layup. Under normal circumstances, it would have called for a dunk, but earlier Wright had been called for a technical foul for hanging on the rim. He was taking no chances.

With Skyline ahead by 12 with 2:52 left in the game, Donlea turned to Nick Wimberly on the bench and said, "We've got a chance to win this game." Wimberly looked at Donlea like he just proclaimed the world to be flat.

"Coach," Wimberly said, "We've got this *shit won*."

Wimberly was right. Skyline won, 75–65, and everything about the game went beyond Donlea's lofty expectations. The scoring was incredibly balanced: Blackwell scored 25, Wright 16, Govan 13, Johnson 9 and Albert 7. They played strong defense and were remarkably unselfish with the basketball.

They had beaten the fourth-ranked team in the Bay Area. They had beaten somebody they weren't supposed to beat. This was what Donlea had been waiting for.

Darren Albert had been waiting for it, too. He walked over to Lamont Brown. They shook hands and hugged. Brown shrugged. Albert resisted the temptation to gloat. It wasn't his style.

"Nah, I wouldn't do that," he said. "He knows we beat 'em good. That was enough."

Blackwell stood underneath the Skyline cheering section, dancing and laughing and whipping his warmup top over his head, like a
rodeo cowboy, playfully threatening to throw it into the stands.
Some of the girls above looked down at him, trying to coax him into
sending it up at them.

"I can't," Blackwell yelled up at them. "One more game."

Donlea congratulated David Strom. Strom looked up into
Donlea's eyes and said, "Good job, coach. That was a good game."

Sophomore guard Rod Ponder shook Donlea's hand and told him,
"You're a great coach, man. You're the best coach in the league."

Some members of the junior varsity team were on the court to
congratulate the players. They told Donlea they couldn't wait for
next season.

The bus headed back to Skyline packed beyond capacity. It was
filled with the girls basketball team, which had lost in the early
game. The cheerleaders were there, along with the boys team, girls
coach Charles Davis, Donlea, two faculty members and two statisti-
cians.

The post-game euphoria wasn't allowed to last long. Donlea hus-
tled the team to the bus, where they were told to hurry aboard and
keep the windows up. There were people milling about outside the
bus, telling Skyline to wait until McClymonds got to them. They
didn't want to hear that, though; they wanted to let the satisfaction
of this win soak in before they thought about their third game
against McClymonds.

The bus was hot and cramped and noisy, the air thick. The players were hot and sweaty, and the windows were fogging up. One of
the cheerleaders in the back of the bus pulled a window down
slightly to get some air. Davis, the girls basketball coach and the
head of Skyline campus security, immediately stood up.

"Ladies, keep the windows up," he said calmly. When it was
clear that he was being ignored, he picked up the volume. *"KEEP
THE WINDOWS UP!"*

"If you're hot, close your mouth," said Beverly Palley, a Skyline
teacher.

Donlea sat in the front row with a drained and dull smile on his face. He looked through the scorebook and nodded, utterly impervious to the clamor around him. Occasionally, he would look up and say something before looking back down. ("Great balance in the scoring." . . . "David really played well." . . . "Will's something else.")

The bus whined its way away from the Henry J. and hit East 14th. Davis stood up and yelled, "You can open the windows. They're not going to throw any rocks at you now."

These buses had trouble climbing the hill to Skyline under normal circumstances. With the load it held now, it struggled to keep moving. Nobody paid much attention, though. The bus was filled with chants and songs and the sounds of pure, undiluted happiness.

Donlea got in his car and drove home, alone, his tie loosened, the windows open and the radio blaring. For once, he allowed the game to stand on its own, completely separate from yesterday or tomorrow. He didn't care that McClymonds—24–0 McClymonds—was next. He didn't care that only one OAL team would advance to the tournament of champions. He had broken through, finally, and that's all that mattered. They *believed*, and it was a sweet moment, unimaginably sweet. It was fitting that he was alone with the wind and the radio. Nobody else could understand the perfection of this moment. Not his friends, not his parents—not even his players.

He had been shackled by his own stratospheric ambitions the entire season. This was vindication. The days of shattered confidence and total disillusionment were swept away with one perfectly orchestrated game plan. Donlea drove and the music played. For this one day, and this one drive, he couldn't imagine being anyone or anywhere else. He was right where he belonged.

EPILOGUE

Skyline's season ended in the Oakland Athletic League championship game, two days after the win over Fremont. McClymonds
won, 77–61, and the result was never in doubt.

McClymonds played perhaps its best game of the season against
Skyline. The Mack players took the floor at the Henry J. Kaiser
Convention Center wearing their OAL T-shirts. The words com-
memorated their 24–0 record, but it wasn't considered the final
statement on the team's season. To them, the regular season was
just a formality, something to do before the games got serious.
Their mission had just begun.

The crowd was bigger this time; the game was televised on a
local cable station. It was another night game, and the security was
airtight.

Before the game, Donlea brought his team into the makeup
room, the bright, bare bulbs casting severe light, creating a sharp
contrast to the dim lighting in the auditorium. Donlea's message
was simple: If you're going to go out, go out hard.

When the game ended, Donlea walked over to congratulate
McClymonds coach Willie Hearnton. The music had started, the
players were dancing on the court and Hearnton was in the middle
of it. Donlea slowly approached, not wanting to interrupt, not wanting to wait around. Hearnton saw him and walked over toward center court. He hugged Donlea—a big, powerful hug—and refused to
let go.

There were fans on the court and McClymonds players were
dancing and shouting and waving their arms. Still Hearnton held on.
Donlea could feel the tears burning their way into his eyes. He tried
to pull away from Hearnton, but he couldn't.

"You're a great coach," Hearnton told him. "I've got all the respect in the world for you. You've done a great job with that team."

"You've done a great job with your team," Donlea said. "Go win the state."

Finally, Hearnton released Donlea, ending the dance. Donlea, still holding back tears, congratulated the McClymonds players. He began to walk back to his team's bench. He looked up and saw Will Blackwell and Jason Wright and David Strom and Eric Govan sitting on the bench. Darren Albert was behind the bench, talking with his brother Eric, who arrived in the fourth quarter and now sat in his wheelchair, with John Beam at his side. As Donlea walked back to his team for the last time, the veneer of composure cracked and broke. He began crying, the tears rushing out in torrents. He hugged Govan and Strom, thanking them and telling them he was glad they were part of his first team at Skyline. He did the same with Blackwell and Nick Wimberly and Damon Gardner and Calvin Wilson. He told Jason Wright and Rod Ponder and Mike Scates that he would see them again.

"I just lost it," he said. "I couldn't hold it in anymore. There was so much built up from the season, so much. I haven't cried like that in years. I can't remember the last time."

Two weeks after the final game of the season, Shawn Donlea moved to an apartment in the lower Oakland hills, about three miles from Skyline.

With the money he earned coaching the basketball teams at Skyline, Donlea purchased auto insurance for his 1985 Volkswagen Golf.

In addition, he was hired full-time at Skyline as the coordinator of the school's in-house suspension program. Donlea's students are those in the most trouble at Skyline. Security officers conduct sweeps of truant students on campus and send them to Donlea. For the first offense, a student must stay in the classroom for the remainder of the period. A second trip calls for a full day in Donlea's room and notification of parents.

The classroom is an old auto shop, and to say it has been converted to a conventional classroom would be too kind. The door is a metal roll-up, and there are hoists in the concrete floor, remnants of oil stains everywhere. Donlea has posted handwritten signs all over the vast room, all in capital letters: NO SLEEPING; NO GUM; NO EATING OR DRINKS; REMAIN SEATED; NO HATS OR WALK-MANS; ABSOLUTELY NO TALKING; DO NOT MOVE DESKS.

Will Blackwell achieved a score above 700 on the Scholastic Aptitude Test and earned the football scholarship to San Diego State University. He was the most valuable player of California's North-South Shrine football game. He caught three touchdown passes and intercepted a pass in the end zone with less than a minute left to give the North a 28–23 win.

A glut of talented receivers made the Aztecs decide to redshirt Blackwell for the 1993 season.

David Strom attends the University of California at Davis. He didn't earn a basketball scholarship to a Division I school, and he didn't receive the financial assistance that would have enabled him to attend the University of Oregon. He worked full-time during the summer and saved enough to afford a four-year college, and he planned to walk on to the basketball team at UC Davis, a Division II program.

"I don't like to blame anyone but myself," Strom said. "If I wanted to, I could have done everything I set out to do. Even if the offense wasn't set up for a point guard, or even if I wasn't supposed to shoot that much, it all came down to me, whether I did it or not. I just didn't."

Darren Albert decided to stay home and help his family care for his brother Eric. Darren attends Chabot Junior College. Eric continues his therapy and says his outlook on life is improving.

Calvin Wilson got the grades he needed to graduate from Skyline.

After the final basketball game of the season, he signed the scholarship papers for the University of the Pacific. He went on to City College of San Francisco, where he needs to pass nine units before entering UOP in the spring.

Jason Wright was named to the all-OAL second team despite leading the league in scoring. He was named first team All-East Bay by *The Oakland Tribune* and received one vote for East Bay Player of the Year. Shortly after the season ended, he began receiving recruiting letters from Division I colleges.

He attended the summer Super Stars camp in Southern California, a showcase for potential college recruits, and was voted one of the top fifteen players in camp. And, of course, he won the slam dunk competition.

Nelson Burns attends Diablo Valley Community College in Concord, California. He worked out hard during the summer and planned to try out for the basketball team. He said he would give himself two years to earn a Division I scholarship. If he fails, he'll put basketball aside and get on with his life.

Bryant Johnson returned to Skyline for his senior year and is expected to be the team's starting point guard.

Eric Govan and Nick Wimberly both attend Patten Academy, a new Christian university in Oakland. Formerly a high school, it opened up to college students for the 1993–94 school year. Patten will have an NAIA basketball team; Govan and Wimberly expect to be a big part of the school's inaugural team.

John Beam returned to Skyline as head football coach. He says senior wide receiver Ron Holmes is the next Will Blackwell.

• • •

The McClymonds Warriors advanced to the Northern California semifinals, where they lost to De La Salle High School, a wealthy Catholic high school in Concord. The game was played at the Oakland Coliseum Arena.

De La Salle's Kevin Groves was an incredible 27 of 30 from the free-throw line in the game. McClymonds shot 25 free throws, De La Salle 51.

"The rich get richer," McClymonds coach Willie Hearnton said after the game.

The gymnasium floor at Skyline was resurfaced during the summer of 1993.

September 6, 1993

INDEX